EUROPE
1715–1919

EUROPE
1715–1919

FROM
ENLIGHTENMENT
TO WORLD WAR

Shirley Elson Roessler and Reny Miklos

ROWMAN & LITTLEFIELD PUBLISHERS, INC.
Lanham • Boulder • New York • Toronto • Oxford

ROWMAN & LITTLEFIELD PUBLISHERS, INC.

Published in the United States of America
by Rowman & Littlefield Publishers, Inc.
A wholly owned subsidiary of The Rowman & Littlefield Publishing Group, Inc.
4501 Forbes Boulevard, Suite 200, Lanham, Maryland 20706
www.rowmanlittlefield.com

PO Box 317
Oxford
OX2 9RU, UK

British Library Cataloguing in Publication Information Available

Library of Congress Cataloging-in-Publication Data

Elson Roessler, Shirley, 1942–
  Europe 1715–1919: From enlightenment to world war / Shirley
Elson Roessler and Reny Miklos.
    p. cm.
Includes bibliographical references and index.
  ISBN 0-7425-2766-2 (hardcover : alk. paper) — ISBN 0-7425-2767-0
(pbk. : alk. paper)
    1. Europe—History—18th century. 2. Europe—Intellectual life—18th
century. 3. Europe—History—19th century. 4. Europe—Intellectual
life—18th century. 5. Europe—History—1871–1918. I. Miklos,
Reinhold, 1943– II. Title.
  D299.E47 2003
  940.2'53—dc21
                                                          2003010251

Printed in the United States of America

♾™ The paper used in this publication meets the minimum requirements of
American National Standard for Information Sciences—Permanence of Paper
for Printed Library Materials, ANSI/NISO Z39.48-1992.

To our parents
Kathleen and Elmer Elson
Alexander and Magdalena Miklos
and
to our children
Anton, David, and Kristin
and
Jill and Bernie

CONTENTS

MAPS

ILLUSTRATIONS

ACKNOWLEDGMENTS

We wish to thank Dr. Frederick de Luna and Dr. Kenneth Munro of the University of Alberta's Department of History and Classics who have given generously of their time and expertise in helping in the preparation of this book. We are grateful to Jeannine Green and John Charles of Bruce Peel Special Collections, University of Alberta Libraries, for their assistance in obtaining pictures, and to Dr. Robert Smith, chair of the Department of History and Classics, for his support. We thank Tara Langlois and Bernie Roessler at *plumbheavy design* for their expert preparation of maps. As well, we are extremely grateful to our families who have borne with us and offered encouragement and whose recent resounding sigh of relief has been duly noted.

INTRODUCTION

In approaching the period in European history that begins with the Age of Enlightenment and ends with World War I, we have attempted to describe, analyze, and interpret the ideas, events, and trends which bear responsibility for the formation of modern Europe and, by extension, for the creation of the modern world. We begin with the premise that the origins of the modern state lie with the ideas of the philosophes, ideas that were eventually diffused throughout the political and intellectual elements of society. During the eighteenth century, their popularization by individuals and groups contributed to the formation of a new society and to an ever-expanding challenge to existing institutions. Gradually, this philosophical expression of a new worldview came to reverberate throughout the cultural, economic, and political realms. As modern Europe took shape, rivalry in various spheres emerged among states and was eventually carried far beyond their boundaries. The great watershed of the French Revolution, which marked an irrevocable break with the past and the beginning of the modern world, was the result of the collision between volatile political, economic, and social dissatisfactions and the new ideas that challenged traditional bastions of privilege and authority. The attempts of neighboring states to quell and contain this upheaval, coupled with the determination of the French to have their revolution succeed, resulted in widespread warfare after 1792. With the emergence of Napoleon Bonaparte, these revolutionary wars continued well into the nineteenth century, until Napoleonic domination and ambitions were finally destroyed at Waterloo in 1815.

The period that followed the Napoleonic era was one of relative peace, as Metternich's balance of power, constructed during the Congress of Vienna, maintained a certain order among the countries of Europe. The Industrial Revolution, taking place first in Britain and some seventy years later on the continent, served to destabilize the European order and led to expanded contact with the rest of the world. In response to new and changing conditions in society, new ideologies surfaced, one of the strongest of these proving to be a conservative reaction to any change in the traditional order. However, by far the most powerful and effective force to emerge was nationalism, which burgeoned during the nineteenth century in the wake of the Napoleonic conquests and which was to spawn rivalry among the newly emerging nation-states, now struggling to match political entities to nationalities. Also, nationalism served to exacerbate hatred and distrust among the various groups within the emerging nation-states. With the rise of science and technology during the Industrial Revolution, a new popular culture developed that helped to diffuse the ideas of nationalism throughout all levels of society with the result that modern states began to compete for hegemony in Europe and beyond.

Increasing bellicosity among nations became the hallmark of the period between 1870 and 1919, as Europeans established global dominance through a new imperialism and as new nation-states attempted to obtain positions of power within Europe. Meanwhile, nationalities within the boundaries of the nation-states continued to express a strong desire for their own political independence. These pressures led to the calamitous reality of 1914, when tensions exploded in the disastrous debacle of the Great War. In the aftermath, Europeans encountered a world transformed and, thus, began their long struggle for security and stability.

Chapter 1

IDEAS SHAPE THE MODERN STATE

THE AGE OF ENLIGHTENMENT

Since historical landmarks rarely coincide with the beginnings of centuries, historians are faced with an ongoing challenge in their attempts to determine feasible divisions of time. The matter is further complicated when single terms become the conventional mantle of an age, era, or century. The eighteenth century and the label "Enlightenment" present such a challenge. Yet, in this case the label is not solely the product of subsequent historical judgment, but has origins in contemporary assessments. The expression "Siècle des Lumières" appeared frequently in France during the eighteenth century in descriptions of new ideas taking hold within the ranks of the European intelligentsia. In Germany, by the latter part of the century, Immanuel Kant (1724–1804) asked, "What is the Enlightenment?" and answered, "Dare to know! Have the courage to use your own intelligence!" This emphatic response summarizes key aspects of the intellectual values and attitudes of the period. To contemporaries, it suggested that in contrast to past practice, the individual must move away from ignorance and incomprehension and take responsibility for his own knowledge and actions. The directive also implied that the individual was equipped for the task; the spirit to undertake such an endeavor and the intellectual tools required for it were already present, having originated and developed in the European past.

Some strands of influence that contributed to the Enlightenment can be traced to the increasingly prominent role that secular interests came to play during the Renaissance of the fifteenth and sixteenth centuries. Attention to the here and now, combined with concerns for the material world, competed with more spiritual priorities. The dominant world view was undetermined. In addition, the unity and strength of the Christian church had been broken by the Protestant-Catholic split of the sixteenth century and by the subsequent religious wars. Secular rulers in many countries had succeeded in asserting the primacy of the state over the church in matters of land control and clerical appointments. At the same time, the more widespread use of the printing press diminished the ability of the church to control what was read and what was taught. By the seventeenth century, the church was no longer in a position to shape and propagate a single worldview for the entire European public. The possibility of an alternate vision was to be found in the scientific and intellectual developments that emerged. It was through the scientific study of nature and the systematic analysis of society that Kant's precursors developed the necessary tools and established a foundation for building new ideas.

In *Novum Organum,* published in 1620, Francis Bacon (1521–1626) set out the procedures for a new method of acquiring knowledge. He argued that the traditional deductive approach by which logical implications were derived from an unquestioned body of principles and sources restricted the expansion of knowledge. Bacon stated that observation and experience were the only sound basis for establishing facts. He maintained that in proceeding from the particular to the general, from the concrete to the abstract, through the systematic use of the senses, one arrives at true knowledge. In this way, preconceived patterns and old prejudices are avoided in the process of determining that which is considered to be true. Although his career kept him in government positions for some time, rather than in science, it was Bacon's formulation of the scientific approach that placed him among the leading exponents of empiricism. His contention was that such an approach to pure science would yield practical benefits for the working world of farming, manufacturing, and trade, and thereby contribute to national wealth and power.

In France, René Descartes (1596–1650), beginning with the postulate, "I think, therefore I am," articulated the principle of systematic doubt. From that position, he used reason to arrive at a number of conclusions. One of these was that there are two kinds of reality in the universe: the realm of subjective experience and the extended, objective world outside the mind. This famous Cartesian dualism, as it came to be called, made available one-half of the universe to a process of investigation in which problems were to be divided into component parts and solved by means of step-by-step mathematical logic. By this means, untenable hypotheses were to be rejected one by one until only the truth remained. This rational approach displaced reliance on established authority, as the material world at least could be measured, quantified, and brought within the grasp of human understanding.

While Bacon and Descartes devised methodologies based on observation and analysis, others were already employing these techniques using new instruments in their study of astronomy and physics. Johann Kepler (1571–1630) and Galileo Galilei (1564–1642) tested the validity of the Copernican hypothesis, which held that the Sun rather than the Earth was the center of the universe, and investigated planetary and terrestrial motion. Their conclusions disturbed the belief in a cosmic order that extended from a creator to the least of his creations in a great chain of being. The Earth was removed from the center of the solar system, man's unique place in the universe was questioned, and human faith in a divine being in constant and direct control of the physical world was undermined.

It remained for Isaac Newton (1642–1727) to provide the synthesis and mathematical explanation of motion that suggested that the whole material universe could be understood using the scientific method. Newton's law of universal gravitation, modified only in the late nineteenth century, held that a precise

1.1. Galileo presents his telescope to the Doge of Venice in August 1609. (Scala/Art Resource, New York)

mathematical relationship described the force by which every body in the universe attracted every other body. It is not surprising that such an assertion encouraged a desire to discover scientific laws in every aspect of the material world.

This rise of modern science coincided with the development of an international scientific community and the establishment of institutions promoting scientific study. Scientists corresponded, traveled, visited, and organized bodies such as the Royal Society of London and the Royal Academy of Science in France, proposed projects, held meetings, and published periodicals. Although applied investigations led to improvements in navigation and weaponry, scientific developments had few consequences for the daily life of the masses in the seventeenth century. The primary outcome was to expand knowledge about nature among the educated and to promote a new way of obtaining knowledge.

The scientific method and its practitioners were highly critical of old techniques that had relied on established authority, sources, and tradition. While some thinkers turned their attention to investigating human society to discover its natural laws and advocate modifications accordingly, scientists usually tended not to take the lead. For example, both Descartes and Newton earnestly wrote in defense of the existence of God and argued for the truth of fundamental Christian doctrines.

Discovery and exploration of the world overseas provided new knowledge about humanity and gave impetus to the direct study of society. The impact of European expansion on other parts of the world was obvious; however, reciprocal influences were also at work. Upper-class Europeans were exposed to a wide range of products from other continents and European material wealth grew. Educated people became aware of an unsettling array of political, economic, and cultural systems abroad. This evidence called into question Europe's assumed monopoly on truth and civilization and led to the emergence of strong currents of skepticism in the sixteenth century.

Michel de Montaigne (1533–1592) exemplified a cautious attitude as expressed in the famous question, "What do I know?" with the implied answer, "Nothing." In his essays, he suggests that no certain knowledge is possible and that beliefs and customs vary with no definitive judgment being possible. In the seventeenth century the questioning became increasingly determined as it broadened in scope. Pierre Bayle (1647–1706) provided in his *Historical and Critical Dictionary* (1690) a compendium of articles that continued as a favorite reference book of Enlightenment thinkers. This collection conveys the message that what was held as truth by tradition and authority may only be opinion or, worse yet, superstition, with no firm basis available for conclusion or resolution.

The most direct attack on the great problem of knowledge was launched by John Locke (1632–1704) in his *Essay Concerning Human Understanding* (1690). He believed that certain knowledge is derived from direct experience through the perceptions of the sense organs and reflection by the mind on these perceptions. At birth the mind is a blank tablet, or tabula rasa, completely open to environmental influences. Knowledge and subsequent human behavior are products of the environment and can be altered by improvements to social institutions. In this way, Locke's theory contributed to the view that planned constructive action for the purpose of changing institutions and altering collective behavior can ultimately result in social progress.

The question of collective action leads to seventeenth-century political theory and another of Locke's works, *Two Treatises on Government.* Locke's perspective on government must be viewed within the context of his time and the concepts of "natural right" and "natural law." As a rational animal, man is able to use the power of reason to understand the natural law that is integral to the structure of the world. This law is not a human invention, and it distinguishes right from wrong, regardless of time, place, or culture. He concluded that by nature humans possess certain rights that individuals on their own are unable to protect. Therefore, they enter into a social contract creating a government charged with the responsibility of ensuring such basic rights as life, liberty, and property. That government is, however, also constrained by the obligation to observe these self-same rights. In the extreme, should a government violate these contractual rights, the people, having created that government, may exercise their sovereign right to rebel against it. As dramatic as these thoughts appear for their time, caution must be exercised in attributing too much modernity to any of the seventeenth-century thinkers. For Locke, full participation in the social contract and exercise of rights was limited to those possessing wealth and status. Although his examinations of the analogy between family and government led him to view marriage as a form of social contract, he rejected the equality of women in everyday life.

From these antecedents stemmed belief in reason, natural law, and progress. They brought with them the assumption that human reason was capable of discovering the natural laws that governed existence and that structuring a society in accordance with these laws would ensure unending progress. A mechanical interpretation of the universe, along with skepticism and optimism, served to challenge established authority.

The Philosophes: The Inner Circle

The eighteenth-century intellectuals to whom the spread of Enlightenment ideas is attributed were the French philosophes. Few possessed extensive academic credentials. Many were journalists, publicists, freelancers, even economic and political reformers. Their goal was not the development of systems of thought for the purpose of investigating ultimate questions of existence. Rather, like the thinkers of the Renaissance, they placed man at the center of intellectual activity and sought to understand the complexities of the world in which they lived.

To this task they brought the knowledge provided them by Newton, Locke, and other figures of the previous centuries. Their goal was to pursue the implications of the knowledge that emerged through sense perception and reflection rather than continually to accept the dictates of established authority. In the same way that the Marquis de Laplace (1749–1827), French mathematician, astronomer, and physicist, rounded out Newton's investigations into celestial mechanics, they wanted to complete the journeys begun in the seventeenth century by using rational analysis to solve the concrete problems of their time. They turned their attention to problems arising from economics, justice, education, religion, and politics. In so doing, policies and institutions were scrutinized in the confidence that natural laws could be discovered and used to implement constructive reforms. Such activities soon brought them into conflict with authority, with the result that the intellectual freedom needed to realize their objectives was hindered by censorship and defensive measures taken by church and state in most European countries.

This challenge to the established beliefs and institutions, aimed at achieving progress, was not based on uniformity of mind and conformity of effort. While the philosophes shared a style of thinking amplified by a critical spirit, there were variations in attitude and vision arising from differences in class, generation, and nationality. Not all were steeped in an optimistic outlook. Despite the attention directed to practical problems and issues, they were not revolutionary crusaders seeking to usurp authority. The philosophes were thinkers and communicators who established a "republic of letters." This consisted of a loose coalition of literary men and women scattered across western Europe, and while membership in this international family, with its cosmopolitan program, spanned the continent, its headquarters remained in France. France was still the wealthiest and most populous country in Europe, and French remained the international language of the educated classes in the eighteenth century. It is, therefore, not surprising that the Enlightenment was centered in France.

This intellectual leadership is clearly evident in the early stages of the eighteenth century as the prominent figures of Baron de Montesquieu (1689–1755), François Marie Arouet (Voltaire) (1694–1778), and Denis Diderot (1717–1784) dominated the discourse with a surge of new ideas about society, religion, and politics. To avoid censorship, imprisonment, or the exile that could result from criticism of church and state, the philosophes resorted to spreading their message through subtleties, satires, and double entendres in the content of their novels and plays, as well as through their histories, dictionaries, and encyclopedias. A brilliant example comes from the early works of Montesquieu, who was a presiding judge in the Parlement of Bordeaux, a position inherited from an uncle. In addition to his judicial function, he also engaged in business and academic activities. His views were at times questioned by fellow philosophes for too strongly representing the interests of his social class, but nonetheless the ideas he popularized were fundamental to the Enlightenment. In *Persian Letters* (1721), he satirized European customs by exposing existing practices and beliefs to the critical eye of supposed Persian travelers. Their political and religious comments include the observations that monarchy invariably deteriorates into despotism and that religious wars are the product of intolerance on the part of those who believe in the superiority of their own faith. In early eighteenth-century France, such views constituted an affront to the state and church and were unbecoming enough of a magistrate to require their publication under an assumed name. However, *Persian Letters* served to bring the young writer to the attention of the Parisian elite and provided, in the form of letter writing, a model that would be used frequently throughout the century for the presentation of controversial views.

In his most famous work, *The Spirit of Laws,* Montesquieu turned his attention to government and politics (see appendix, Document I). Applying critical inquiry and historical study to political institutions, Montesquieu concluded that climate and geography determined social customs and forms of government. He attributed vigor, courage, and virtue to people in colder climates and deemed warmer zones more conducive to passion, vice, and cunning. It was because of climate, he suggested, that in hot regions women were marriageable as children and usually aged rapidly. This fact justified the practice of polygamy. According to his theory, more temperate climates ensured slower aging, preserved individual charm, and were conducive to monogamy. These views appear absurd to us, but Montesquieu's efforts to identify regularities in human society and their causes illustrate the Enlightenment quest for natural laws. As Montesquieu began his search for common elements, he proclaimed, "Laws, in their most general signification, are the necessary relations arising from the nature of things."

The influence of geography on government, Montesquieu argued, is more complex than is its impact on social customs. In his view, political systems were the product of the national culture and character. These had been previously determined by physical factors that included, among other things, the total area of the territory governed. Montesquieu concluded that monarchy passes into despotism as its area increases and that democracy is best suited to small city-states.

These hypotheses, of course, did not stand the test of time or experience. Montesquieu's most famous and influential proposal was for separation of powers and a system of checks and balances. Reflecting on Locke's ideas and his personal experiences in England, he believed that a separation of the executive, legislative, and judicial functions would prevent the undue abuse of power by any one branch of government. Montesquieu admired the balance that England appeared to have achieved since the latter part of the seventeenth century in distributing power among monarchy, Parliament, and independent courts. He suggested that a similar result could be achieved in France by using the regional *parlements*, which were dominated by the aristocracy, to check the legislative and executive prerogatives exercised by royal absolutism. These *parlements* were courts of law, located in Paris and twelve provincial cities, which administered royal justice and served as courts of appeal. In addition, they had the power to register edicts of the king. By refusing to register a royal decree, a *parlement* could block actions of the monarch and thereby influence law making. While certainly not democratic, and while viewed as conservative even by some contemporaries for his support of a strong role for nobility in preventing royal despotism, Montesquieu, like Locke, held that the ultimate source of political authority was popular sovereignty and not divine right.

The name Voltaire has come to be almost synonymous with the Enlightenment. The son of a notary, he was sent as a child to Paris to be educated by the Jesuits in preparation for a career in the law. Voltaire instead made a name for himself as a poet and dramatist while still a young man. In his early works, the wit and sarcasm of his social commentary produced controversy in society and turbulence in his life. Since publication and distribution of ideas in all forms in the eighteenth century was construed to be a political act, it is understandable that Voltaire's literary gifts, while securing him entrance into the

fashionable salons of the Parisian elite, also resulted in his exile and imprisonment. At twenty-one he was briefly exiled from Paris for an insult to the regent. This was compounded by another published attack, attributed to
Voltaire, which sent him to the Bastille for eleven months, followed by further
banishment. At this time he began using the name Voltaire. Subsequent public acclamation, including royal acceptance for his poetry and plays, was followed by yet another controversy, a dispute with a nobleman that resulted in
three years of voluntary exile in England. His return to France marked
Voltaire's first major published contribution to the Enlightenment, *Letters on
the English* (1733). He acknowledged the intellectual debt his generation
owed to Locke and Newton, praised English economic achievements, and admired the tolerance evident in religion and the press. Voltaire did not share
Montesquieu's hope that a system of checks and balances similar to that
found in England, but dependent on the *parlements,* could serve to counter
monarchical power in France. While he approved of popularly elected representative bodies, he nevertheless had strong doubts about the wisdom of involving the masses in government. Voltaire placed his faith in the education of
enlightened monarchs who, ruling with knowledge of and adherence to the
principles of natural law and natural rights, would provide for government action in the best interests of the entire population. He also suggested that each
state needed to develop a political system best suited to its history.

Voltaire's return to France also coincided with the beginning of his association with the Marquise Emilie du Chatelet (1706–1749). Their initial
meeting arose from Voltaire's business dealings, but their intellectual collaboration and romantic interest lasted until her death in 1749, with the knowledge of her tolerant and frequently absent military husband. Because she was
a woman, the Marquise was restricted in her academic endeavors and access
to publication opportunities, but she nevertheless succeeded in translating
Newton's *Principia Mathematica* into French and publishing an essay, *Exposition Abrégée du Systeme du Monde.* She also contributed to the debate
raised by the new scientific ideas in her *Institutions des Physiques,* an essay
published in 1740. Her chateau near the Lorraine border afforded Voltaire
an easy escape from French authorities when circumstances warranted, and
it also contained an extensive laboratory where she and Voltaire conducted
experiments in chemistry and physics. Her devotion to science was unquestioned, and in unpublished manuscripts, as well as in private and salon con-
versations, she contributed to the philosophes' understanding of recent scientific developments. Voltaire's interests and inclinations took him in other
directions. After the death of the Marquise, he spent almost two years in the

court of Frederick II of Prussia, whom he labeled "the Great," probably because he came closest to Voltaire's ideal of an enlightened ruler. Nor did he neglect the French monarchy, completing in 1751 his *Age of Louis XIV*, a history in praise of the achievements of the Sun King. Although critical of despotic and arbitrary monarchical actions, he did not condemn the institution of the monarchy and had even gained enough court support to have himself appointed royal historian (1745).

The cause of religious tolerance rather than that of political reform consumed his greatest energies. In early dramas and poems and in *Letters on the English*, he had denounced the narrow imposition of belief and the harsh intolerance of the church. During the second half of his life, he went on to become a vocal and determined crusader for tolerance. During the 1760s he took up the cause of a Protestant, Jean Calas, who had been wrongly convicted and tortured to death for the murder of his son. The father's awareness that the younger Calas intended to convert to Catholicism was the apparent motive. Supporters of Jean Calas maintained he was guilty only of attempting to cover up the son's suicide to prevent public scandal and financial ruin. Voltaire launched a campaign to reopen the case, lending not only his pen and finances to the cause but requesting funds from foreign heads of state. He highlighted the case as an atrocious example of religious fanaticism, part of a long history of Christian intolerance and persecution encompassing Catholic and Protestant faiths alike. Four years after the initial trial, the king's council proclaimed Jean Calas innocent. Voltaire's famous cry of "crush the infamous thing" (*écrasez l'infâme*) arose from the tribulations of the Calas affair. Despite his strong stand, Voltaire did see value in religion and retained a belief in God. Like many of the philosophes, Voltaire's religious views may be regarded as deist. Deists maintained that there were a few common religious principles that could be arrived at through reason alone. There was in essence a natural religion that included the ability to distinguish between good and evil and a belief in a supreme being. This God, however, was not an interventionist being who worked through mystery and miracles in everyday life. In place of such "superstition," the Newtonian world implied the existence of a creator who had set the universal machine in motion and was not concerned with the day-to-day affairs of humans, although he might preside over his creation at the Last Judgment.

Voltaire accepted these rational tenets, and in the *Philosophical Dictionary* (1764), he subjected Christian belief and practice to scrutiny, identifying contradictions and absurdities. Like Bayle's, Voltaire's dictionary became a cherished source of argument for philosophers, while authorities in a number of major European cities responded by burning available copies. Earlier, in *Candide* (1759), the most enduring of Voltaire's works, he entertained his generation with another satirical work that not only assailed superstition and fanaticism, but questioned the optimism so frequently portrayed by writers of the time.

In 1751 Denis Diderot and Jean le Rond d'Alembert (1717–1783) began collaboration on the twenty-eight volume *l'Encyclopédie*, which was to become the Enlightenment's largest project. The backgrounds of these two men were ideally suited to the compilation of material for such an endeavor. Diderot had written plays and articles on a variety of topics, translated major works and tutored pupils, and had gained extensive writing and editing experience. D'Alembert was a respected mathematician who held a position in the Academy of Sciences in Paris. Their collaborative effort was an attempt to produce a compendium of scientific and social knowledge, not only for the sake of compiling information in a single reference, but, in Diderot's words, to "change the general way of thinking." With contributions from many of the philosophes, including Montesquieu, Voltaire, Rousseau, and d'Holbach, as well as Diderot, it reflected the spirit of the age in its skepticism, rationality, and scientific orientation. In addition, it presented knowledge in a manner critical of existing society and institutions. More than any other work of the age, *l'Encyclopédie* was a storehouse of knowledge and ideas created by the philosophes and widely read by a growing literate public. Thus, it not only described and reflected the character of the era, but contributed to the impetus for change. That it was regarded as a threat is substantiated by its official suppression in France, but Diderot continued to publish the work abroad.

The Philosophes: A Widening Circle

Around the midpoint of the eighteenth century, the circle of intellectuals who contributed to Enlightenment ideas increased in number. The currents of thought set in motion during the first half of the century continued; they were broadened in some respects, more thoroughly explored in others, and presented new and interesting challenges. Jean-Jacques Rousseau (1712–1778) represents both continuity and change in Enlightenment thought. Although he gained entry into the intellectual circles of Paris, his origins and temperament contrast with those of his contemporaries. Born in Geneva, Switzerland, his youth was an unhappy one; his mother died in childbirth and his father left him from the age of ten to be brought up by relatives.

Rousseau wandered from Switzerland to Italy and into France in his youth, working at odd jobs, until he gained access to upper-class gatherings in Paris, becoming friendly with Diderot, and in 1749 winning an essay contest sponsored by the Academy of Dijon. Although his subsequent publications were a literary success, his private life and associations with other philosophes remained difficult. He maintained a lengthy relationship with a mistress, Thérèse Levasseur, fathering five children, all of whom were sent to orphanages. In the intense atmosphere of Enlightenment society, he remained an outsider. His lower-class origins, his ideas, and his behavior explain this in part; however, he frequently distanced himself from others through distrust and suspicion. Regardless of the role played by social maladjustment or personality traits, it is certain that his writings had an immediate impact on society, as well as a profound continuing influence. His prize winning essay, published in 1750, paid tribute to "the achievements of minds and men which had succeeded in dissipating by the light of reason all the thick clouds by which [man] was by nature enveloped." Such a perspective won the applause of his fellow students, and yet the work also presented a challenge, for it asserted that civilization and apparent human progress had corrupted the essential goodness of natural humanity. Rousseau attributed the best human traits of compassion, honesty, understanding, and sympathy to nature. All of these, he maintained, had been corrupted by the existence and growth of social institutions. His attack on these endeared him to other philosophes, but his injection of feeling and intuition as part of the solution was regarded as "primitivism," or as an "idealization of the uncomplicated." In other words, it lacked intellectual sophistication.

In the 1760s Rousseau moved from social criticism to revealing his prescription for humanity. Although the original, uncorrupted state of nature could not be recaptured, it was necessary to move beyond the man-made restrictions of civilization. The nature of these human possibilities was made clear in two novels, *Julie, or the New Heloise* and *Emile*. In the former, he presents the ideal picture of a happy marriage of fidelity, devotion to children, economic efficiency and justice, religious tolerance, and sensitivity to the beauty of nature. It was a popular success, but his fellow philosophes were less enthusiastic about the novel because its rural setting and its idealization of nature, emotions, and the senses did not fit with the order and reason of the world of the philosophes. In *Emile*, Rousseau turned his attention to the type of education that would ensure a young child's proper development, despite an imperfect environment. Under the guidance of a moral adult, Emile is tutored in surroundings that allow little contact with family members. Rather than teaching from books, the tutor uses nature, example, and instinctive conscience to achieve his goals. The whole issue was rather a thorny one for Rousseau who found himself pondering the question of whether a man who had abandoned his own children could credibly discuss education. However, *Emile,* controversial as it was in its own day for its views, which included the portrayal of women as having the capacity for intellectual development, proved inspirational to later generations as well.

The opening statement of Rousseau's *The Social Contract* (1762), "Man is born free and everywhere he is in chains," remains one of the most stirring passages in Western literature. This work also presents one of the greatest problems of interpretation in political theory. In it Rousseau appeared to contradict his earlier assertion regarding the goodness of man in a state of nature by contending that society was necessary if human progress was to take place. The need for structures posed the problem of how the liberty accorded to individuals by natural right was to be reconciled with the institutional limitations imposed by the existence of government. The solution was embodied in Rousseau's conception of a social contract, which for him was not just an agreement between ruler and ruled, as Locke supposed. Rather, Rousseau seemed to regard the contract as constituting a consensus, or rational unity, among the people themselves, leading to an alternative application of popular sovereignty. From this consensus, a government is elected that possesses the authority to enact the "general will." This general will does not necessarily represent the wishes of the majority, nor the sum total of individual desires, but the fulfillment of the best interests of the community. This could even be at variance with the wishes of any one person or even of many people. An individual can only be truly free when acting in accordance with the welfare of the collective entity. This led Rousseau to state emphatically that government must at times "force" its citizens to be free.

This controversial formulation has given rise to varied interpretations. Some have followed or extended Rousseau's argument to justify complete subordination of individual interests to the common good. Since Rousseau doubted the readiness of people to participate fully in democracy, this could be the common good as defined by an elite. Others have found in the concept an argument for economic equality, seeing it as a prerequisite for participation in the general will, since only then could private interest be transcended. Although the impact of *The Social Contract* was minimal at first, it became a standard by which to critique contemporary politics. And after the tumultuous events of the French Revolution, it emerged as a source of intensive debate.

Some Enlightenment writers, particularly in the last quarter of the century, focused their attention on specific policy issues. In Milan, Cesare Bonesana, Marquis of Beccaria (1738–1794), a professor and civil servant who was well versed in the writings of the French philosophes, published *On Crimes and Punishment* (1764) (see appendix, Document II). His ideas were to have a direct influence on the policies of a number of European states. Beginning with observations made by Montesquieu on penal policies, Beccaria enlarged a debate that continues to this day. He held that the actions of the state in respect to justice must not only protect society, but respect the dignity of individuals, including criminals. In his analyses, Beccaria identified some principles based on natural law. These included his assertion that the purpose of punishment is to deter others from committing crime. In addition, he believed that justice must be achieved quickly and that the certainty of punishment, rather than its severity, serves the primary purpose of deterrence. He thus held that punishment should be commensurate with the injury done to society and must not be based on its association with sin. Torture, capital punishment, and barbarous treatment, he believed, all undermined public support for the law. Beccaria wanted public trials to be held in accordance with consistent standards and equitable treatment for all before the law, regardless of social origin. "Justice," he argued "is the hand which is necessary to keep the interests united, without which men would return to barbarity," a problem often associated in his eyes with public executions.

At this time in Europe, the prevailing economic theory was mercantilism, which maintained that wealth was to be measured by the possession of gold and other finite and fixed precious metals. This encouraged nations to pursue prosperity by achieving the most favorable balance of trade at the expense of competitors. The granting of monopolies, establishment of state enterprises, and expansion of colonies were all part of this economic program. In France, a group of thinkers known as *physiocrats*, who were more closely associated with government and policy implementation than were the philosophes, joined the quest to discover the natural laws governing economic behavior. They attacked the theory of mercantilism, and François Quesnay (1694–1774), a physician to Louis XV with a lifelong interest in economics, provided a whole new perspective in a series of articles that included contributions to *l'Encyclopédie*. The *physiocrats* contended that land, not gold, was the basis of wealth. Prosperity, they maintained, follows the establishment of conditions under which the people are able to use their labor and resources to create and exchange products freely, unhindered by government intervention. In an article on grain in *l'Encyclopédie*, he maintained that government controls supported arbitrary prices, thus undermining efficient production and distribution. The economic well-being of a nation could best be ensured if the people were able to trade products of land and industry without interference. This laissez-faire, hands-off approach would allow unencumbered natural processes to operate.

In Great Britain, the Scottish moral philosopher Adam Smith (1727–1790) formulated the classic statement of laissez-faire economics in his *Inquiry into the Nature and Course of the Wealth of Nations* (see appendix, Document III). Placing greater significance on commercial and industrial activities, Smith held that all components of economic endeavor contributed to progress and growth as long as the role of government was minimized. In an unregulated market, capital and labor, attracted by rising prices, would produce whatever was in short supply. Increases in supply would, in turn, lead to reductions in prices, thereby stimulating demand. Providers of goods and services who sought to maximize their profits and gain a competitive advantage would become more efficient to lower their costs. Consumers would reap the benefits of this competition through further reductions in prices. All parties, acting out of self-interest, would thus be guided by an "invisible hand" to serve the interests of the common good while maximizing their own goals. The same principles, Smith argued, applied internationally. Specialization of production and the unrestricted exchange of products would lead to increasing benefits for all countries. Here was an economic theory that assumed no apparent finite restrictions on economic potential. In place of the mercantilist threat of economic warfare, nations could be competitive partners in mutually beneficial exchanges, not unlike citizens within a country. These arguments, which maintained that freedom and abundance were not mutually exclusive, made Smith the prophet of the free market and free trade.

Although many women writers had published works in the eighteenth century, including Mary Astell with *Some Reflections on Marriage* and Christine McCauley with her eight-volume *History of England*, the scarcity of women in Enlightenment discourse is indicative of the limitations imposed by society, rather than a reflection of ability or effort. Similarly, the issues raised by the philosophes rarely focused on matters that incorporated concerns pertaining to the lives and status of women. In *l'Encyclopédie*, Diderot had recognized marriage as a contractual arrangement and subjected it to some rational analysis, noting that women had been victimized not only by pain in childbirth, but by defective education and a flawed legal system as well. However, in practice there remained the attitude that women by "nature" were morally inferior to men. Rousseau, in *Emile*, did not allow the prospective bride to read books prior to marriage lest she become knowledgeable and less docile.

It remained for Mary Wollstonecraft (1759–1797) to make the strongest argument of the time in Britain for logically extending natural rights and equality to women. In 1792, writing in the context of the tumultuous political developments taking place across the channel in the form of the French Revolution, Wollstonecraft published *A Vindication of the Rights of Women* (see appendix, Document IV), in which she argues that contemporary distinctions made between men and women are irrational. In addition, she calls for female suffrage

1.2. Mary Wollstonecraft, an early advocate of the rights of women (Tate Gallery, London/Art Resource, New York)

and granting of the right to hold elected office, thus precipitating a significant step in the discussion of the role and status of women in British society.

As already demonstrated by the experience of Rousseau, the primacy of reason was not unanimously accepted in the eighteenth century. As the century drew to a close, other complex currents of thought contributed to the Enlightenment. For example, the Scottish philosopher David Hume (1711–1776) examined the limits of reason as a means to practical knowledge. His persistent skepticism led him not only to criticize existing institutions, but to question whether reason and nature alone account for human knowledge and actions. Hume concluded that the simple ideas humans derived from sense impressions are combined into complex ideas that do not necessarily correspond to objective reality. This was due, he said, to the fact that their formulation is a product of habit rather than logic. While committed to the use of reason to analyze human behavior, Hume did not believe that immutable laws of nature were waiting to be discovered. When he turned his attention to religion, Hume found that the human need for gods originated in the fears experienced by primitive peoples in threatening environments. Polytheism developed over time into monotheism, which, in his view, did not herald progress but gave rise to division, dispute, and intolerance. Hume decided that neither reason nor progress was evident in the history of religion. Neither the established church nor deists were spared his criticism.

Even deeper criticism of religion came from the pen of Baron Paul d'Holbach (1723–1789), whose philosophic circle had briefly included the visiting Hume. D'Holbach deemed the origin of all religion and its primary human motivation to be the human need to avoid pain. In his *System of Nature* (1770), he extended his argument to develop a determinism that rejected all belief systems that were not guided solely by reason, experience, and nature. D'Holbach wrote:

> The enlightened man is man in his maturity, in his perfection, who is capable of pursuing his own happiness, because he has learned to examine, to think for himself, and not take that for truth upon the authority of others, which experience has taught him examination will frequently prove erroneous.

Such views, while not contrary to mainstream Enlightenment thought, carried d'Holbach to a rigid atheism that other philosophes found to be as dogmatic as church intolerance.

In Germany, the Enlightenment produced a number of intellectual variants of which the school of German idealism is the best known and Immanuel

Kant the most renowned proponent. The man who summarized the challenge of his era with the motto "Dare to know" thoroughly investigated how the individual can acquire knowledge. His answer did not provide comfort to those that placed supreme value on human reason. In contrast with the prevailing Enlightenment tendency to believe that knowledge reflects the objects of perception, Kant held that our minds are actively involved in creating knowledge, maintaining that the structure of the external world conforms to concepts present in the mind. These concepts are the products of individual experiences so that universal reason alone cannot be the basis of knowledge. In addition, Kant argued that there were some questions, such as the existence of God, which reason could not adequately address and would result in logical contradictions. In his mind, reason was capable of proving both thesis and antithesis. Kant was, in fact, asserting that the capacity of human reason to address the problems posed by life was not unlimited.

SOCIETY AND CULTURE

The philosophes constituted an elite component of the social, economic, and cultural milieu during the eighteenth century. The unique status of these writers and intellectuals and the bonds between them are captured in the expression associated with them, the "republic of letters." These individuals regarded themselves as part of a cosmopolitan group whose intellectual prowess cut across existing political and geographical boundaries. Those with the advantages of economics, education, and opportunity participated directly through the written word and through travel. In France, intellectuals eagerly read the journal *Nouvelles de la République des Lettres* produced by Pierre Bayle. From the British Isles, many undertook the continental "grand tour," and from the mainland, sojourns, whether voluntary or forced by political exile, were frequent.

Enlightenment Thought and the Public

Central to the discussion and dissemination of enlightened ideas were the salons, academies, and Masonic lodges of the eighteenth century. Salons, gatherings of the social and cultural elite presided over by a host or hostess, had become part of urban life in the preceding century and provided contact between intellectuals, including foreign visitors, thereby adding to the exchange of new ideas. Participants could express themselves without fear of reprisal from authorities; however, they were required to do so in a manner that made their ideas understandable, thus increasing their potential for wider dissemination and influence. An important opportunity provided by the salons was that of making contacts that could result in official appointments or financial support.

Although such gatherings occurred in all of the major cities of Europe and many provincial towns, the most famous were held in Paris. There, as elsewhere, the salons were conducted mainly by women from noble or wealthy bourgeois families, although some of the philosophes themselves, like Voltaire and d'Holbach, also hosted sessions. The Parisian salons of greatest repute were those frequented by the renowned French philosophes and visiting intellectual and cultural dignitaries. Louis XV's mistress, the Marquise de Pompadour, was perhaps the most notable of the social elite to preside over such assemblies. However, the best-known hostesses included Marie Thérèse Rodet Geoffrin (1699–1777) and her rival Marquise Marie de Vichy-Chamrond de Deffand (1679–1780). Geoffrin, wife of a bourgeois merchant, conducted artistic gatherings on Mondays and reserved Wednesdays for literary discussions. At various times, the guests included Montesquieu, Voltaire, d'Holbach, and occasionally foreign figures, with King Gustavus of Sweden and the English philosopher David Hume among the most prominent. She also provided financial support for some philosophes and secretly gave money to Diderot's *l'Encyclopédie* when the project encountered financial difficulties in 1759. The Marquise de Deffand, separated from her military husband, also welcomed Voltaire, Montesquieu, and d'Alembert, but eventually became an antagonist of the encyclopedists. These and others like Madame Helveticus (1722–1780), wife of the French philosopher, and Julie-Jeanne de Lespinasse (1732–1776), one time companion and assistant to du Deffand, demonstrate the significance of women as protectors and facilitators of Enlightenment thought and art. One of the earliest salons was hosted by Anne-Thérèse de Marguenat de Courcelles, the Marquise de Lambert (1647–1733). In her youth, she had been encouraged in her literary interests at home, and she went on to publish works on education. De Lambert attracted to her circle a number of women who were also strongly dedicated to intellectual pursuits. This, however, was the exception in the salons, as men played the dominant role in conversation under the skilful guidance of their hostesses.

In addition, through the learned academies, eighteenth-century ideas reached a wider audience. The most prominent were institutions that had been established in national capitals such as the French Academy of Sciences, the

1.3. The reading of Voltaire's tragedy *L'orphelin de la Chine* at the salon of Madame Geoffrin (c.1755) (Réunion des Musées Nationaux/Art Resource, New York)

Royal Society of London, and the Berlin Academy. However, the number of these institutions increased markedly throughout the century, particularly in France, where there were academies in more than thirty provincial cities. These academies promoted intellectual activity by providing an institution where people interested in science and philosophy could gather regularly for discussion, debate, and lectures. Unlike the universities, which with few exceptions remained enclaves of established thought and doctrine, the academies encouraged the exploration of new ideas and began to contribute to a climate favorable to a wide range of reforms.

The Masonic lodge was a third formal institution that made possible the wider dissemination of Enlightenment ideas. This fraternal organization of the Freemasons probably originated out of seventeenth-century stonemasons' guilds, but a century later in England, the order aimed to bring people together around a set of universal religious beliefs that cut across conflicting dogmas and diverse socioeconomic backgrounds. The ideas of the early Enlightenment, which valued tolerance, reason, and progress, were welcomed, and Masonic organizations spread across Europe and North America. Although practices and beliefs were not uniform from one Masonic lodge to another, their humanitarian and educational activities made them effective organizations for spreading the messages of the Enlightenment.

The coffeehouses of the eighteenth century, although not formal organizations like academies or lodges, also played a significant role in the spread of new ideas. These establishments had originated in the previous century, when coffee had gradually become the favorite drink in England. This enthusiasm spread to the continent, and by 1715 there seem to have been more than 3,000 coffeehouses in London, where merchants in particular met for conversation and increasingly to conduct business. In the lively atmosphere of these public meeting places, informed discussion contributed to an increasing familiarity with new ideas and to their wider dissemination. Some establishments included intellectual figures among their clients. In London, Samuel Johnson's Literary Club met in a coffeehouse and Voltaire frequented the Café Procope in Paris, where many lively discussions took place.

Participation in salons or access to the academies was restricted by custom, if not by law. The popularity and activities of Masonic lodges and coffeehouses indicated that the greatest potential audience for the philosophes lay in the increasingly literate and growing middle class. The growth in literacy between the sixteenth and eighteenth centuries is attributed by many historians to the religious competition between Protestant and Catholic reformers, who were hoping to use reading as an effective means of proselytizing. The largest gains in literacy were made in the eighteenth century with 50 to 60 percent of males becoming literate in some regions of England and France. Although literacy among women was also increasing, a variety of social and cultural obstacles accounted for the fact that literacy rates for women were less than half those for men. To meet the demands and take advantage of the opportunities presented, the number of periodicals published in the eighteenth century increased significantly in England, where there were approximately twenty-five journals and newspapers in 1700 and over 150 a century later. These ranged from the famous *Spectator* of Joseph Addison and Richard Steel, specializing in single-issue essays, to erudite journals that featured critical articles on science and philosophy. In addition, larger circulation newspapers intended originally for entertainment were also beginning to report political news.

The book trade expanded dramatically. In France, it appears that the ownership of books may have increased as much as tenfold during the eighteenth century, and a major shift occurred as the number of secular titles grew more rapidly than the previously dominant religious ones. Erratic efforts at censorship presented obstacles; however, these did not stop the flow of critical books into France and other states as publishers smuggled works in through neighboring regions. While the writings of the philosophes certainly reached the general public through the great cultural project of *l'Encyclopédie*, which appeared between 1751 and 1782, it was nonetheless political and economic thought and social criticism in more popularized versions that had the widest readership. For example, a Swiss supplier receives the following request from a French bookseller: "Please send the invoice in advance: *Venus in the Cloister* or *The Nun in the Nightgown, Christianity Unveiled, Memoirs of Mme la Marquise de Pompadour, Inquiry on the Origin of Oriental Despotism, The System of Nature, Theresa the Philosopher, Margot the Campfollower.*" If the scarcity of recognizable philosophical titles is an indication, it seems that the reading public was not focused on abstract questions. Rousseau's most widely read works were his novels, not *The Social Contract*.

Beyond the popularization of scientific, historical, and philosophical writers lay the publishing world of the "scribblers," as Voltaire aptly named them. These individuals worked in a competitive journalistic milieu known in England as Grub Street. To survive, desperate writers and unscrupulous booksellers produced pamphlets that contained no abstract ideas, followed few principles, and provided no program. Depending on scandals, real or fabricated, sensational gossip, and scurrilous attacks, the pamphleteers criticized all aspects of the social order. Clergy, nobility, and royalty were favorite targets of this printed venom, which vulgarized and demeaned individuals by means of a combination of pornography and dubious moral innuendoes. The quantity of the material produced leaves no doubt as to the extent of its readership; however, its impact remains a matter of speculation. Although such attacks and criticisms did not disseminate ideas as such, their continuing influence did contribute to a progressive undermining of the existing social order. The exact extent to which printing and reading changed people's ideas and influenced their behavior is debatable. The presence of alternative literature suggests there were limits to the influence of secular thought. Many of the philosophes, in attempting to reach the educated public, did not believe they could have much impact on "the blind and noisy multitude." Some historians argue that differences between the upper and middle classes of society were not extensive, but that dramatic distinctions remained between the educated and privileged and the masses. In addition, the growth of libraries and the increasing popularity of reading clubs assisted in the spread of literacy among the commoners.[1]

Among the urban artisans and poor, as well as the peasants of the countryside, oral culture predominated, but there did exist a literature quite distinct from the reading material of the upper classes. Small books and pamphlets, usually written anonymously and printed on cheap paper, circulated and were read aloud to those who were illiterate. A large portion of this literature was religious and included Bible stories, catechisms, devotional manuals, and accounts of the lives of saints. Many were almanacs with practical information or instructional pamphlets that gave advice on daily living or health. Still other publications relayed a variety of tales, fables, or mixtures of fact and fiction that provided entertainment. Many historians regard this literature as having been escapist, or at least as having prompted acceptance of the status quo mainly because it did not confront problems with new ideas. Among the social groups who formed the audience, it is certainly more likely that the material supported tradition rather than promoted change.

Popular Culture and Religious Revival

In addition to the differences in literature, which indicate that the philosophy of the Enlightenment was far removed from the life and work of peasants and urban laborers, other aspects of popular culture suggest the social distance involved. As a counterpart to salons and coffeehouses, there existed local taverns where common people gathered for socializing and merrymaking, often with alcoholic beverages. Although the reform-minded artist William Hogarth (1697–1764) did not spare the English aristocracy in his visual social commentaries, the etching *Gin Lane* perhaps typifies the attitudes of the educated elite toward popular culture in the eighteenth century. Hogarth shows the results of excessive gin drinking by common people, in contrast to the desirable moderation evident in the companion piece *Beer Lane.*

Social interaction and recreation tended to bear the strong marks of tradition, as family gatherings and festivals combined with religious celebrations and popular recreation in the formation of common patterns. These provided occasions for socializing to take place between boys and girls, as well as ritual observations of the church calendar. Local soccer matches were becoming popular in England, but more commercially oriented recreation like traveling shows, horse racing, and boxing were also gaining importance. Blood sports remained popular. In bull baiting, a pack of dogs would attack a tethered steer that an innkeeper had usually provided, along with the site and the refreshments. This form of entertainment, as well as cockfighting, was increasingly denounced by the educated elite. Members of this class were in the process of embracing enlightened attitudes and, as a result, were experiencing a reduced enthusiasm for such pastimes.

1.4. *Gin Lane* by William Hogarth (Giraudon/Art Resource, New York)

The strongest indication that the common people were receptive to calls
for change was evidenced not by their response to intellectual appeals, but
by the religious revival of the eighteenth century. In the continental heartland
of the Reformation, the well-established Lutheran church was being viewed
by some of its members as having itself become hierarchical in structure and
complacent in its mission. The Protestant revival began in northern Germany with a movement known as Pietism. In place of theological concern
and doctrinal disputes, Pietists placed emphasis on Bible study, prayer, and

Christian rebirth in everyday life. They engaged in these activities, reasserted the priesthood of all believers, and went beyond personal inner renewal in the demonstration of their commitment. Pietists established schools, orphanages, and other charitable institutions within their communities. The majority remained members of the established churches; however, in a few instances differences gave rise to new sects, such as the Moravian Brethren founded by Count Nicholas Zinzendorf (1700–1760) in Saxony. Strongly influenced by these examples, John Wesley (1703–1791), a minister in the Church of England, launched a crusade to reinvigorate personal worship with emotional commitment and enthusiasm for good works. Labeled "methodists" by their critics for their constant devotional expressions, Wesley and his followers eventually broke with the Church of England in 1784 and established a new denomination in 1789. The message of Pietists and Methodists appealed least to the elites of their societies and gained the largest following among the lower classes, who felt their plight and position had been ignored by the religious hierarchy. Nevertheless, these Protestant religious movements were consistent with the call for less reason and more passion which occurred during the late Enlightenment.

It is more difficult to assess the strength of religious revival in Catholic regions of Europe. Roman Catholicism had earlier experienced resurgence, partly in response to Protestantism, but in the eighteenth century it was strongly attacked by many of the philosophes. The campaign led by Voltaire during the Calas affair was one of a number of instances in which repression and intolerance were publicly criticized. Despite such revelations, attacks, and anticlericalism, Catholic belief remained strong. Religion and the local parish church continued to play integral roles in community life. In some areas, clergy attempted to reduce or eliminate aspects of religious practices that were more associated with folklore or pagan ritual than with Christian belief. For example, it was difficult to dissuade peasants from the expectation that special blessings, saints' relics, or sacred springs would provide higher crop yields, physical healing, or family well-being. In any case, Catholics continued to attend church on major feast days in massive numbers. The piety of the common people was not diminishing, however confused their beliefs may have been.

High Culture

Scholars differentiate between popular culture, which is the written and unwritten culture of the common people, and high culture, the literary and artistic culture of the wealthy and educated segment of society. While popular culture remains essentially traditional, trends and shifts in high culture can be more readily associated with different time periods. However, such developments in eighteenth-century Europe were varied in nature, with continuity and change evident according to geography and tradition. The seventeenth century had witnessed a major surge of creative activity in the visual arts, producing the dominant baroque style of art and architecture. In the latter, the use of curved, flowing lines created a sense of motion, as is evident in the Bernini's colonnade in front of St. Peter's Cathedral in Rome and the papal throne he designed for the interior. In art, combinations of diagonal and curved lines and strong primary colors similarly evoked motion and drama. Artists of the seventeenth century like Caravaggio, Rembrandt, and Rubens are regarded as outstanding representatives of this style. In part, the baroque style had evolved to satisfy the aristocratic and royal patrons of the era, and the pattern continued into the early eighteenth century, but by the 1730s and 1740s, a new style known as rococo emerged. Derived from the French word *rocaille,* which referred to an elaborate decoration of rocks and shells frequently found in the grottos of baroque gardens, this style combined shell motifs with other scroll and ribbon elements to give an expression of lightness and gaiety. Paintings tended to explore pleasurable feelings and frequently included pastoral themes or simple daily activities. Interlaced designs with delicate and graceful contours contributed to an effect of softness and charm. This occurred concurrently with the prevalent concept of sensibility stemming from the psychology of Locke, which focused on sensation and experience as the basis of understanding.

In France, where the rococo style emerged, Antoine Watteau (1684–1721) revealed early in the century a world of aristocratic elegance and refinement, tinged with the recognition of the fragile nature of joy and pleasure. His *The Pilgrimage to Cythera,* which depicts upper-class pilgrims about to leave the island of Cythera after having paid homage to Venus, the goddess of love, illustrates this sensibility. Toward the end of the century, Watteau's countryman Jean Honoré Fragonard (1732–1806) depicted in *The Swing* a world of dreams, showing adults abandoning themselves to play in an enclosing landscape that shuts out the realities of life. The pastel hues and arrangement of trees focus attention on the delights of the young baron who commissioned the work and accentuate the charms of his mistress.

In architecture, rococo style was more conducive to interior decoration; ornamentation of the ceilings and walls and integrated paintings were intended to delight the eye with a sensual appeal. In France, the Pompadour rooms at Versailles serve as one example, but it was in the smaller chateaux

1.5. *The Pilgrimage to Cythera* by Antoine Watteau (Réunion des Musées Nationaux/Art Resource, New York)

and townhouses of the nobility where such decoration often occurred. In southern Germany and Austria, the relatively lengthy peace that followed extended religious conflicts provided an opportunity for new buildings that exemplify the complexity of rococo style. Two pilgrimage churches in southern Germany suggest the high point of rococo. Near Bamberg, the church of the Vierzehnheiligen (Fourteen Saints) designed by Balthazar Neuman (1687–1753), although displaying a relatively simple exterior, houses an interior of elaborate decoration. The ornate ceiling spills downward in a seemingly unbroken flow past a hidden conjunction with the walls. A series of curves then carry the viewer's eye to the floor. Outside the village of Wies, a pilgrimage church designed by Domenikus Zimmerman (1685–1766) presents even greater richness of detail. In a contemplative setting of meadows, distant forests, and mountains, the interior design is meant to evoke a joyful love of God.

A style in which artists competed with the exuberances of rococo emerged by the middle of the century. Classical models and themes had never been totally ignored or submerged in any of the visual arts, and by the 1750s general interest in antiquity and the unearthing of the ruins at Pompeii and Herculaneum renewed enthusiasm for ancient culture. In addition, the eighteenth-century emphasis on reason contributed to a preference for simplicity, order, and geometric form. These elements combined to favor compositions in paintings and building designs that incorporated more linear forms, restrained appeals to sentiment, and were subtler in their use of color. The style in which the artist expected to appeal more to intellect than the senses is known as neoclassicism. An architectural example is the portico of the Pantheon in Paris designed by Jacques Germain Soufflot (1755–1792), whose use of columns and pediments was inspired by ancient Roman temples. In painting, the style and content of *Oath of the Horatii* by Jacques Louis David (1748–1825) clearly contrasts with the lush and effete world of rococo artists. Making use of new knowledge of dress and style gained from excavations, David draws upon a Roman story to appeal to the civic virtues and honor of the viewers, rather than to their sentiments.

In England, Sir Joshua Reynolds (1723–1792), famous for his portrait paintings, introduced neoclassical restraint and calm into his work, frequently using elements derived from antiquity. His *Discourses to the Royal Academy,* dedicated to the institution of which he was to become president, presented a firm defense of eighteenth-century neoclassicism. Reynold's main rival, Thomas Gainsborough (1727–1788), is less open to categorization. His portraits rarely include classical elements, nor do his landscapes bear the lush marks of rococo. His work exhibits a straightforward quality that is relatively free of dramatic effect and embellishment.

Another English artist whose work was popular with contemporaries and defies easy classification is William Hogarth. His famous series of prints provides insightful observations and satirical comment on aspects of eighteenth-century English life. In addition to *Gin Lane* and *Beer Street,* Hogarth created a series entitled *The Harlot's Progress* (1732), *A Rake's Progress* (1735), and *Marriage à la Mode* (1745), among others. In true Enlightenment form, he drew upon varied sources for inspiration in his satirical and moral commentary on the frivolity, extravagance, and decadence of the privileged classes. He was internationally renowned and popularly favored by the middle class, among whom his works sold well.

The novel as a literary form gained popularity and experienced rapid development in the eighteenth century, reaching far beyond the merely romantic or picaresque as was characteristic of earlier works. Late in his career, Daniel Defoe (1660–1731) published *Robinson Crusoe* (1719), which became a success with middle- and lower-class readers, as well as a favorite of Enlightenment readers. The natural common sense, self-reliance, and independence demonstrated by the protagonist when confronting dangerous situations emphasized values prized by various elements of the reading public.

In 1740 Samuel Richardson (1689–1761) published his first of a number of sentimental novels, *Pamela, or Virtue Rewarded,* in which the author intimately and extensively describes private emotions and lauds the simple virtue of a heroine who contends with a scoundrel lover and his family. While it was an immediate success, there was also a negative reaction to the simplistic vision of morality presented in the novel. Henry Fielding (1707–1754) published a burlesque entitled *Shamala,* followed by *Joseph Andrews* (1742) and his masterpiece, *Tom Jones* (1749). Fielding's depictions of English life from the alleys of London to the stately country houses of the upper classes depicted characters enmeshed in believable, real-life experiences that gave his novels a complexity appreciated by the critical Enlightenment mind.

Similar in manner to Richardson's sentimentality were the novels of the French writer Antoine-François Prévost (1697–1763). But perhaps Rousseau's *La Nouvelle Heloise* and *Emile* are better examples of novels that portray love and duty in the same spirit. Prior to the end of the century, Johann Wolfgang von Goethe (1749–1832), in his short novel *The Sorrows of Young Werther* (1774), provided a critical examination of the young German's society. However, themes of self-pity and self-loathing were more prominent in the romantic movement, which was to assert itself in the nineteenth century.

Literary landmarks outside the realm of the novel in England include the work of Samuel Johnson (1709–1784) and Edward Gibbon (1737–1794). Johnson, striving to create order out of linguistic disarray, wrote his *Dictionary of the English Language* between 1747 and 1755 and, thus, ensured his position as "a Newton of the English language."[2] Classical interest and neoclassical temperament combined in Gibbon to produce the account of the glories and disintegration of the great Roman Empire. The final volumes of *History of the Decline and Fall of the Roman Empire* were published in 1788. The work was subjected to strong criticism from religious quarters as a result of his placing a significant part of the blame for the demise of the empire on Christianity. However, his critiques of intolerance, the prominence he gave to reason, and his commitment to freedom were welcomed by enlightened circles. This work has remained one of the masterpieces of eighteenth-century prose and a landmark of historical writing.

Music in the eighteenth century underwent perhaps the most significant development of all the arts. Audiences beyond the bounds of the privileged classes, which included mainly the courts of the monarchs and the homes of the wealthy, were introduced to the beauty of music. The traditional patronage of the elite in sustaining creative artists slowly gave way to public concerts, and public concert halls were built in major cities. Whereas changes in painting and literature are most strongly associated with France and England, it was in Austria and Germany that music flourished. In the early decades, baroque themes remained in the forefront. Johann Sebastian Bach (1685–1750), more famous as an organist and improviser than as a composer in his lifetime, was ultimately regarded as one of the greatest composers who ever lived. In comparison with other major musical figures, he lived a rather provincial life in Germany, but his prolific output includes a variety of forms. He favored the fugue, and his achievement in that style is best appreciated in a collection of works called *The Well-Tempered Klavier*. Throughout his compositions the single strongest theme is his deep religious faith, as exemplified in the powerful oratorio *Saint Matthew Passion*. Bach did not ignore the secular world. In the *Coffee Cantata* he satirized societal concerns about the new drink gaining popularity in Europe. His best-known works, however, are the six *Brandenburg Concertos* originally written for the private entertainment of one of his patrons, the Margrave of Brandenburg.

In contrast to Bach, George Frederich Handel (1685–1759), also born in Germany, gained early fame in Italy and later settled permanently in England. His most imposing efforts were his operas and oratorios, of which *The Messiah* became the best loved and most celebrated. The presence of 3,000 people at his funeral service attests to his having reached a musical audience in the middle class, far beyond the privileged circles of nobility and royalty.

The classical music that emerged in the second half of the eighteenth century shared with neoclassical art and literature a preference for clarity, balance, order, and a measure of intellectual weight. During this period, Franz Joseph Haydn (1732–1809) composed operas, string quartets, and piano sonatas, but made his greatest impact through his symphonies. The changes to the symphony, many of which were initiated by Haydn, are sometimes equated with the development of the novel in the eighteenth century. Haydn routinely wrote in four, rather than in three, movements and preferred to incorporate the newly developed pianoforte instead of the harpsichord. His innovations earned him the title "father of the symphony."

Haydn had a strong influence on Wolfgang Amadeus Mozart (1756–1791), whose contributions to music, frequently referred to as the classical synthesis, gave expression to the unity of reason and sensitivity:

[P]assions, whether violent or not, must never be expressed in such a way as to excite disgust, and music, even in the most terrible situations, must never

offend the ear, but must please the hearer, or in other words must never cease
to be music. . . . Melody is the essence of music.[3]

Such universality emerges in his compositions, which include all forms, but
personal emotions are also explored. He achieved this with a mastery of
technical skill recognized by Haydn, who remarked to the young man's father, "Before God and as an honest man, I tell you that your son is the greatest composer known to me either in person or by name."

Mozart applied his craft to a variety of musical forms including symphonies, masses, and string quartets, but of particular excellence were his series of concertos written for the piano. The rich themes that characterize
each work complement one another and leave the listener with a strong impression of coherence. Many regard Mozart's operas as his greatest achievements and as representing the best of human sensibility and aspiration. The
Marriage of Figaro expresses in restrained and classical form the varied feelings of the age, ranging from protest against the abuse of human rights to the
very personal emotions of resentment and pleasure.

Although Mozart experienced early recognition and acclaim, his brief life
sadly fell into increasingly difficult financial and personal circumstances.
However, to the end, his music continued to express the faith in humanity so
characteristic of the attitudes of many of the philosophes.

SOCIETY AND ECONOMICS

While science and thought had changed by the beginning of the eighteenth
century, everyday life had not. Reason and progress were still concepts for
the privileged few, and European society was largely agrarian, as it had been
for hundreds of years. It is little wonder then that the physiocrats responded
to the mercantilist argument with a focus on land rather than on commerce.
After all, land remained the economic basis of life. In all countries, more than
80 percent of the population lived in the countryside and depended directly
on the soil for a living; furthermore, most of the remainder relied to some degree on agriculture for their roles in the economy.

Land and Agriculture

Agricultural practices had changed very slowly since the Middle Ages. The
work of ploughing fields, sowing seed, and harvesting grain had not been

substantially affected by technological innovation, and the yields were little more than those of earlier centuries. In good years, enough food was produced to sustain the rural family, but poor harvests due to bad weather could result in rapid depletion of meagre reserves. This led to crises in which famine was compounded by illness and disease. Even when not severely affected by the whims of nature, peasants were subject to the impact of price fluctuations, with any change in supply or demand tending to affect the rural poor sharply, because crises in the countryside could be worse than in urban centers where local authorities usually provided stores of reserves.

The traditional open-field system was an important factor limiting agricultural production in much of western Europe. Peasants living in villages worked large fields in the surrounding areas that were divided into long, narrow strips, with individual families, either as owner-producers or tenant farmers, working patches scattered in the communal area. Whether they owned the property themselves or it was held by nobility, clergy, or wealthy townspeople, the pattern of farming was similar. To combat the problem of soil exhaustion, a three-year rotation system had developed in which two years of cropping were followed by a year of fallow for each strip. Each year at least one-third of all cropland lay idle. In addition "common" lands were set aside for hay making and grazing, and these remained unaltered over time. This system provided barely adequate supplies for the existing population and did not allow for potential increases in production. The precarious nature of this farming system was captured in Jean François Millet's famous nineteenth-century painting *The Gleaners*, which depicts impoverished French peasant women searching amidst stubble for grain and stalks the harvesters have missed.

Circumstances for peasants in eastern Europe, where many were still bound by the restrictions imposed by serfdom, were even harsher and more oppressive. Land ownership could entitle the lord to require hereditary service of peasants, as was the case with the *robot* in Austria; this amounted to forced labor. In Russia it was customary to enumerate property holdings by counting the number of male serfs or "souls," rather than by giving the size of land holdings. Because these serfs and their families could be sold with or without the land, the differences between serfdom and slavery were minimal.

Although social conditions for peasants in western Europe were better, and they were free to own land, daily life was still very harsh. The economic uncertainties resulting from weather and farming practices were compounded for the peasantry by their low status in the social hierarchy. In Britain and the Netherlands, serfdom had been replaced with landlord-tenant arrangements; however, in France in the eighteenth century, despite significant land ownership by peasants in some regions, vestiges of serfdom remained. Peasants who owned their land could still be legally required to pay a variety of feudal dues (for use of mill, wine press, and oven) and perform work on the land of the local lord. The state imposed additional burdens: property taxes, further work requirements such as the *corvée* (two or three days' road maintenance or monetary equivalent) in France, and taxes on essential commodities, particularly the *gabelle* (salt), were all inescapable.

The peasantry was not in a position to challenge the formidable political forces successfully to improve its condition. In Russia, dozens of peasant revolts in the eighteenth century culminated in a rebellion led by Emelyan Pugachev (1726–1775), who promised freedom and land to his followers. Like previous uprisings, this one was brutally crushed and its leader executed. Smaller revolts occurred in Bohemia, Transylvania, Moravia, and Austria. In western Europe large-scale protests generally did not occur. Whether violent or not, rural protests are regarded as having been conservative in nature, taking place in opposition to current reforms, which were perceived as threatening the precarious stability of the food supply.

Nonetheless during the eighteenth century new farming methods were introduced that in the view of some historians constituted an agricultural revolution. Slow implementation of technological innovations rather than radical political action brought about improvements in production. Many of the new methods originated in the Netherlands. This more densely populated region, with a higher degree of urbanization stimulated by commerce and trade, created pressure and markets for foodstuffs. Marshes and swamps were drained to increase the area under cultivation. The practice of fallowing land was replaced by continuous rotation of alternating grains, which served to rejuvenate soil and increase production. Well-established crops such as peas and beans were systematically rotated with newer varieties from overseas such as turnips, potatoes, and clover. Some of the new crops served as animal feed, allowing farmers to maintain cattle and sheep through the winter. This provided not only an improved diet for people, but more manure for fertilizer, which further enhanced crop yield. While the Dutch provided initial leadership, the English quickly took advantage of Dutch expertise by employing engineers and workers from the Netherlands to carry out drainage projects, which brought new fertile land under cultivation. Dutch precedents were also significant in the introduction of new crops to eastern England by Charles Townsend (1674–1738). Enthusiastically using clover and particularly turnips in crop rotation, he earned the nickname "Turnip" Townsend, as production on his estates increased substantially.

This motivation to improve farming methods was also evident in the contributions of Jethro Tull (1674–1741). With an enlightened attitude, Tull conducted research and experiments in ploughing and seeding, the use of horses as draft animals, and selective livestock breeding, all with considerable success. New methods of animal breeding were also pioneered by Robert Bakewell (1725–1795), resulting in larger and more productive livestock and more meat and milk on English tables. Advances in English agriculture were noted with satisfaction by agronomist and traveler Arthur Young (1741–1820), who commented in his *Travels in France* that the average yield of wheat and rye was twenty-four bushels in England, but only eighteen in France. He also maintained that the quality of wheat and corn in France was inferior to that of England. More significant than Young's strongly biased observations is his attribution of the French disadvantage to the continuation of leaving a field fallow each year and the small size of landholdings.

The gains made in England through technological innovation and land reorganization entailed costs, which fuelled controversy at the time and contribute to historical debate today. The traditional open-field system, with its multiple strips, the practice of fallowing, and the provision of "commons" for pasture imposed production limits. Yet, in the experience of peasant farmers, any proposed changes appeared to threaten the tenuous stability of the peasants' lives. It is then not surprising that the initiative for agricultural change came from those able to bear the risk of innovation and investment in new technology. The large landowners used legislation as a basis for enclosing lands to engage in large-scale enterprises. And since they also controlled Parliament, "enclosure acts" were passed, which authorized the enclosure of land that was rented to tenant farmers.

The debate surrounding the impact on peasants and tenant farmers of blocking fields for innovative large-scale production remains unresolved. Some historians focus on the injustice of large landowners with economic and political power forcing the fencing of open fields and the division of "commons." The latter were divided in proportion to property held in open fields. The extensive costs resulting from surveying and legal procedures were divided among all landowners, forcing many peasants to sell out simply to cover their share of the expenses. Those already landless no longer had access to the commons where they had been able to raise an animal or two while working for others. Other historians maintain that the consolidation not only provided the benefit of increased food production, but that it did not significantly increase the proportion of landless laborers dependent on farming. While acknowledging that the rate of enclosure increased in the second half of the century, they note that much land had already been consolidated as early as the sixteenth century, when sheep pastures were enclosed in response to the increasing demand for wool in textile production. The number of small independent peasant farmers simply continued to decline in the eighteenth century.

What perhaps can be said is that the changes constituted a slow process of commercialization of agriculture in England and Scotland. Increasingly, large landowners held most of the agricultural property, leasing the land to tenant farmers who produced for cash markets and relied on landless laborers for their workforce. More production was estate based and market oriented to maximize profits. Many peasant farmers became landless rural wage earners; however, the countryside was not depopulated, nor were large numbers forced into towns. Nonetheless, traditional communities and existing social patterns were disrupted, producing a degree of unrest. Protests escalated to riots in some areas, and Parliament responded by passing the Waltham Block Act in 1723. This legislation created new categories of crime, which allowed for conviction of individuals who appeared to have suspicious intent while in forests or enclosed lands. Landlords used their political power to ensure the security of their productive estates.

Although the early efforts and inspiration for agricultural change are usually traced to the Netherlands, reforms elsewhere on the continent were slow and minimal. In France much was published about new farming techniques, including articles in *l'Encyclopédie*. However, ideas tended to remain matters for discussion rather than implementation. As Young noted in his observations, traditional practices predominated into the 1780s. Further to the East, limited improvements occurred in production by increasing the amount of land under cultivation. As the emphasis shifted to profit-oriented agriculture in eastern Europe, landlords tended to place greater pressure on tenants and serfs rather than modify existing technology to improve productivity.

Population and Production

The slowly expanding food supply, which resulted from farming innovations, contributed to the growth of the European population in the eighteenth century. Population increases alternating with periods of stability and even decline had characterized the uneven demographic pattern in previous centuries. However, in the eighteenth century the increase from about 120 million to 190 million was noticeable, even if the statistics were unavailable

1.6. New farming techniques as illustrated in Diderot's *l'Encyclopédie* (Courtesy of Bruce Peel Special Collections, University of Alberta Libraries)

at the time. Thomas Malthus (1766–1834) in his *Essay on the Principle of Population* extrapolated from limited empirical evidence that an increasing food supply was responsible for the population growth. However, since the food supply grew arithmetically while the population multiplied exponentially, famine was a natural check on population. Other factors, Malthus noted, were plague and disease, war, and infant mortality. Subsequently, with more complete data available, it became apparent that he was describing conditions that more appropriately applied to earlier centuries. The diminishing impact of these Malthusian death-rate factors was allowing the population to increase. The gradual disappearance of the bubonic plague in Europe was a critical component and largely a consequence of chance: the black rat, which carried the flea that transmitted the bacillus to humans, was driven out by a competing brown rat for unknown reasons. Other factors that reduced disease and epidemic were improvements in water supply and sewage in towns and the drainage of marshes and swamps. The former reduced the incidence of typhoid and typhus, while the latter reduced insect populations that transmitted disease. The nature of warfare changed as more professional armies employed strategies with less impact on civilian populations. The result was a reduction in casualties and fewer epidemics. These, in addition to an increasing food supply, contributed to population growth as the death rate declined, while the birth rate remained unchanged. What Malthus could not have predicted, rendering his view quite pessimistic, was the vast increase in productivity that was to take place with the mechanization of agriculture. This provided a food supply that more than kept pace with population growth.

Population increases and agricultural transformation contributed to another economic development during the nineteenth century: the growth of industry in rural areas. Although based on agriculture, peasant communities had always produced some manufactured goods on a small scale, primarily out of necessity. Large-scale handicraft production was controlled by craft guilds and merchants in urban centers, who regulated production and distribution by means of monopolies. In the eighteenth century, the rural poor, seeking to supplement meager farming incomes, provided an opportunity for urban textile merchants to bypass the control of guilds. Under the putting-out system (also called domestic or cottage industry), textile merchants contracted with peasants to spin and weave finished products from unfinished fibers. The merchants then sold the goods and paid the workers. Various arrangements between merchant capitalists and rural workers appeared in England and then spread gradually and unevenly across western and central Europe. Sometimes spinners and weavers worked independently, obtaining their own materials and equipment, but merchants were usually in a better position to acquire raw materials and purchase machinery. Whatever the relationship between capitalist and worker, this unregulated form of production outside the jurisdiction of urban guilds provided essential earnings for rural families. Frequently, the work was apportioned among men, women, and children so that all contributed to the family enterprise. Although textiles predominated, other goods such as various housewares or even luxury items for the wealthy were produced.

The introduction of technological inventions, commonly associated with the beginnings of the Industrial Revolution, began to transform the process before the end of the century. John Kay (1704–1764) invented the flying shuttle in the 1730s, and its introduction into the industry after 1750 created a production bottleneck. This invention increased the speed of loom operation and the productivity of weavers. The imbalance was addressed in the 1760s when James Hargreaves developed the spinning jenny, which allowed simultaneous spinning initially of sixteen and then of increasing numbers of spindles of thread. Acquisition of the new equipment increased capital costs, but they continued to be operated on a cottage basis or sometimes in small rural workshops. In the last decades of the eighteenth century, cotton textile manufacturing began to move from the cottage to the factory, following the invention of the water frame by Richard Arkwright (1732–1792), which allowed the use of waterpower to drive spinning frames. The imbalance shifted in favor of spinning with the development of the spinning mule by Samuel Compton. Now the demand was for faster weaving, a need filled by Edward Cartwright's water-powered loom in 1785. Since these processes now had to be located by streams, the initial factories remained part of the rural landscape, close to the source of cheap labor.

During the eighteenth century, the continent remained predominantly rural, with less than 20 percent of the European population living in urban centers. Although the urban population was now growing more rapidly than its rural counterpart, towns and cities were not yet the sites of factories or large manufacturing enterprises. Cities and towns could be divided into two general categories. The most common were regional towns, which served as the seat of provincial administration and as market centers where area goods were exchanged. Population varied, with the average center having fewer than 60,000 people. The second category included the seaboard and river ports, which were large commercial centers and national capitals. The latter were the largest, with London reaching a population of one million by 1780, Paris over half a million, and Berlin just under 200,000.

Relationships between town and country were intimate and complex. Dependent on the surrounding region for much of their food supply, towns shared the crises of shortages with their rural neighbors, although urban authorities attempted to keep adequate supplies of grain in reserve against the threat of famine. The livelihood of many in the towns depended on the processing and distribution of agricultural products. Nobility who owned large tracts of land maintained residences in urban centers and frequently owned income property there as well. Wealthy middle-class town dwellers were landlords of nearby farmers. Not only did the merchant capitalists engage in cottage industry venture into the countryside, but so did many rural day laborers who lived in town and traveled daily to work. As the century progressed, there was the continued movement of men and women to the towns seeking employment as servants or hoping to learn a trade.

The small elite at the top of the urban social structure usually included members of the nobility and the clergy, government officials, and the wealthiest merchants, bankers, and financiers. They dominated the economic affairs of the towns and controlled political life through the monopolies they held on municipal positions. The group traditionally regarded as middle class, or bourgeois, consisted of the less-prosperous merchants, bankers, independent tradesmen, and professional people. Members of this segment of society were an increasingly dynamic feature of eighteenth-century town life. The European economy was expanding. The impact of increased output from agriculture, cottage industry, and urban workshops placed greater demands on banks to provide capital and credit. The flow of trade within Europe accelerated, and global trade, particularly transatlantic commerce, was becoming more important. The enhanced activity raised the profits of people engaged in banking, insurance, investment, and the law. Understandably, these middle-class citizens chafed at the restrictions imposed by mercantilist programs and aristocratic privilege, demanding in their place more rational economic policies and access to power and prestige.

In addition to the urban elite and the middle class, a third category comprised the largest and most diverse socioeconomic segment of the urban population: the journeymen and craftsmen, shopkeepers and diverse wage earners (laborers), as well as the vagrants and the city poor. In many cases, the artisans, as the skilled tradesmen were called, continued to use guild organizations to control entry into crafts and training for members from apprentice through journeyman to master. Guilds also assisted members in time of family need and protected them against the economic threats posed by the encroachments of the commercial market. In guild economics, the value of a product was determined by the "just price," not by the fluctuating interactions of supply and demand.

Objections to price increases were a common occurrence. In the most severe cases, protests turned into riots when the price of bread or other food essentials increased in response to merchants' attempts to take advantage of market opportunities. Diverse groups within this third category, unable to earn enough to pay for bread and other necessities, responded by confiscating bread or grain and selling them at just prices to the crowds. These bread or food riots, like the peasant revolts in the countryside, were efforts by the poor to retain stability in an economy in which daily life was a constant struggle for subsistence in the face of scarcity.

SOCIETY AND POLITICS

Domestic politics in the early years of the eighteenth century were marked by monarchical succession crises in major countries, including France, Britain, and Prussia, while internationally, the treaties of Utrecht (1713) and Rystaadt (1714) signaled the conclusion of conflicts referred to as the War of the Spanish Succession (see chapter 2). The later stages of the century witnessed further uncertainties as the American colonies gained their independence from Britain and the consequences of revolution in France were felt far beyond the borders of that country (see chapter 2).

Despite the convenience of these chronological markers, generalizations that apply to the political status of all European states are difficult to formulate; however, it can be stated with assurance that during the eighteenth century, the major countries of Europe did not yet constitute nation-states. A process of centralization had been well underway in the previous century, and with the exception of Britain, greater power was now concentrated in the hands of the monarchy. In most countries the monarchy and the state were still synonymous. The justification for absolutist royal authority was, however, shifting from the theory of divine right to more utilitarian considerations. The need for an administration more effective in collecting revenue, building professional armies, and maintaining peace and security increasingly provided the impetus and rationale for monarchical state authority. Many of the arguments came from the philosophes, who subjected the state to harsh scrutiny, but whose distrust of the masses led them to call for strong rulers as the only hope for implementing reforms. This increasing consolidation of power undermined, but did not destroy, the aristocracy. The institution of the monarchy gained in strength on the continent, but the nobility continued to retain nonpolitical privileges and to exercise strong political influence on the ruler and the court. In the relative peace of the quarter century following the Treaty of Utrecht, domestic, social, and economic factors came to the fore, placing stress on the existing political structures. As a result, a variety of political paths emerged.

France

In France, which was regarded as the model for absolutism, the authority of Louis XIV, the Sun King, passed to his five-year-old great grandson, who reigned as Louis XV (r. 1715–1774). Within two years, his elder cousin, Philippe, Duc d'Orléans, had consolidated his position as regent at the cost of sharing power with the aristocracy. The regent initially attempted to work through committees of noblemen, but these were abandoned, and the nobility began to reassert some traditional authority through the old *parlements,* which had been silenced by Louis XIV. In particular, the Parlement of Paris led the way in regaining the authority to assent to royal edicts prior to their implementation. Thus, an aristocratic resurgence began as the more privileged groups in society sought to check the absolutist power of the monarchy.

In addition to this political ferment, economic problems arose. France, like other nations in that postwar period, had to contend with a large public debt and a troubled economy. Under the mercantilist principles of the time, government financial policies and private entrepreneurship were closely linked. In France, the two came together in a program formulated by John Law, a Scottish financier, mathematician, and gambling partner of the regent. Law established a French central bank and then also organized a monopoly trading company, popularly called the Mississippi Company, for trade with Louisiana. This company soon extended its control beyond its initial jurisdiction of Louisiana to encompass all French colonial trade. The next step in the project, with the regent's approval, was to have the company assume the entire government debt. Individuals possessing certificates of royal indebtedness could exchange them for shares of company stock. The company's profits would be used to retire the debt. A flurry of speculative purchasing of stock raised prices; however, it also generated investment concerns when investors began to sell stocks and attempted to obtain gold for currency from the new central bank, which did not have sufficient gold to redeem all the money presented. Gold payments were halted, many suffered severe losses in savings, and Law fled the country. This financial debacle came to be known as the Mississippi Bubble. Not only were the regent and John Law discredited, but suspicion of royal authority was widespread and attempts to impose financial reform were increased.

Following the resignation of the Duc d'Orleans, Cardinal Fleury, chief minister, provided stable political leadership and economic policies, which solved some of the financial problems. Louis XV finally assumed personal control of the government when Fleury died in 1743. It is a measure of the king's lack of dedication and his mediocre skills that his period of rule is better known for the presence, tastes, and foibles of his mistress, Madame de Pompadour. However, personal failings were not solely responsible for, but augmented, the problems and obstacles that plagued the regime.

This can be seen in the revenue problems of the French government. Some revenue was derived from the sale of offices and privileges, but the main source of government funds was the *taille*, a tax on property. The burden of this direct tax, variously applied according to location, fell almost entirely on peasants, because, for the most part, the nobles were exempted by law and the bourgeois property owners were generally able to obtain exemptions. Church property was not taxable, but the monarch was accorded a periodic gift, or *don*, in place of payment. A system in which the privileged classes were able to enjoy prosperity while the government constantly sought revenue was inherently unstable and was viewed as such by many officials. In 1726 an attempt to introduce a poll (head) tax, which would have required an assessment proportional to income, failed. A further effort in the 1740s to impose a 5 percent tax, the *vingtième*, on income from all forms of property, fell victim to the *parlements*, who ruled that such unilateral actions were contrary to the fundamental laws of France. The aristocratic members of the *parlements* put Montesquieu's arguments to use. In the early 1770s, Louis XV's first minister, René-Nicolas de Maupeou (1714–1792), replaced the existing *parlements* with new ones with limited authority. This move, along with proposals for further administrative and judicial reform, was applauded by people who, like Voltaire, were constantly struggling to obtain a fairer society. However, another attempt at tax reform ended when Louis XV was succeeded by his grandson, Louis XVI, in 1774. Louis XVI (r. 1774–1793) was twenty years old when he ascended the throne, and in an attempt to secure the support of the nobility, he restored the power of the *parlements*, which had been suspended by Louis XIV. To his credit, the new king, who had good intentions, but was of a weak nature, appointed a physiocrat, Robert-Jacques Turgot (1727–1781), as finance minister. Some of

Turgot's reforms included restricting guilds and implementing a freer grain trade. These were accepted, but his plans to replace the *corvée* with a money tax applicable to all classes, along with a general tax-policy review, incurred an immediate strong opposition from the Parlement of Paris, the church, and the provincial estates, precipitating his resignation. Therefore, in France, the cradle of enlightened political thought, the institutions that supposedly worked toward balance and reform instead served to bring about stalemate and tension.

Britain

Britain, too, underwent a succession crisis early in the eighteenth century as the last Stuart, Anne (1665–1714), died without an heir and the throne passed to George I (1660–1727) of the House of Hanover. In this instance, simple succession by lineage was not the case. The Act of Settlement passed by Parliament in 1701 ensured that only Protestants could succeed to the throne. In direct contrast to French absolutism, a number of events had occurred in Britain, particularly the Glorious Revolution of 1688, which had taken the country along the path of constitutionalism, limiting the powers of the monarchy with an elected, effective parliament. However, this was not yet a modern democracy with entrenched rights and institutions following clearly defined roles. Development over the next few decades began to shape some of these institutions, including political parties, the cabinet, and the office of prime minister.

The new Hanoverian ruler was not unanimously accepted in his new kingdom. Some claimed that a son of James II, the Catholic Stuart king who had been deposed in 1688, was the legitimate heir to the throne. An uprising by his supporters, Jacobites, in Scotland was quickly suppressed by troops loyal to George I. Neither this monarch nor his successor George II (r. 1727–1760) was proficient in English, and both tended to show greater concern for their continental possessions than for British interests. These factors contributed to the growth in parliamentary authority and the increasing importance of royal ministers.

A financial scandal similar to that of the Mississippi Bubble in France aided the rise of Sir Robert Walpole (1676–1745) to political prominence as a royal minister. In a project similar to John Law's plan, the South Sea Company assumed a large portion of England's public debt by receiving government bonds in return for shares in the company. In anticipation of profits to be made by the company in Spanish America, the demand for company stock rose rapidly. However, when stockholders began to doubt the viability and promises of the company and various similar speculative enterprises that had developed, a market value crash precipitated losses of savings and inheritances. In the aftermath, Walpole, who had been critical of the scheme, became principal minister to George I. Although the major participants were temporarily discredited, Walpole's actions in Parliament saved and gradually reformed England's financial institutions.

England's more successful recovery from her bubble crisis is attributable more to the effectiveness of parliamentary government by the middle of the eighteenth century than to the work of a single individual. The government debt in England was regarded as a national responsibility. None of it was repudiated, as had occurred in France, and there was a willingness to levy and collect taxes from all propertied people. All landowners paid a share of the tax because it was through Parliament, which they controlled, that policies could be effectively influenced or determined. The consent of the gentry, even if not enthusiastic, could be obtained when the national good and self-interest coincided, as they did in matters of economic strength. The elite that ruled Britain was made up of all those who had large land holdings, whether they were noble or not. Gentry status at the beginning of the century was claimed by about 4,000 families who, by the end of the century, owned about 25 percent of the land. Since only the eldest could inherit the father's land and title, the younger sons sought careers and income elsewhere. Thus, higher positions within the Church of England came to be held mostly by sons of the nobility. Increasingly, economic opportunities were to be found in alliances with urban commercial interests. The resulting relationships with the rising middle class created a group known as the "funded gentry." Seats in the House of Lords were reserved for the titled nobility and bishops of the Anglican Church, while the House of Commons was the preserve of members of the landed and funded gentry. This ruling elite, however, did not speak with a single voice. Two collections of interest groups labeled Whig and Tory defined alternate political paths. They were far from disciplined political parties with consistent policies and are best regarded as shifting factions whose differences varied in accordance with the circumstances and issues involved.

The electoral system, which determined seats in the House of Commons, was not representative of the general population in numbers or opinion. The approximately 500 members of the House of Commons were elected from historic counties and boroughs (districts) in which voting practices varied, but wherein the franchise, restricted to males, was determined by ownership of property and compromised by patronage, bribery, and corruption. In many instances wealthy members could assure their reelection through patronage. In "rotten" boroughs a single landowner purchased all the land that entailed voting rights. This produced situations like the infamous "Old Sarum," which had no inhabitants, but sent two members to the Commons. Another borough, which had been under water for some time, was also represented. In addition, there were many pocket boroughs where elections remained uncontested or never doubted for the same reasons. At the same time, many of the growing industrial towns, such as Manchester and Birmingham, remained without representation.

From this unstable, unsatisfactory, and unjust situation, there emerged new institutions: the office of prime minister, political parties, and the concept of opposition. The king's first minister, Robert Walpole, is sometimes regarded as England's first prime minister, but the position did not formally exist in the eighteenth century. Walpole emerged from the scandal of the South Sea Bubble to gain prominence and respectability. The king's unfamiliarity with the English language, the political environment, and Walpole's effective use of patronage served not only the interests of the Whig factions for which Walpole spoke, but also increased the importance of his position as the king's primary adviser. He was instrumental in defining British policies for twenty years and was succeeded by a fellow Whig, William Pitt (1708–1778), "the Great Commoner," who came to power in the 1760s. The king had come to depend on the ability of a minister sitting in the House of Commons to guide the legislative agenda and gain support for executive policies in the lower chamber. When George III (r. 1760–1820) assumed the throne, it appeared that he wished to rule without consultation with Parliament and to create a government above the factions and groupings in the legislative body. To this end, he appointed a chief minister who was not a member of Parliament. This action gave impetus to the development of clear ideological distinctions in the Commons, as the Whigs strongly protested the king's persistence in asserting the independence of the monarch. Whigs viewed themselves as defenders of parliamentary rights and even began to use the term *party* to distinguish themselves from the Tories, whom they claimed gave unquestioning support to the monarchy. The Tories, of course, denied this, but nevertheless were associated with the prerogatives of the throne. Out of these disputes, the embryonic concept of the political party began to take shape, along with the concept of ministerial responsibility, which required members of the Crown to be chosen from Parliament. In addition, the idea of parliamentary opposition took hold, which allowed members to be loyal to the Crown, yet disagree with and criticize the government. The gradual emergence of a new relationship between the monarchy and Parliament is evident in Pitt's resignation and subsequent return to power. King George had come to rely upon him to provide national political leadership.

Not all of the political activity of the day was within the confines of the formal institutions or the theoretical commentary provided by the Enlightenment. Public protest concerning government policies occurred in opposition to Walpole's proposed excise tax in 1733 and in other subsequent controversies. As the reading public expanded, the demand for systematic reform arose, and in the 1760s opinion coalesced around the controversial figure of John Wilkes, a middle-class member of Parliament arrested when he attacked the government ministers and the king in his newspaper, the *North Briton*. Wilkes regarded his arrest as an arbitrary act of government that violated the principles of English liberty. Although subsequently freed from jail, Wilkes feared further action and fled to France. When he returned he was immediately rearrested, being in the eyes of the king "that devil Wilkes," but for thousands of common people and dozens of reformers "Wilkes and liberty" became a battle cry. Although convicted, he was released due to public protests and demonstrations, but Parliament did not allow him to take another seat despite a number of reelections.

Reformers' demands came to include annual meetings of Parliament, residency requirements for members of Parliament, publication of parliamentary debates, and greater freedom of the press. The increase in daily newspapers in major cities and provincial towns and the spread of political ideas through literary and political clubs, salons, coffeehouses, and taverns not only spread ideas of reform, but helped to extend political life and culture far beyond the traditional political arena. Although some minor adjustments occurred in response to popular concerns, such as in the abuses of patronage, the landed ruling class still maintained its privileged political position to the end of the century.

Continental Variations

Political engagement, which involved reform from above and demands from below occurred in most other European countries as well. The United Netherlands (Dutch Republic) had tended to alternate between periods of centralization and local autonomy owing to its unique political structure.

The regents of Dutch towns defended republican federalism in the Estates General in opposition to the House of Orange, which exercised national executive power through the *stadholder* office. This position was left vacant during the first part of the century, as the local oligarchies sought to reduce the centralizing power. But by midcentury some middle-class merchants, shopkeepers, and artisans, demanding democratic reforms, formed a radical Patriot Party, which threatened existing political power. With assistance from a foreign power, Prussia, the regents and House of Orange reestablished the old system, which combined the tension of monarchical executive power with provincial authority.

On the Iberian peninsula, Spain entered the century with a dynastic change as the Bourbons of France replaced the Spanish Habsburgs in accordance with the Treaty of Utrecht. The change seems to have provided Spain with a rejuvenated monarchy, as the Bourbon rulers, Ferdinand VI (r. 1746–1759) and then Charles III (r. 1759–1788), asserted their authority in relation to the nobility through administrative reforms and curtailing the powers of the church. The Inquisition was limited but not abolished, and the Jesuits were expelled from the country. In the second half of the century, additional policy changes resulted in tax reforms, the encouragement of industry, and a revision of the school system. In neighboring Portugal, significant reforms occurred at midcentury during a time when the Marquis of Pombal served as chief minister. He curbed the Inquisition, placed the property of the Jesuits under state control, and expelled them from Portugal and its territories. In pursuit of economic revival and modernization, the tax structure was reorganized, a new school system introduced, and efforts at a general modernization were initiated. In the Iberian states, where there existed a cautious admiration for enlightened administrative thought, reform was implemented in an authoritarian manner by regimes attempting to consolidate monarchical power and centralize the administration of government.

In the northern corner of Europe, Sweden, while losing prestige on the international scene, experienced an aristocratic resurgence early in the century. However, factional disputes enabled Gustavus III (r. 1771–1792) to reassert the power of the monarchy. During his reign a number of reforms were implemented by decree that reflected fundamental Enlightenment values. Gustavus established freedom of speech, religion, and the press and instituted a system of justice that eliminated the use of torture. His economic policies reflected laissez-faire principles, as he reduced tariffs, abolished tolls, and encouraged trade and agriculture. Other legislation made judges permanent and protected the rights of the accused. To protect his reforms and in his determination to pursue both his domestic and foreign policies, Gustavus imposed a new constitution, which gave him virtually absolute powers. The opposition and outrage of the nobility led to his assassination by a masked aristocrat at a masquerade ball in 1792.

By 1700, the Hohenzollern family of Brandenburg had fashioned the state of Prussia from an inherited collection of north German possessions. Frederick William I (r. 1713–1740), intensely attached to military values, created the best army in Europe and entrenched absolutist rule in his country. The king's devotion to the military expressed itself in his own highly disciplined personal life, which dictated that he always appear in an army uniform, maintain a rigid schedule, and impose specific standards on all subordinates. He organized an entire regiment of tall grenadiers (over six feet), recruiting them throughout Europe, and even resorted to kidnapping men who met the criteria for this special, imposing troop. His most impressive achievement was the expansion of the regular standing army, which he more than doubled in size to over 80,000 during his reign, making it the fourth largest land force in Europe. This highly skilled and disciplined force made Prussia a major military power, despite its limited economic resources.

The second institution that gave Prussia its strength was a highly centralized administrative apparatus supervised by the General Directory, a central government agency. Charged with the responsibility for overseeing the domestic affairs of state, it maintained an efficient bureaucracy of civil servants that consistently and rigidly applied a common framework of policing, economy, and finance on Prussia's varied territories. The combined authority of army and bureaucracy reinforced an already rigid class structure. The landed aristocracy, or Junker class, monopolized the officer corps of the army, while peasants, being accorded very few rights, spent their lives as serfs and soldiers. The middle class could only aspire to social prestige through loyal service in the bureaucracy. Such focused attention on military matters and state values gave rise to the conventional image of Prussian militarism.

The reign of Frederick the Great (II) (r. 1740–1786) brought a continuation of policies, combined with some administrative reforms. A well-educated monarch familiar with Enlightenment thought who played host to Voltaire, Frederick introduced judicial reforms that unified the legal code, limited the use of torture, and provided some freedom of speech and of the press, as well as full religious tolerance. At the same time, he reinforced the hierarchical structure of Prussian society by excluding all but the nobility from the highest positions in the bureaucracy, thereby binding the interests of the landed aristocracy even more closely to those of the state. In military affairs, he extended the policies of his predecessors by further enlarging the force to 200,000 men. His willingness to use this force and the efficiency of the state bureaucracy placed Prussia among the great European powers by the latter part of the eighteenth century.

By the beginning of the eighteenth century, the Austrian Empire had emerged in central and southeastern Europe under the Habsburg dynasty. In addition to the traditional Austrian provinces, Bohemia had been incorporated during the Thirty Years' War (1618–1648). Hungary was added as Ottoman power was successfully challenged. Unlike Prussia, the Austrian Empire did not develop as a centralized state; rather, the Habsburg emperor held together the various possessions through his position as archduke of Austria, king of Bohemia, and king of Hungary. The treaties following the War of the Spanish Succession (1701–1714) added the Spanish Netherlands and former Spanish possessions in Italy to the empire, making Austria a state of considerable potential strength.

However, it remained a collection of territories held together by a dynastic union. Landed aristocrats throughout the empire tended to form the officer corps and hold bureaucratic positions, but there were few other common institutional bonds. Under circumstances of extensive linguistic, cultural, and even religious diversity, the Habsburg rulers had to devote considerable energy and domestic policy to maintaining political unity. To this end, agreements with the nobility of the varied territories, continued recognition and maintenance of regional estates, and the persistence of local laws took precedence over establishing a common legal code and a centralized administration.

Empress Maria Theresa (r. 1740–1780) initiated a reform program to strengthen the Habsburg empire. Administrative changes subjected Bohemia and Austrian possessions to a central bureaucracy. Provincial diets, local committees, and chancelleries made up of landed aristocrats were replaced with salaried officials responsible to Vienna; however, Hungary, the Austrian Netherlands, and the Italian possessions were excluded. Policies to increase the empire's economic strength were based in large part on the central-European mercantilist doctrine. Tax collection came under the jurisdiction of royal officials making it difficult for clergy and nobility to avoid payment. Guild monopolies were checked, and effective policing made movement on the roads less hazardous. Internal tariffs were reduced, particularly benefiting the slowly growing cotton manufacturing industry in Bohemia. Maria Theresa initiated reforms to the traditional institution of serfdom from a combination of humane and economic motives. Laws were

introduced to check the direct abuse of peasants, regularize labor obligations, and limit the taxes and services required of them. This direct intervention also made more men available for military services as the army was
enlarged and modernized. Remaining a devout Catholic, Maria Theresa also
limited the power and influence of the church. She not only imposed heav-
ier taxes and confiscated some monastic properties, but also expelled the Jesuits.

Her son and successor and coregent for the last fifteen years of her life,
Joseph II (r. 1780–1790), extended these reforms far beyond the limits approved by his mother. Joseph's impatience and determination produced
6,000 decrees and 11,000 laws in his ten-year reign. "The state," said
Joseph, "must ensure the greatest good for the greatest number." While not
holding the philosophes in high regard, he nonetheless exemplified some of
the basic principles and values of the Enlightenment. He sought to create a
uniform and rational empire guided by a centralized state. Remaining measures of regional and local self-government were swept away, and a single administrative structure was imposed, even in Hungary. The bureaucracy was
modernized with training courses for officials, promotion schedules, and efficiency reports. German became the language of the administration.

Joseph went far beyond the regulation of serfdom, retaining only a few elements, like the *robot*. Subsequently, he attempted to effect its complete abolition and to introduce a single land tax. The latter measure had to be withdrawn due to strong opposition not only from the nobility, but from the
peasants as well. The peasants lacked the money to make payments and resented the changes in traditional agricultural practices that would be required; the nobility objected to the loss of power, revenue, and status imposed by equality of taxation. Justice, too, was to meet the criteria of equality,
and many of Cesare Beccaria's proposals were implemented. Equal punishment for equal crimes was instituted, so that aristocrats were subject to the
pillory and to street sweeping, as were common criminals. Other aspects of
Beccaria's program were introduced to abolish torture and to make physical
punishment less cruel in general.

In religious reforms, Joseph exceeded the initiatives taken by Maria
Theresa. He introduced an edict that granted Protestants (Calvinists and
Lutherans) and Orthodox Christians legal equality and the right to receive
education, enter professions, and worship privately. Similar rights were also
accorded to the Jews, making the Austrian Empire the first European state to
introduce such a law. The principle of tolerance was certainly a motive, but
practical considerations also played a role, as Joseph believed it would en-

courage immigration, enhance economic development, and increase social harmony. Other aspects of Joseph's religious policies centered on practices within the Catholic Church, which he deemed superstitious or unnecessary, as well as on the controversial issue of church-state relations. He supported Febronianism, a movement that proposed more national independence of German bishops from Papal authority. He reduced the authority of the church in the Austrian Empire by removing its capacity to censor and close monasteries, confiscating property, abolishing tithes, and making priests salaried civil servants.

It is perhaps in social and educational reform that Joseph's goal of ensuring that "the state [provide] the greatest good for the greatest number" was advanced. Money obtained from the dissolution of monasteries was used to fund orphanages, hospitals, maternity facilities, and medical schools, as well as institutions for illegitimate children, unmarried mothers, and those with various physical disabilities. Children of primary-school age were required to attend state-operated schools. Secular teachers were trained and instruction was delivered in the local language with the intent of providing a practical education. The most able boys would become civil servants, and the remainder would be farmers or soldiers. Girls received training only in domestic skills, but any provision at all for state schools for girls was unique in Europe at this time.

Despite his good intentions, Joseph's reforms were strongly opposed. The aristocracy and church resisted. Fears of assimilation were aroused among the religious minorities, and peasants perceived threats to cherished institutions and practices. In the final years of his reign, Joseph implemented the features of a police state to force compliance with his reforms and consequently had to contend with rural uprisings. He moderated some of his reforms, and his brother and successor, Leopold II (r. 1790–1792), while personally supporting the changes, faced increasing opposition. During the reign of Francis II (r. 1792–1835), most of Joseph's efforts were undone.

Russia entered the eighteenth century under the rule of Peter the Great (r. 1682–1725). Determined that Russia was to play a major part in eastern Europe, Peter introduced reforms to modernize the army, centralize administration, and promote economic development. Although he co-ruled with his half-brother, Ivan, until the latter's death in 1696, Peter dominated the government after 1689, at which time his followers overthrew his older sister, Sophie, who was serving as regent. He had long admired or been fascinated by aspects of European culture, which he encountered in the foreign suburbs of Moscow, and in 1697 the physically imposing tsar (he was about seven feet tall) made his famous tour of Europe, frequently attempting to use ineffective disguises. Peter was most fascinated with the practical aspects of European society, those that could be copied, imported, or adapted from abroad to make Russia a great power.

He borrowed from Western practices in reorganizing the central government and consolidating power in his own hands. The landholding class, or *boyars*, who had played a major role in succession and governing through consultative bodies, were no longer summoned. In place of individual ministers, administrative bureaus or colleges were given responsibility for departments such as justice, foreign affairs, and war. All noblemen were required to serve either in the army or civil service for life. In 1722 Peter established a table of ranks for civil offices, which allowed non-nobles to serve the state and achieve noble status. Similar opportunities were available in the military. By requiring all to start at the bottom and work their way up, the old nobility was tamed, and the new nobility rose on the basis of merit. However, after his death, the new upper class, becoming hereditary itself, merged with the old.

State control of the Russian Orthodox Church was achieved when Peter abolished the traditional position of patriarch and established a holy synod to rule in his place. The head of the synod was a layman through whom Peter was able to ensure that the interests of the state remained paramount. Peter's reforms placed demands on the lives of Russia's peasantry. A regular standing army of more than 200,000 men was created, consisting mainly of peasants, who were drafted for twenty-five years. The peasantry also bore the brunt of the cost, as taxes were more than tripled during Peter's reign and individuals, or "souls," became the main unit of taxation. Other aspects of Peter's economic reforms extended serfdom as an institution. While capable young Russians were required to attend schools or go abroad to acquire technical and managerial skills, serfs provided the "unfree labor" for early steps in industrial development. Serfs could now be sold without land or moved from agricultural tasks into mines or factories. Mercantilist policies, which protected and encouraged Russian economic development, went hand in hand with a more oppressive serfdom.

The vast majority of government revenue and efforts were expended in almost constant warfare during Peter's reign. The most significant of the modest territorial gains came with the victory over Sweden at the end of the Great Northern War (1700–1721). With the acquisition of present day Estonia and much of Latvia, Russia was not only dominant in the Baltic region, but became as well a European power. In 1703 Peter had already begun his ambitious project of constructing a new city, St. Petersburg, which was to be his "window to the West." Peter has for a long time been labeled as a Westernizer owing to the nature of the changes he introduced in Russia. Whether his intention was modernization or simply power for Russia and absolutism for the tsar remains debatable. His policies not only built a window, but also opened a door through which foreigners and ideas flowed. Customs and manners forced upon Russia's elite by Peter included shaving heads and shortening coats in accord with Western practices. Etiquette now prohibited spitting on the floor or scratching oneself during dinner. Aristocratic women

1.7. An equestrian portrait of Catherine the Great in military regalia by Vigilius Erichsen (Giraudon/Art Resource, New York)

CHAPTER 1

could now remove their traditional veils and mix socially with men. Although aristocratic reaction undid some of his work, these developments contributed to further changes later in the century during the reign of Catherine the Great.

Peter's commitment to Westernization was so extreme that he had his eldest son beheaded for opposing it. Following Peter's death in 1725, the palace guard, which he had attempted to curtail, proved instrumental in determining who was to reign. When his successor, Peter III, was murdered in 1762, stability returned to the government with the accession of Catherine II (r. 1762–1796), a German princess, whose mother's relationship to the Romanovs had provided her the opportunity to marry into the Russian court. Known as Catherine the Great, she proved an intelligent and determined person and an industrious and able ruler. She had read extensively in literature of the Enlightenment and began her reign determined to rule in a manner that was enlightened and that would Westernize and modernize the country. She was very willing to import Western talent and ideas to Russia. In 1767 she summoned a consultative assembly called a legislative commission for which she wrote a set of instructions drawing upon the ideas of the philosophes who had anticipated the implementation of enlightened reforms. In her guidelines to the commission, Catherine questioned serfdom, capital punishment, and torture and raised the possibility of legal equality. Some reforms in education were introduced, but ultimately no new legal code was produced, and the deliberations of the commission were inconclusive. Catherine disbanded it within eighteen months, and subsequent policies were reactionary in nature, to the great disappointment of those who had been anticipating more enlightened measures. These policies strengthened the landholding class at the expense of the Russian serfs. A program of administrative reorganization, which divided Russia into fifty provinces, each further subdivided into districts, placed power in the hands of the local nobility. In addition, the gentry received special legal privileges, including exemption from personal taxation and corporal punishment. Peasant resentment and unrest culminated in the massive Pugachev rebellion, which swept across southern Russia in 1773. After its brutal suppression, all rural reform efforts ceased, the nobility regained absolute control over serfs, and serfdom actually expanded to newer parts of the empire. In 1785, a *Charter of the Nobility* formalized the special social and legal status of the aristocracy in Russia.

The efforts at "reform from above" as attempted by various eighteenth-century rulers, particularly the prominent central and eastern European monarchs, gave rise to considerable debate at the time and to subsequent historical controversy. During the period, political theorists recognized the contradiction inherent in the idea of an enlightened despot. The ideal of individual rights and liberties seemed to be violated by the presence of unlimited power in the hands of a hereditary monarch. However, many accepted the latter because they believed the general populace to be in need of humanitarian and utilitarian reforms, such as literacy and rational governance, even against their immediate wishes. The long-range goals of the individual and society would be served. Thus, Frederick the Great, Joseph II, and Catherine the Great were initially applauded by Voltaire and Diderot, but as the eighteenth century progressed, most philosophes supported limitations on the monarchy. By the nineteenth century, when the term *enlightened despotism* was coined, many believed that the major absolutist rulers had introduced dramatic changes based on Enlightenment principles. Some historians regard the practical result as modest and question the sincerity of the monarchs, whereas others emphasize the difficulty of the task given the entrenched interests of the powerful nobilities. More recently, an interpretation has emerged stressing that the reforms gave priority to the utilitarian needs of state building over humanitarian social concerns. State power was best served by administrative reorganization and military strength, but the welfare of the state was also served by reforms that introduced practical education, made uniform legal codes, and provided for tolerance of minorities. It is certain that the monarchies of Europe worked to change the social, political, and economic realities of their realms in the years between the close of the Seven Years' War and the upheaval of the French Revolution and that they did so in the Enlightenment spirit of innovation.

NOTES

1. Robert Darnton, *The Literary Underground of the Old Regime* (Cambridge, Mass.: Harvard University Press, 1982).
2. Robin Winks et al., *A History of Civilization: Prehistory to the Present,* 7th ed. (Englewood Cliffs, N.J.: Prentice Hall, 1988), 479.
3. As quoted in Henry Vyverberg, *The Living Tradition,* 2nd ed. (New York: Harcourt Brace Jovanovich Publishers, 1988), 33.

Chapter 2

WAR, REVOLUTION, AND THE MODERN STATE

INTERNATIONAL RIVALRY IN THE EIGHTEENTH CENTURY

In Europe, the eighteenth century opened with conflict in the West and in the East. While Russia and Sweden battled in the Great Northern War, western nations were embroiled in the War of the Spanish Succession (1701–1713). The former saw Russia emerge as a European power, a power with interests in Europe, and the latter is regarded as marking a failed attempt by France to gain continental hegemony. The eastern power struggle concluded with a devastating blow to Swedish power and the signing of the Treaty of Nystadt (1721). Russia obtained Estonia and the southeastern part of Finland. With these lands on the coasts of the Gulfs of Riga and Finland, Russia now controlled the eastern Baltic. Tsar Peter declared his expanse of lands to be the Empire of All the Russias, and with water access to the West, it was a power that could potentially be more closely associated with European affairs.

In western Europe the conflict and the settlement that followed it involved more nations and was more complex. The War of the Spanish Succession had been triggered when France moved to take advantage of the absence of a direct heir to assume the Spanish Habsburg throne. The French goal was to join the two kingdoms by placing a single monarch on both thrones. The treaties signed at Utrecht in 1713 and 1714 confirmed Louis XIV's grandson, Philip V, as king of Spain on the condition that he renounce all claims to the throne of France. In addition, the major portion of Spain's holdings in the Mediterranean (Milan, Naples, and later Sicily) were passed to the Austrian Habsburgs, as were the Spanish Netherlands, or Belgium, thereafter called the Austrian Netherlands. In addition, the Duke of Savoy was granted the island of Sardinia. Spain retained its New World possessions, but Britain kept Gibraltar and Minorca, which it had taken during the conflict. The French nation, financially exhausted and denied its goal of controlling Belgium, had to surrender its holdings in the New World. Newfoundland, Nova Scotia, and the Hudson Bay Territory were relinquished to the British. The only areas gained were Alsace and the Franche-Comté. The Dutch, while their security was ensured by a system of forts along the Belgian border, had also been financially strained by the war.

Great Britain emerged from the war as a great power. England and Scotland had united in 1707. She was now more prominent as a naval nation than the Dutch Republic, had gained territory in North America at the expense of France, and was strongly positioned in the Mediterranean. In addition, the British negotiated the legal right to provide Spanish America with African slaves, and while permitting only one shipload of British goods to be sold in Panama each year, the agreement gave British merchants the opportunity to smuggle and compete aggressively with the French in the area. Thus, both in Europe and the Americas, Great Britain's position was favorable. A final element in these early eighteenth-century political rearrangements entailed the minor territorial gains of Brandenburg-Prussia, whose ruler was also recognized as a king by the other European states.

Warfare and Balance of Power

The system of relations among this collection of European states formed, for the remainder of the eighteenth century, a pattern of diplomacy and warfare aimed at preserving a balance of power. Neither the concept nor its practice was new, but the term first gained common usage at this time. The idea certainly appealed to the philosophies as consistent with the view that balance was, according to David Hume, "inherent in the operation of the universe," or as part of the Newtonian view presupposing order and regularity in the physical universe. No one assumed a mathematical precision or that there was a "built-in equilibrium," but it was accepted that interaction among states should ensure that no one power could attain hegemony. To this end, cooperation among states, as had occurred in the War of the Spanish Succession, could be expected. Otherwise, individual states would continue to act in their own best interests against the international status quo.

Diplomacy and warfare were recognized as the two avenues of foreign policy and were expected to result in the desired balance of power. The origins of the practice of modern European diplomacy can be traced to the Italian Renaissance, but by the eighteenth century, it had developed into a profession whose growth paralleled that of standing armies. Most states now included a foreign ministry in their capitals, staffed with experts and ambassadors who resided in permanent embassies in foreign capitals. For the most part this diplomatic corps drew its membership from the nobility, which, along with the use of French as a common language, provided the appearance of a fraternal association. However, the interests of the personnel remained those of their respective states and monarchs, with the result that the practice of diplomacy could be as duplicitous as war might be brutal.

The increasing prominence of diplomacy in the eighteenth century cannot be attributed to a distaste for military alternatives. Although the number of international congresses designed to settle differences increased, so did the size of standing armies and the expansion of military technology. In fact, wars were commonplace and extensive, including the Seven Years' War (1756–1763), which was the first global conflict. Yet these wars are regarded as limited in nature when compared with the earlier religious wars of the seventeenth century or the subsequent national and ideological clashes of the nineteenth and twentieth centuries. While the intellectual elite, including Diderot and Voltaire, strongly denounced war, the primary cause of the diminished intensity of conflict lay in more mundane factors.

The growth in the size of armies with the accompanying costs compounded by the investments in new technology led to tactics that served to limit their use and reduce the devastation of warfare. Standing armies of increasing size required investment in equipment, training, and maintenance, and countries were not inclined to place such an investment at risk. Much cautious consideration was given before war was declared. The infantry used a smooth bore musket with a range of up to 200 metres, a weapon that was severely limited in battle because it was not reliably accurate, except at relatively short range. Battlefield encounters required well-trained and disciplined soldiers to be arranged in linear formations, firing volleys and then quickly reloading. To achieve this in battle required considerable prior investment in training. In addition, the strategies that developed were based on maneuvering and firing in a fashion designed to force an opponent to abandon a position, rather than to pursue the opponent with the goal of destruction. The basis of victory was the withdrawal of the enemy and not unconditional surrender. A final tactical factor was the dependency of armies on supplies maintained in fortresses. Since armies could not function at great distances from their supply depots, many battles focused on the siege of fortresses.

The social composition of armies also contributed to limited conflict. Officers were predominantly from the landed aristocracy, and due to their position in society, they obtained their positions as sinecures for which only a small number were well suited since ability and merit were not a consideration. Some wealthy middle-class individuals were able to purchase commissions, but they were rarely able to rise above the middle ranks of the military hierarchy. The competence of aristocratic officers was frequently in doubt, and they tended to have more regard for their opposing counterparts than for the men under their command. Recruitment of rank-and-file soldiers varied, but the majority, whether conscripts or volunteers, comprised peasants and artisans. With the exception of France, mercenaries still provided a significant portion of the army. Under conditions of brutal discipline, commitment in battle was questionable and desertion a major problem.

Naval warfare experienced developments parallel to the land-based capabilities. The British navy extended its advantage by increasing its size to almost 200 ships by 1790, while France attained less than half that number. Technological improvements in sails and rigging increased the size and quality of ships, while navigational techniques and cannon accuracy improved their combat effectiveness. However, conditions for sailors were dreadful and desertions common. Volunteers did not fill the required needs, and the press gangs apprehending idle males were a common sight, especially in Great Britain. The cost of building, maintaining, and manning vessels for battle readiness tempered inclinations to place such investments at risk. Naval encounters in many cases tended to be skirmishes rather than battles.

Another factor that served to limit conflict was the nature of the alliances, which were the products of diplomacy. Alliances were readily arranged and terminated. This lack of permanence and commitment meant that the military actions of apparent allies were rarely effectively coordinated.

As a consequence of these factors, civilian populations in Europe were not greatly affected by battles compared with the devastation inflicted during the religious wars of the seventeenth century. With strategic maneuvering rather than annihilation as a common military objective, civilians were spared the direct impact of war as they had experienced it during the previous century, particularly in central Europe. Yet, however limited the nature and impact of eighteenth-century warfare may have been, conflicts did occur. Their causes were rooted primarily in the developing global economy and continuing dynastic struggles.

Transatlantic Economy

Transoceanic communications, which brought America, Africa, and Asia within reach of Europe, led to an expanding Eurocentric global economy. By the eighteenth century, Spain and Portugal still had overseas empires, but France, Britain, and the Dutch Republic were the primary colonial competitors. However, the continued growth of the rival British and French economies overshadowed attempts by other powers, particularly those of the Dutch, to establish global trading companies. Britain and France had the advantages of growing domestic production and national governments able to protect and guide merchant activities abroad according to mercantilist principles. Mercantilism assumed that a nation's power and prestige was dependent upon a favorable balance of trade, which was reflected in a constant surplus of precious metals. In the context of the further assumption that wealth was finite, mercantilism contributed not only to the drive for economic expansion, but to the major conflicts of the eighteenth century.

Each continent had a unique role in this Eurocentric global economy. Asia, from first contact, had minimal value as a market for European goods, but was the source of many commodities in high demand in the West, particularly spices, porcelain, tea, and silk. But the lack of a reciprocal demand in Asia resulted in a drain on European coffers and led eventually to the Opium War with disastrous results for China. In West Africa, the search for gold was one element in the European presence, and included the region that was known for some time as the Gold Coast. Most global trade conducted by western Europe was aimed at North and South America. The primary commodity, sugar, was responsible for the establishment of a plantation economy in the West Indies–Caribbean region. Cotton and tobacco were crops of secondary importance. Production of these items required a significant investment of capital and cheap labor. The latter was found in Africa and fuelled the slave trade, which reached its peak in the eighteenth century. Black Africa had been a source of slaves for Europeans and Arabs for centuries, but as slavery became institutionalized in the plantation economy and in the system of trade, the numbers of Africans transported from their homelands rose dramatically. Exact figures are difficult to ascertain, but it appears that the number of Africans taken to America as slaves between the sixteenth and eighteenth centuries may have been as high as twenty million. This deplorable trade and exploitation of human beings resulted in the deaths of an estimated 50 percent of those captured. The voyage taken by the captives is well known as part of the golden triangle of trade. Slaving ships sailed from

Great Britain and western Europe to the African coast, where manufactured goods and alcohol were exchanged for blacks who had been captured by African middlemen. The captives were packed together and chained in prone positions for the two-month crossing, which became known as the middle passage. Some died of initial wounds, others on the long journey to

2.1. The slave trade in Africa (Réunion des Musées Nationaux/Art Resource, New York)

the coast, some in the stockades awaiting shipment. The voyage itself took a heavy toll on the Africans with 10 to 30 percent dying in transit. From the Caribbean and the colonies on the mainland, ships would pick up plantation products and other goods for the return voyage to Europe, thus completing the last leg of the golden triangle of transatlantic trade. This system was primarily practiced by and beneficial to the British who had, in addition to their West Indies positions such as Jamaica, a relatively densely populated string of colonies on the east coast of America. The French had Haiti (then San Domingo), but their remaining colonies in North America, Canada, and Louisiana lacked the population necessary to produce commodities, although they did provide raw resources such as furs, timber, and fish. The economic impact of transatlantic trade did not end in western Europe. The products obtained from the Americas and Asia were sold not only to their own people by the British, French, and Dutch interests, but also to those of central and eastern Europe. From these latter areas, agricultural products moved westward, contributing in the East to the growth of large-scale estate farming, which tended to entrench serfdom for the masses, while the upper classes became more "Europeanized."

Continental and Colonial Conflict

Rivalry between European countries became the hallmark of the interlocking mercantile system. In an effort to ensure a favorable balance of trade, navigation acts were passed by the British and French governments to regulate economic relations with their respective colonies. At the same time, merchants, trading companies, and governments sought to take advantage of opponents whenever possible. The sequence of events leading to the conflict between Britain and Spain in 1739 is one such case. The Treaty of Utrecht (1713) had given the British the right to furnish 4,500 slaves (*asienta*) to the Spanish in the Caribbean and also to send one trade ship each year to a Spanish Caribbean port with manufactured goods. The Spanish diligently attempted to exploit these provisions as British merchants attempted to smuggle and circumvent the limitations of the treaty. In a boarding operation in 1731, the ear of an English captain, Robert Jenkins, was cut off by a Spaniard. Jenkins apparently preserved the ear in a jar of brandy and used it in his appearance before a parliamentary committee seven years later when pressure was being exerted by British merchants to counter Spanish actions in the West Indies. Political opponents of Prime Minister Walpole attempted to use the issue to

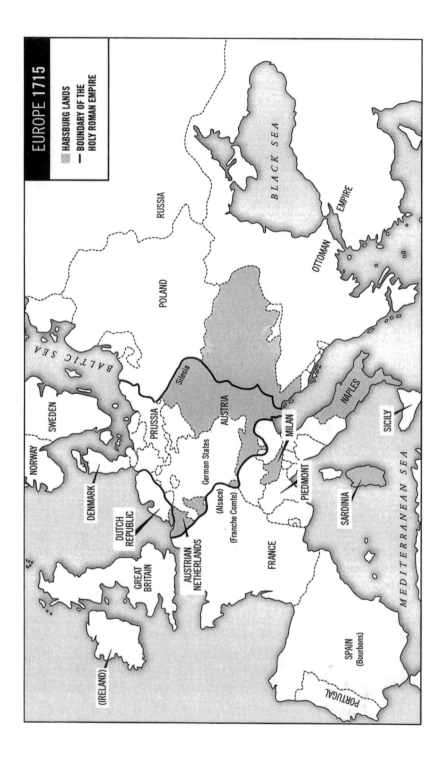

EUROPE 1715

HABSBURG LANDS
BOUNDARY OF THE
HOLY ROMAN EMPIRE

NORWAY

SWEDEN

BALTIC SEA

DENMARK

RUSSIA

POLAND

PRUSSIA

German States

Silesia

AUSTRIA

BLACK SEA

OTTOMAN

EMPIRE

(IRELAND)

GREAT
BRITAIN

DUTCH
REPUBLIC

AUSTRIAN
NETHERLANDS

(Alsace)

(Franche Comte)

FRANCE

MILAN

PIEDMONT

NAPLES

SARDINIA

SICILY

MEDITERRANEAN SEA

SPAIN
(Bourbons)

PORTUGAL

drive him from office, and the result was a British declaration of war on Spain in 1739, which came to be known as the War of Jenkins' Ear. Although France hoped to gain from this colonial struggle, other powers were not inclined to become involved in an issue of concern only to the combatants. From 1713, diplomacy had arrested war among the major powers, or at least had localized conflict on the continent. However, the war broadened in scope the following year when dynastic ambitions threatened the balance of power. In 1740 the colonial conflict between Spain and Britain became linked in a continental struggle that involved all the major powers following the death of the Austrian (Holy Roman) emperor. Charles VI (r. 1711–1740) had hoped to secure recognition and guarantees from the European powers for his heir apparent, daughter Maria Theresa, through his 1713 declaration, the Pragmatic Sanction. Upon Charles' death in 1740, Frederick II of Prussia, hoping to take advantage of Maria Theresa's lack of experience and the fact that she was a female monarch, offered a series of flimsy excuses to justify seizing the Habsburg province of Silesia. He invoked "reason of state," meaning the welfare and expansion of the state he ruled, in an attempt to validate his actions. Frederick was joined by other German states, in particular Bavaria, whose ruler, Charles Albert, also claimed the throne of Austria and managed to have himself elected Holy Roman Emperor as Charles VII.

Other countries, including Spain, became part of the anti-Habsburg coalition with the goal of regaining lands in Italy and Piedmont-Sardinia and in hopes of obtaining the duchy of Milan. France was looking at the Austrian Netherlands with acquisition in mind. The latter in particular, if achieved, would have upset the continental balance of power. That threat initiated Great Britain's entry into the conflict as Austria's ally. In addition, George II wished to protect the dynastic territory of Hanover. Austria was also supported by Russia, Sweden, and Denmark, although this support was largely nominal since these three states had little impact on military developments.

On the continent, Prussia held Silesia, despite the forces arrayed against her, which, in addition to Austria, included Denmark, Sweden, and Russia. Her ally, France, occupied the Austrian Netherlands. Overseas, the conflict was a struggle between British and French forces in North America, the Caribbean, and the Far East. The British captured the strategic French fortress of Louisbourg, which guarded the Gulf of St. Lawrence, while France took Madras from the British in India. The conflict began to wind down when Prussia made peace with Austria in 1745, and by 1748 all combatants, feeling the economic impact of the struggle, agreed to end the fighting. The subsequent peace treaty of Aix-la-Chapelle (1748) restored most of the occupied territories to their previous rulers; however, Austria lost some territories on the Italian peninsula and could not obtain the return of Silesia. While the outcome ensured the survival of the Habsburg domain, the loss of Silesia was a severe blow to the dynasty and confirmed Prussia's status as a major power in central Europe. The acquisition of Silesia doubled Prussia's population and added rich deposits of coal and iron to her resource base, in addition to bringing her an established textile industry. There was now a dual power situation in the German states. The old balance of power had shifted, and the struggle was not over. Austria did not regard the loss of Silesia as final, nor was the mercantile conflict between Britain and France concluded.

Prior to the resumption of the conflict in the following decade, a diplomatic shift occurred. The Austrian foreign minister, Count Kaunitz, saw in Prussia's rise not only the loss of Silesia, but the uncertainties of a destabilized status quo. Kaunitz used his diplomatic skills to find common ground with France, Austria's centuries-old rival. Meanwhile Britain, dissatisfied with Austria's lack of commitment to its continental interests in Belgium and Hanover, had by late 1756 concluded a defensive alliance with Prussia. This action gave Austria the opportunity to persuade France to end the Bourbon-Habsburg rivalry and enter into a working partnership. This diplomatic revolution was completed when Russia, concerned about isolation and the potential threat of Prussia, joined the Franco-Austrian alliance.

The renewed war once again witnessed land conflicts in Europe and colonial territories and a series of naval engagements. In Europe, hostilities began in August 1756 with Prussia invading the Kingdom of Saxony in an act that Frederick II regarded as both defensive and preemptive and undertaken to forestall a French and Austrian conspiracy to destroy his state. This placed Prussia at war not only with those three states, but also with Russia, Sweden, and the smaller German states as well. Using Prussian resources to their full potential and employing brilliant strategies, Frederick won a number of battles, but the combined forces of his opponents proved a difficult opposition until 1758 (see appendix, Document V). Despite a combined population advantage of fifteen to one, the Austrians, French, and Russians were never able to conclude effectively any final military success. In addition, Prussia's effectiveness and the ineptitude of its opponents constituted two other factors that served to save Frederick's state: the British war effort intensified when William Pitt the Elder became prime minister, and in Russia the death of Empress Elizabeth I brought about a change in policy. Her son and successor, Peter III, an admirer of Frederick the

Great, withdrew from the coalition and placed his forces at the Prussian king's disposal. The outcome was a peace settlement, the Treaty of Hubertusburg (1763), which concluded hostilities in Europe and, while resulting in no significant territorial changes, confirmed Prussia's hold on Silesia.

In North America, the conflict had begun earlier as raids and skirmishes occurred in frontier areas. War was declared in 1756 with the British on the defensive as the French with their Indian allies harried them from positions that stretched from the St. Lawrence River and the Great Lakes down the Ohio and Mississippi Rivers. However, in 1758 the French lost naval battles off the European coast and were thus unable to supply and maintain their colonial efforts. In 1759, the British general Wolfe defeated his French counterpart, General Montcalm, on the Plains of Abraham outside the Quebec fortress, and the French were unable to prevent the capture of Montreal the following spring. The colony of Quebec fell to the British. Superior British naval power also led to the occupation of French islands in the Caribbean. In India as well, French ports were cut off from Europe, and the British were able to use a limited land force to maximum advantage. In addition to having isolated France from its overseas world, British forces had also defeated the Spanish. France and Spain had been allies since 1761, as the result of heightened Spanish concern for their American empire following the British victories over the French at Quebec and Louisbourg.

The Peace of Paris (1763) did not fully reflect the extent of Britain's victory. Changes in the British cabinet and skillful French negotiations allowed France to keep the sugar plantation islands in the Caribbean, as well as retain slave stations in Africa and commercial installations in India. The French did, however, relinquish Louisbourg, Quebec, and all territorial claims east of the Mississippi to the British. Spain transferred Florida to Britain, but reclaimed French holdings at the mouth of the Mississippi River and territories west of the river as well. This peace settlement, which concluded the Seven Years' War, marked a turning point in European power politics. Britain was now firmly established not only as a European power, but as a global force. France, despite having lost her North American colonial possessions, remained a major player in the growing global economy. Prussia's position in Europe and as Austria's rival for German leadership was confirmed. This new international balance of power, although subject to threats and crises, was to last until the French Revolution.

In eastern Europe, Tsarina Catherine intervened in a succession controversy in Poland to place her favorite, Poniatowsky, on the Polish throne, one of a series of expansionist actions that alarmed other powers in the region. In 1768 the

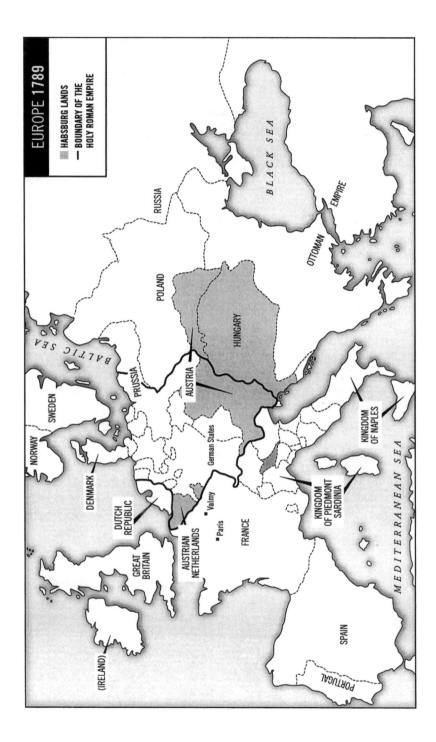

HABSBURG LANDS
— BOUNDARY OF THE
HOLY ROMAN EMPIRE

BLACK SEA

RUSSIA

POLAND

HUNGARY

OTTOMAN EMPIRE

BALTIC SEA

PRUSSIA

SWEDEN

NORWAY

AUSTRIA

German States

Valmy

Paris

FRANCE

DENMARK

DUTCH REPUBLIC

GREAT BRITAIN

(IRELAND)

AUSTRIAN NETHERLANDS

KINGDOM OF PIEDMONT SARDINIA

KINGDOM OF NAPLES

SPAIN

PORTUGAL

MEDITERRANEAN SEA

Ottoman Empire declared war on Russia. Russia's victories aroused Austria, and by 1771 open conflict appeared imminent. Frederick of Prussia promoted a proposal by which all three countries (Russia, Austria, and Prussia) would annex Polish territory, rather than court a general war. The First Partition of Poland, concluded in 1772, divided about one-third of Poland's territory and one-half of her population among the three neighbors (see appendix, Document VI). Meanwhile, the Russo-Turkish war ended in 1774 with Russian gains in the Crimean region and navigation rights in the Black Sea.

A general European war had been averted, but difficulties were not at an end. All nations had experienced financial exhaustion from the quarter century of war, which ended in 1763. The powers pursued various paths in the hope of replenishing their treasuries; however, it was Britain that first experienced strong political consequences. The military and financial efforts of British American colonists in the midcentury wars had been very limited at best. It had been regular British forces financed by the British government treasury that had driven the French out of North America. After that victory, British army units contended with Indian uprisings that threatened frontier settlements. The British government then attempted to make the colonial subjects pay a greater share of the past and current expenses. Those who in the past had only paid local taxes, the lowest of any European nation or colony, had now to endure the taxation expected of all loyal British subjects. Passage by Parliament of the Sugar Act (1764) and Stamp Act (1765) was met by refusal to pay and claims by colonists that they could not be subject to taxation without political representation. Although the British government relented on the tax-collection issue in 1766, Parliament passed a declaratory act affirming its right to impose such laws. Further attempts by Parliament to impose revenue-collection legislation met with further resistance (see appendix, Document VII).

The American Revolution

In 1773 an attempt to force the sale of tea imported by the British East India Company led to the famous Boston Tea Party incident in which chests of the commodity were dumped into the harbor. The British government responded with the Coercive Acts (1774), which included closing the port of Boston to trade and suspending local elections in the colony. In the same year, the British government was addressing the problem of administering land and peoples previously under French rule. Implementation of the Quebec Act angered colonists by restricting westward expansion, and they responded by sending delegates to a continental congress in Philadelphia and organizing a boycott of British goods. In April 1775 clashes occurred when British troops were dispatched to disarm colonists. Tensions increased, and although delegates to the congress were not seeking to break with Britain, public opinion was shifting toward independence. One contributing element was the publication of a pamphlet in January 1776 entitled *Common Sense* by the recently arrived English radical Thomas Paine, who argued that the cause of the American colonists was no less than the struggle for liberty in the face of tyranny. In July 1776 the congress adopted the Declaration of Independence, which echoed the natural rights and republican principles embodied in the works of many Enlightenment thinkers.

At the outset of the dispute, other European nations remained officially neutral, although military supplies were quickly provided to the colonists by the French government, which sought to revenge the losses of the Seven Years' War. French volunteers were in the colonies within a year and France formally declared war in 1778, followed within the next two years by Spain and the Dutch Republic. Britain once again faced encounters at sea, in the West Indies and India, as well as in the newly formed United States. By 1783 Britain and the United States were negotiating and soon signed the Treaty of Paris by which Britain recognized the independence of the thirteen colonies and ceded all territory east of the Mississippi River.

The political theory and principles upon which American leaders drew to justify their actions and to frame the constitution of the new state stemmed from the Age of Enlightenment of which they were a part. The ethos the leaders hoped to put into practice included elements derived from Locke and Montesquieu. Their newly written republican constitution was in effect a new social contract that put lofty ideals into concrete practice. Those in Europe who sought reform were encouraged, while those protective of privilege were, with good reason, deeply concerned. The most immediate impact of revolution in America was felt by the government of France, which, to subsidize American efforts and finance its own involvement, had added further debts to an already overburdened economic system. These consequences were part of a complex constellation of factors that would contribute to an unprecedented upheaval in Europe beginning in France in 1789.

OLD REGIMES UNDER STRESS

While Europe in the eighteenth century witnessed a rapid growth in overseas commerce, internal trade remained relatively backward. Food shortages were common and largely the result of a lack of agricultural progress in the face of a rapidly expanding population. However, the growth of industry played an increasingly important role in the economic life of the various countries as the century progressed. Such growth affected, to some extent, the moribund economies that were restricted by a system based on privilege and tariffs. The essentially hierarchical social structure to be found in most European countries rested on the twin pillars of heredity and privilege. Members of an aristocracy of birth, wealth, and legal status occupied a position of superiority over their countrymen. Among this group were to be found governors and magistrates, high army, state, and church officials, or the ostentatiously wealthy. The order of society was "fixed" and had been since the Middle Ages. It was believed to be sanctioned by God and was securely rooted in tradition. The individual had a duty to fulfill the obligations of his estate or order and to be satisfied within it. Those of the lower estate, of whom the majority were peasants, had a responsibility to accept and therefore, to maintain the order of society. Between the aristocracy and the peasantry stood a middle class of urban dwellers, the upper echelons of which consisted of bureaucrats, bankers, merchants, and professionals. The lower middle class included artisans, shopkeepers, and small traders. Below them were laborers, or the working class, and on the fringes of society, the landless, the homeless, and the destitute subsisted.

By the eighteenth century, some differences did exist in the zeal with which this traditional organization was maintained. The exemptions and privileges of the nobility in the West tended to be less clear-cut than in the East, where nobles and commoners were distinctly separated. For example, in Poland until 1768 the nobles retained the powers of life and death over their serfs; in Hungary only nobles could own land, and after the mid-eighteenth century, they were totally exempt from paying taxes. In western Europe, France serves as an important case study of the structure and function of European society under the Old Regime, for without doubt, the Revolution, which began there in 1789, had its origins in the realities of the Old Regime, although it may have come as a surprise to Louis XVI. At the time there was a shortage of neither criticism nor proposals for change. Many people, when reflecting upon their immediate concerns, were able to use a variety of intellectual tools and concepts arising from the Enlightenment. These included the ideas of tolerance and social equality, as well as the principles of free trade and the separation of political powers. In addition, for more than a century, developments across the Channel in the English political system had significantly limited the power of the monarchy, while more recently the American Revolution had served to topple the existing order within a colonial empire. Although ideas stemming from intellectual ferment and models arising from revolutionary change suggested alternatives, it is within the complex interplay of social conditions, economic problems, and political responses that the origins of the French Revolution are to be found.

The Orders, Monarchy, and Crisis

The principles of privilege and inequality formed the basis of French society prior to 1789, and the population of about twenty-six million was legally divided into three estates, or orders: clergy, nobility, and commoners. The social and political status of the individual, as well as his economic obligations and opportunities, were defined by the order to which he belonged. The respective roles of members of the three estates were traditionally characterized as representing those who prayed, those who fought, and those who paid.

The First Estate consisted of the clergy, who numbered about 130,000 people (slightly less than 0.5 percent of the population) and who, through the Roman Catholic Church, controlled about 10 percent of the land. Members of the clergy were exempt from paying all taxes, although the church made a voluntary contribution to the government every five years. In addition to the revenue from land, the church levied its own tax, or tithe, on church members. This amounted to about one-tenth of a household's annual income. From this revenue the church supported hospitals and charities, provided education, and kept registries of births and deaths. But much of the wealth was channeled to the higher clergy, leaving local parishes and the lower clergy in poverty. The aristocracy of the church, the bishops, archbishops, and abbots, were mostly of noble birth. They benefited personally from this transfer of wealth and held positions that allowed them to exercise considerable political influence. This distanced them from church members, whose resentment they tended to earn. As recipients of tithes and defenders of church property, local priests could also be at odds with the populace, but in rural areas they were the primary contact with the outside world, sympathetic to the peasants, and quite frequently their spokesmen and leaders.

The nobility, about 390,000 people (approximately 1.5 percent of the population), comprised the Second Estate and owned about 25 percent of the land. United in privilege and status, they filled most of the leading positions in government, military, the courts, and the church. Yet, the nobility, too, was divided. Members of the nobility of the sword traced their origins to medieval ancestors who had achieved title and property through service to the monarch in time of war. The nobility of the robe had generally acquired title through royal appointment to office, and its growing ranks were regarded with suspicion by the former. Many members of the nobility of the sword had experienced a decline in their standard of living due to the continued division of property through inheritance, which had reduced the amount of land and income enjoyed by individual family members. Despite their differences, the nobility generally remained a closed group, as it tended to marry within its own ranks, protect its privileges, and attempt to expand its influence and power at the expense of the monarchy. Their most useful privilege and the one most resented by their fellow citizens was their near total exemption from the payment of property taxes and the tithe. Thus, despite its ownership of one-quarter of the land, the nobility paid only a small proportion of the total taxes. Its income from land was supplemented through feudal obligations, which still allowed for collection of dues and fees from the peasants, the exercise of exclusive hunting and fishing rights, and monopoly on essential activities like grain milling. The nobility was also accorded certain traditional honors such as taking precedence at public functions and the wearing of swords. All of these, whether economically useful or merely honorary, made members of the nobility socially and legally conspicuous, regardless of their wealth or lack thereof.

The remaining 98 percent of the population made up the Third Estate. This vast population of commoners, united in their inferior legal status, was socially and economically diverse. The order was composed of three distinct groups, although the divisions were neither formally defined nor always socially and economically obvious. The upper portions of the Third Estate, comprising about 8 percent of the population, or 2.5 million people, were the bourgeoisie, or middle class. Merchants, bankers, and industrialists, who controlled trade, financing, and manufacturing, were included in this social class, as were professional people such as lawyers, doctors, and some civil servants. To achieve security and status, some had been able to buy property with the result that this class owned about 20 to 25 percent of the land. Those engaged in business activities felt hampered by restrictive government regulations and practices, laws that varied from region to region, and the inequities of the tax system. Tolls between regions served as internal trade barriers and greatly increased costs for merchants, as well as resulting in higher prices in towns and cities where the cost of bread was a frequent issue. In the urban centers, guild monopolies persisted, making it impossible for independent entrepreneurs to establish new businesses. While having a greater capacity to absorb and in some cases avoid tax payments, this growing middle class looked upon itself as economic victims of the Old Regime no less than other members of the Third Estate. Credited with creating much of the new wealth responsible for France's economic growth in the first half of the eighteenth century, the bourgeoisie regarded itself as enlightened, progressive, and worthy of social recognition and political participation.

The majority of the Third Estate's population lived in towns and cities and included the shopkeepers, artisans, and wage earners, skilled and unskilled. These were the "little people," or the *menu peuple,* some of whom later constituted the revolutionary group known as the *sans-culottes.* This label referred to the fact that they did not wear the fashionable knee breeches of the upper classes; rather, they wore a simple style of long pants. Their main concern was economic survival. This diverse collection of urban workers had to contend with a rising cost of living while their wages lagged behind. At times the cost of bread, the dietary staple, would consume one-half of a Parisian worker's daily income. In the absence of any other means to exert economic or political influence, public demonstrations frequently erupted, focusing on demands for stability of bread prices and not infrequently such occasions developed into riots.

The single largest portion of the Third Estate was the approximately twenty-one million peasants who constituted 80 percent of the total population of France and owned about 40 percent of the land. The proportion varied greatly from region to region and more than one-half had little or no land. Although serfdom no longer existed, the peasants were subject to feudal or manorial dues and fees. These required payments *(banalités)* covered the use of such facilities as the village mill, oven, and wine press and obliged them to work on the nobleman's land for a set number of days each year, although payment in cash or goods could be made in lieu of labor. In addition to the *taille,* which was a direct tax paid to the government with its application varying in diverse areas of the country, peasants could be required to provide labor for road maintenance each year *(corvée).* The poll tax, from which only the clergy were exempt, and salt tax *(gabelle)* added to this burden of repressive taxation, which in some parts of France consumed one-half of the income of a peasant household. Although there was a small number of relatively prosperous peasants, the accumulated taxes and obligations constituted a heavy financial burden and reduced many to meager levels of subsistence.

The inequities among the social orders and classes were the subject of much analysis and discussion, as the observations and criticisms of the philosophes began to reach a wider audience. No longer confined to the salon or café society, discussion of these vital topics was part of daily interaction, particularly in the cities. In densely populated Paris, the more literate bourgeoisie frequently lived at street level in buildings that housed artisans and tradespeople on the floors above. Their daily encounters led to exchanges not only about work or family, but involved questions relating to broader economic and political issues. As the 1780s progressed, the number of concerns that fuelled these discussions did not diminish. The unavoidable confrontations and frustrations with prices, taxes, regulations, and social barriers were also an object of criticism in the numerous pamphlets published by the underground press. The contents of these pamphlets included concise summaries of the ideas of the philosophes, sensationalist and gossipy news stories, and a steady stream of satirical cartoons. It seemed that almost every person, regardless of social status, had a political opinion and wished to share it.

The social structure of the Old Regime and its numerous pressure points created a potentially explosive political environment, which has occasioned much debate. Long-term causes of the French Revolution have commonly been attributed to growing antagonism between a rising middle class in competition with a privileged nobility. However, many historians have recently emphasized views and goals held in common by the wealthy nobility and upper bourgeoisie. Both were influenced by Enlightenment ideas and united in their frustration with the inability of the traditional political machinery to adapt itself to changing economic circumstances. Without a doubt, the monarchy constituted an integral part of the problems confronting the French people. Political power was vested in the hands of an absolute monarch who ruled by the theory the divine right of kings, which maintained that the authority of the monarch derived from God and was, therefore, to be obeyed without question by all citizens. The gradual implementation of this political theory had served to diminish the power of the traditional nobility, which had to resort to currying favor at the royal court to maintain its influence. For a century the center of court life had been the lavish palace at Versailles, thirty kilometres west of Paris. This enormous complex served as the royal residence and the center of political operations, but also housed hundreds of nobles. There to seek favor and advancement, aristocrats vied with one another for royal attention in the midst of elaborate and intricate rituals that dominated the court. Participation was the means by which access to power, in the person of the king and his advisors, was achieved at Versailles. Few could bear the cost or time to create such opportunities and, thus, only members of the first two estates were in position to influence royal decision making directly.

In 1774, the nineteen-year-old grandson of Louis XV succeeded to the throne as Louis XVI (r. 1774–1793). He was a well-meaning, if indecisive, individual ill suited to his role as king. A man of moral commitment, genuine religious conviction, and deep affection for his family, Louis preferred tinkering with locks, working with masonry, and hunting to the responsibilities of the monarchy. He was not highly intelligent, and certainly he was not equipped to meet the challenges that confronted him. The influence exerted by the queen, Marie Antoinette, on Louis' decisions should not receive undue emphasis, yet she certainly was a controversial figure. The daughter of Maria Theresa, the Austrian Empress, she was betrothed to Louis to strengthen the emerging alliance with Austria in the 1760s. Neither Marie Antoinette nor the alliance gained much popular support in France. A determined person in comparison to Louis' weak and vacillating personality, her impact on royal decisions was generally perceived as willful interference.

Although the king was the focus of political attention, political practice did not accord completely with the theory of absolutism and at least one other institution had in recent decades been able to play a significant role in government. The French *parlements,* thirteen regional law courts, could prevent royal decrees from being implemented by simply refusing to register them. Since each *parlement* was composed of members of the nobility, these bodies were vehicles through which the Second Estate could protect or further its interests. Its members could force the modification of royal decrees or block reforms such as those related to taxation. Clashes between the *parlements* and the king had occurred with increasing frequency during the reign of Louis XV, and as Louis XVI took his place on the throne, many wondered how he would deal with the power of the aristocracy. It was not long before the king was tested. A half century of almost continual economic growth was interrupted in 1787 and 1788 by bad harvests and the start of an economic depression in manufacturing, which led to food shortages, rising prices, and unemployment. The rural and urban poor suffered the most, and a demand for government action erupted quickly. Food riots, a traditional form of protest in times of shortage, became commonplace. Bakers' shops were often the targets of the hungry crowds, and the bakers themselves were sometimes dragged to the lamp posts and hanged. Women were usually in the forefront of these activities because feeding their families was their first responsibility and concern.

Simultaneously, the French government was facing a financial crisis. Involvement in a number of major European wars during the first half of the eighteenth century and the substantial support provided to the American revolutionaries during Louis' reign had significantly increased expenditures. The costs of these conflicts, aggravated by royal extravagance, had been financed by loans from domestic and foreign banks that were becoming increasingly reluctant to extend further credit. Payments on this accumulated debt were taking up about one-half of annual budget expenditures by 1788. While other major powers such as Great Britain and the Dutch Republic also had large debts, France struggled with the problem of generating sufficient increases in revenue. Fear of inflation and adherence to gold coinage made it impossible even to attempt printing more money to meet budget demands and the only other alternatives were to default on loan payments or to raise taxes. The first of these was summarily rejected by Louis XVI as dishonorable and, therefore, unacceptable.

The tax problem was complex. In addition to placing the tax burden almost completely on the commoners through exemptions for the first two estates, the system of collection was chaotic and corrupt. A significant portion of tax collection was contracted or farmed out to individuals (farmers-general), who submitted bids for specific regions. The competition was fierce, and contracts were frequently obtained through bribery of government officials. Much tax revenue never reached the treasury, as it was possible to purchase further evasions. Some Farmers General manipulated accounts, thus forwarding to the government only a fraction of the anticipated income. Various efforts at reforming the taxation system were attempted, particularly by Turgot and Necker, two finance ministers whose efforts displeased the royal household, were opposed by the nobility, and were ultimately blocked by the *parlements*. Obviously, the search for solutions had to be expanded. In the hope of persuading the first two estates to pay an increase in their share of taxes, Louis XVI and Calonne, his finance minister in 1787, convoked an assembly of notables, which consisted of the highest aristocrats of the nobility and clergy. Their response at the meeting was to make demands for political power, which resulted in the dismissal of both the notables and Calonne. The king then attempted to impose a uniform property tax by decree, but the Parlement of Paris declared it illegal and asserted that only the nation as a whole through the Estates General could implement such changes. In July 1788 Louis had run out of options and was pressured by public opinion and advice to call a meeting of the Estates General to be held in the following spring. Such a gathering of delegates representative of all three estates had not occurred since 1614. The convocation of this body was an indication of the inability of the Old Regime and its absolute monarch to cope with the problems facing them and to govern the country. It was obvious that the system as it existed was no longer functioning, and the archaic machinery of government had creaked to a halt.

CHAPTER 2

The Collapse of the Old Regime in France

The calling of the Estates General raised the hopes and expectations of government and populace alike. The king hoped that this action, taken as a last resort, would be the means by which the financial crisis could at last be resolved. The nobility, intent upon preserving its privileged status, sensed a further weakening on the part of the monarch and saw an opportunity to assert political power. A generally cautious church was determined to prevent the erosion of its influence and control in such matters as education and public morals. Neither of these estates spoke with a single voice. Many of the younger, urban members of the nobility, influenced by the ideals of the Enlightenment, and members of the lower clergy, exposed to the lives of ordinary parishioners, wished to implement reforms that would undermine the Old Regime. The Third Estate, with its diversity of social classes, desired a wide array of changes ranging from political participation to economic reforms and an end to social privilege.

Since the Estates General had not met for 175 years, there was much uncertainty and debate about its organization and procedures. The Parlement of Paris ruled that each estate was to have an equal number of members who would meet and vote separately. The consent of two estates and the approval of the king would be required for any measure to pass. Not surprisingly, this was denounced by members of the Third Estate, who demanded a proportional representation that would reflect the fact that it comprised 98 percent of the population. These same delegates also wanted voting to be by head and not by order, since its members were well aware that the privileged first two orders would always stand together and outvote the third. By December 1788, the king, accepting the advice of Necker who had been reinstated as financial advisor, doubled the representation of the Third Estate. This meant that its representation of about 600 was now equal to the total of the clergy and nobility combined. In the event of voting by head, the Third Estate, with the support of reform-minded clergy and nobility, could dominate the Estates General. The king, however, did not rule on the method of voting until the meeting of the Estates General had begun.

During the severe winter of 1788–1789, which followed upon poor harvests, the people met to select delegates to the Estates General. The selection procedure and the desire for articulate and educated spokespersons resulted in complete domination by the bourgeoisie of delegate selection for the Third Estate. At the same time, *cahiers de doléances* ("compendiums of grievances") were compiled. These were lists and statements expressing the grievances of each

2.2. The opening of the Estates General, May 5, 1789 (Réunion des Musées Nationaux/Art Resource, New York)

estate for the purpose of submission to the government. Those of the first two estates, while critical of absolutism, tended to defend privilege. In the *cahiers* of the Third Estate, the diverse voices and demands of the commoners found expression. In some cases the voices of the women, angry and plaintive, were clearly heard. The flower sellers of Paris expressed both suffering and hope in their submission, explaining that the oppressive silence and *froideur* ("coldness") of the king's ministers had combined effectively to suppress the concerns of the women. Now, however, the hope was expressed that "a better order" was imminent and that women would receive justice from the king and the Third Estate.

Armed with the results of the most comprehensive survey of public opinion conducted prior to the twentieth century, delegates of the three estates began their formal sessions at Versailles on May 5, 1789. However, problems and proposals could not be discussed until questions of procedure had been resolved. The Abbé Siéyès, a priest, expressed the determination of the Third Estate to play a role befitting the size of its population. In a pamphlet entitled *What Is the Third Estate?* his response to the question was, "Everything." He went on to ask, "What has it been in the political order up to the present?" "Nothing." "What does it ask?" "To become something." He further argued that only the commoners truly represented the nation, stating that "if the privileged orders were abolished the nation would not be something less but something more." Such strong views supported the stand by the Third Estate that voting in the Estates General must be by head. Debate on this issue kept matters at a deadlock. Then on June 17, members of the Third Estate took the first step beyond the legal framework to initiate change. The representatives of the Third Estate voted to declare themselves as constituting the National Assembly, and they invited delegates from the other two orders to join with them. A small number of reform-minded nobility and some lower clergy accepted. The king's response was to bar the commoners from their usual meeting place on June 20. Led by Jean-Sylvain Bailly (1736–1793), distinguished mathematician and astronomer, the Third Estate delegates assembled in a nearby indoor tennis court and swore not to disband until they had written a constitution for France. This event is remembered in history as the swearing of the Tennis Court Oath.

In response to this challenge, the king ordered each estate to resume separate deliberations. When the Third Estate and some supporters from the first two continued to disobey, he wavered and then directed all delegates to join the group now known as the National Assembly. However, at the same time troops began to take up positions near Versailles and on the outskirts of Paris. Combined with the dismissal of Necker, whose economic proposals appeared to provide relief from rising food prices, these troop movements added to the volatile situation in the capital. Demonstrations, protests, and riots had continued throughout the spring. Added to the demands of the crowds was the fear that the king would use troops to disband the National Assembly and reimpose complete royal control. In Paris on July 12 and 13, a new city government and a new citizens' militia, the National Guard, were formed, pledging support to the National Assembly. Crowds roamed the streets demanding cheaper bread, but also in search of arms in anticipation of action by royal troops. On July 14, one such organized crowd seized arms from government buildings, and in the hope of obtaining additional weapons, marched on the Bastille, a former fortress that had become a prison. In the struggle that followed, close to 100 people were killed before Governor de Launey surrendered the Bastille. Little practical value came of the crowd's success, as the Bastille yielded few firearms and only seven inmates, none of whom was a political prisoner. However, the capture of the Bastille and the decapitation of the governor were regarded as symbolic of the triumph of liberty over despotism.

Louis' power waned. On July 15 he traveled to Paris in response to demands for his presence there. At the Hôtel de Ville (city hall), he fastened to his hat the tricolor cockade (blue and red as the colors of the city and white as the color of the Bourbons), already a symbol of the Revolution, which was now generally accepted to be in progress. In addition, he accepted the citizens' militia formed in Paris as the National Guard and appointed the popular French participant in the American Revolution, the Marquis de Lafayette, as its commander. For a third time he appointed Necker to the post of finance minister. The National Assembly was no longer threatened, and its deliberations continued, but the drama was not yet over. Throughout France, royal authority collapsed as local committees and militia were formed in cities. In the countryside peasant rebellions erupted in a number of areas. Nobility were forced to renounce feudal dues and privileges. They watched as the hereditary charters and even buildings were burned. Such actions contributed to a state of "panic terror," known as the Great Fear, that swept through rural France in late July and early August. Rumors about aristocratic plots and foreign troops spread. Attacks on the property of the nobility intensified, and wealthier peasants prepared to defend themselves against armed bands of ruffians rumored to be roaming the countryside.

These circumstances formed the background and gave impetus to the series of reforms that the National Assembly, now called the National Constituent Assembly, initiated at the beginning of August. The first major reform began on the night of August 4 when a nobleman, Vicomte de Noailles, who was Lafayette's brother-in-law and had fought with him in America, rose in the Assembly to renounce his feudal rights (see appendix, Document VIII). He was followed by Duc d'Aiguillon, one of the greatest landowners in France, and over the next few hours these voluntary renunciations became a flood, washing away the rights and privileges so despised by the commoners. Doubts and debates continued over the next week as the declarations of intention were refined and became law. By August 11, tax exemptions, tithes, sales of government office, and restrictions on holding office based on social class had all disappeared. The Assembly now set about drafting a document that would establish the principles upon which a subsequent constitution and future legislation would be based. On August 26, 1789, the Declaration of the Rights of Man and Citizen was adopted. Drawing upon English experience with the Bill of Rights, the ideas of the Enlightenment, and the recent American Declaration of Independence, it asserted a number of fundamental rights. Primary among these were individual freedom and equality. The declaration guaranteed freedom of expression, press, and religion, as well as protection against arbitrary arrest and punishment. Taxation would now only occur with the consent of the people, and all laws would be the product of popular participation and not the decrees of a divine right monarch. The inclusion of property as a basic right reflected the interests of the bourgeoisie, as such a provision would significantly limit the capacity of any government to intervene directly in the economy. While general and abstract in its expression, the most practical impact of the declaration was to assert the legal equality of citizens and identify the people as the ultimate source of power in society. However, women, with only limited property rights and denied the franchise, were excluded from full rights of citizenship. The declaration quickly became a popular document, which was printed, posted, and read throughout France and even beyond its borders. Other monarchical governments on the continent took note of how rapidly the ideas contained therein were spreading. In addition, some members of the French nobility reacted to the uncertain political atmosphere at home by leaving France. They became political refugees, for the most part taking up residence in bordering German states. These émigrés sought to gain sympathy and support from other monarchs both for themselves and for the plight of the French king. Although no immediate action occurred, many European heads of state viewed developments in France with alarm.

Meanwhile, Louis quarreled with the Assembly and refused to sign the reforms passed during the summer. This raised suspicion that he was still planning to use force to reimpose royal power. Although the 1789 harvest was an improvement over recent years, distribution problems contributed to further increases in the price of bread. Hunger, combined with a growing anger, which was fuelled by rumors of hoarding, caused agitation in crowds waiting at bakeshop doors, and at least one baker was hanged in Paris. On October 5, a large group of women set out for Versailles determined in their belief that political action was necessary to bring about economic relief. On the road they expressed their feelings toward the queen, who, more than the king, was the object of their hatred. Late in the afternoon of October 6, the group arrived at Versailles in pouring rain, disrupted the Assembly, and demanded to see the king. A delegation of five women was eventually received by Louis in his chambers, where he was informed that people in Paris were starving. He promised to ensure that grain and flour would reach the city. The next morning, October 6, a crowd of women stormed into the royal apartments, seeking the queen and shouting, "Death to the Austrian whore." The queen managed to escape and later in the day the royal family, accompanied by a crowd of women, the National Guard, and wagonloads of wheat and flour, left Versailles for the last time. The royal household set up residence in the Tuileries Palace, and the Assembly followed them to Paris within days. As a result, the people of Paris were able to keep a closer watch on the king and his court and on the Assembly as it attempted to shape a new era in France.

One of the first tasks addressed by the National Constituent Assembly upon resuming business in the new location was the continuing financial crisis. The new government had yet to find a way of solving the debt problem of the Old Regime. It could have repudiated the debt; however, a significant portion was owed to members of the bourgeoisie who dominated the assembly. The day-to-day operation of the government had to be carried out but under the circumstances, it was next to impossible to collect taxes, and the revenue problem remained unresolved. The wealth of the church presented an attractive practical resource and not all ecclesiastics were unconditionally opposed to a new arrangement by which the religious institution could provide assistance to the state when the need arose. On October 10, 1789, a young bishop, Charles Maurice de Talleyrand (1754–1838), proposed the nationalization of church property and following the assembly's approval in early November, church holdings, comprising approximately 10 percent of the nation's land, were offered for sale at auction. To facilitate the purchase and to raise funds immediately, special bonds in large denominations were offered for sale. These were the *assignats,* which began functioning as a currency and were subsequently issued in smaller bills. This action did not cure the country's economic ills, but it did bring about a measure of stability. Some peasants were able to increase their holdings and many bourgeois purchased land for purposes of speculation. But many peasants were not in a position to profit or were only able to benefit from the sale of church lands indirectly through dealings with middlemen. The members of the social class that dominated the Assembly were perceived to be the main beneficiaries of these sales.

The loss of property was but the first in a series of actions that was intended to redefine the relationship between church and state in France. In February 1790, religious orders were abolished, and in July the Assembly passed the Civil Constitution of the Clergy. This document provided for the election of parish priests and bishops, the redefining of diocesan boundaries to coincide with political administrative units, state salaries for all priests, and subordination of papal authority to the French government. This program was met with strong resistance within the church, and in November 1790 the Assembly required the clergy to swear an oath of allegiance to the Civil Constitution and to the Revolution. Just over 50 percent of the parish priests took the oath, but the majority of the bishops refused, and within a few months (April 1791) Pope Pius VI condemned the Civil Constitution. These actions split not only the clergy, but the population as well, with some supporting the "juring" clergy and others favoring the "refractory," or non-juring, priests who refused to take the oath. The latter tended to be dominant in the West and North of France, giving impetus to counterrevolutionary sentiments and actions among the people. Disturbances broke out in the Midi in the spring of 1790 in protest. The Civil Constitution also contributed to further suspicion about Louis XVI as he insisted on receiving sacraments from the refractory priests who were, of course, loyal to the pope.

As the Assembly continued to labor toward a national constitution, further economic reforms were also introduced. The firm belief of the leaders in freedom from government control, as had been favored by the physiocrats and thoroughly articulated by Adam Smith in the *Wealth of Nations,* was demonstrated in policies introduced to minimize interference in free arrangements among individuals. Government regulations were abolished, as were guilds and journeyman associations. Labor disturbances in 1791 led to the Chapelier Law (June 14), which reaffirmed that organization of any special economic interests was prohibited. Workers' associations and coalitions were outlawed and strikes forbidden. Wages and conditions of work were to be a private matter determined by employers and employees. As a result, workers lacked protection, which in part was due to the far-reaching reorganization of the government and administration of France.

The courts and jurisdictions of the Old Regime were abolished and replaced by eighty-three *départements* that were approximately equal in size and population. The *départements* were divided into a total of about 44,000 districts and communes, all of which were supervised by elected councils and officials responsible for administering the laws of France. Implementation was not yet effectively controlled by the central government, which had so many diverse issues to address. It did not wish to return to the traditional despotic pattern having now decentralized government as a direct reaction to Old Regime bureaucratic control. Eligibility for local office was based on property qualifications with the result that exercise of government was largely in the hands of the bourgeoisie. Aristocrats were very rarely elected.

While all of the Consituent Assembly's reforms were aimed at distancing France from the Old Regime, the formal break came with the finalization of the constitution in the summer of 1791. Although support for a republican form of government was expressed in debates in the Assembly and voiced in public, it was a constitutional monarchy, which replaced traditional absolute rule. In June 1791, Louis XVI and his family attempted to flee France, but were apprehended by the National Guard at Varennes in Lorraine and escorted back to Paris. Although his attempted escape turned public sentiment against the king, the majority in the Assembly feared a civil war if a republic were declared, so Louis XVI remained monarch. Tensions rose on July 17 during a celebration at the Champ de Mars when the National Guard opened fire on a crowd, killing about fifty people and wounding approximately a dozen more. Martial law was imposed, and the more radical leaders went into hiding and later fled.

The constitution in its final form provided for a monarch, now called the king of the French, as opposed to the king of France, who retained a suspensive veto, commanded the army, and directed foreign policy. Acts of war and peace, however, required the Assembly's approval. The new National Legislative Assembly, a unicameral body, consisted of 745 representatives, chosen by an indirect electoral system, who would hold office for two years. The assembly made a distinction between "active" and "passive" citizens. All citizens enjoyed the same civil rights, but only active citizens, that is, those over twenty-five years of age and paying the equivalent of three days' wages in direct taxes, had the right to vote. However, these active citizens, numbering approximately four million, voted not for members of the Legislative Assembly directly, but for electors. The electors, who paid taxes equal to ten days' labor, were a relatively small group of about 50,000 who then chose the deputies. To qualify as a deputy required payment of annual taxes equal to forty-four days' labor. These new regulations were formally passed in September, and elections were held in October, after which the Assembly began to function.

In addition to economic, ecclesiastical, and political reforms, the Assembly enacted social reforms according to which Protestants and Jews were granted civil and citizenship rights. Reforms that affected the family included the establishment of civil marriage, provisions for divorce, the lowering of the age of consent for marriage, and the institution of requirements for dividing inheritances equally among children. Slavery was abolished in France but not yet in the colonies.

Within France and abroad, these revolutionary events were celebrated by some, condemned by others, and regarded by still others as a starting point for more reforms. Most regarded the revolutionary changes as unfinished and requiring further attention. For example, Olympe de Gouges in her *Declaration of the Rights of Woman and Citizeness* (1791) called for the extension of the Declaration of the Rights of Man and of the Citizen to women as a fulfillment of their natural rights, including control of property within marriage and equal access to higher education and public office, at a time when the full rights of citizenship had never been considered possible for women.

The wealthy bourgeoisie looked favorably upon the achievements of the Revolution and anticipated a period of stability. It soon became evident, however, as illustrated by the disturbances at the July 14 celebrations of 1790 and 1791, that no consensus had been reached. By the latter date, resistance to the Revolution by nobles, royalists, and supporters of the refractory clergy led to open confrontations in the South and West and in Alsace.

Revolutionaries demanded more radical changes, particularly in reaction to growing resistance to the Revolution. The lower classes felt themselves hurt by inflation and became more and more vocal and active but did not speak with a single voice, as evidenced by the diversity of political clubs that developed as like-minded deputies formed alliances and distinguished themselves from others. Among the most prominent was the Society of the Friends of the Constitution, known popularly as the Jacobin Club. It took its name from the place where it met, the former monastery of the Dominicans (or Jacobins) on the Rue St. Honoré in Paris. This group wanted to abolish the monarchy and establish a republic based on universal male suffrage. The Jacobin members debated and sought to achieve political results, and before long they had the support of a nationwide network of affiliated discussion groups that numbered around 1,000 by 1791. Although some of its members were tradesmen and artisans, the majority came from the rising professional bourgeoisie. The more moderate supporters of a constitutional monarchy gathered at the Club of the Feuillants, while the Cordeliers Club often challenged the influence of the Jacobins. Political activity was not confined to the clubs but permeated the meetings of the sections as well.

In Paris the strongest supporters of the Revolution were the *sans-culottes,* who were identified not only by their long pants, but also by the red Phrygian caps they wore, decorated with the tricolor cockade. These were distinguishable from the three-cornered hats of the nobility. This group was composed of tradesmen, artisans, small shopkeepers, and workers, whose primary concern was the cost of living, particularly the cost of bread. The *sans-culottes* expected that the popular sovereignty achieved by the Revolution in the first two years would lead to concern for this basic issue, and further economic and social reforms would logically follow.

THE FRENCH REVOLUTION

It was in this political atmosphere that new individuals rose to prominence and carried the Revolution forward. Their methods were often at odds.

Moderates like Bailly, now mayor of Paris, Lafayette, commander of the National Guard, and Count Mirabeau, foremost orator of the assembly, shared leadership with republican Jacobins whose support came from the Parisian population. Men like Georges-Jacques Danton (1759–1794), a lawyer and member of the Cordeliers Club, Camille Desmoulins (1760–1794), a journalist and Cordelier, Maximilien Robespierre (1758–1794), an early member of the Jacobins, Jean-Paul Marat (1743–1793), a physician and editor of *L'Ami du Peuple,* were all revolutionaries of a more radical stripe.

These leaders and their supporters played an increasingly significant role as the newly elected Legislative Assembly met on October 1, 1791. All the representatives were new, since the National Constituent Assembly had prohibited the reelection of its members. Although lacking national political experience, many had participated in their local areas in varied elected offices, the Jacobin Clubs, or the National Guard. In the Assembly, the republicans grouped themselves to the left of the president as he faced the deputies, while the monarchists were on the right. Within a few months the power struggle between the two was to favor the former.

Constitutional Monarchy to Republic

Meanwhile, the king had reluctantly ratified the new constitution and now appeared to make a genuine effort to work with the Assembly, but reaction to the Revolution beyond the borders of France contributed to a change of direction within. In Britain, as in parts of western Europe, the educated applauded the abolition of feudalism, the economic reform, the reduced influence of the Catholic Church, and the establishment of a constitutional monarchy. However, in 1790 British writer Edmund Burke, in his *Reflections on the Revolution in France,* maintained that by destroying the Old Regime, the revolutionaries were undermining the very institutions that allowed the nation to continue its natural and historic evolution. Thomas Paine (1737–1809) soon replied in defense of the Revolution in his pamphlet entitled *The Rights of Man* (1791–92). At the same time, Mary Wollstonecraft, as noted previously, expressed approval of the Revolution in her *A Vindication of the Rights of Woman* (1792). She demanded equal rights for women, but her efforts were condemned as having been influenced by the "pernicious" French Revolution. These controversies contributed to the debate on the need for further political reform in Britain. For many people, the Revolution affirmed the dangers of social upheaval and contributed to a growing British nationalism. Throughout the debate, the British government watched developments warily.

The continental powers in closer proximity to the upheaval were, of course, more threatened by the opposition to monarchical rule. Aware of the danger posed to their own regimes, they reacted much more strongly. The Prussians, although inclined to take advantage of any possible opportunity to weaken Austria's position, made common cause with their recent enemy, and on August 27, 1791, Frederick William of Prussia and Leopold of Austria (brother to Marie Antoinette) issued the Declaration of Pillnitz, which expressed concern for the safety of the French king and queen and stated the desire of the other crowned heads of Europe to see order restored in France. Their action was applauded by the many émigrés who had left France and taken refuge in friendly neighboring countries. They impressed upon the nobility and rulers that spread of revolutionary ideas posed great dangers and that preemptive action was in their own interest. Among these émigrés was the king's brother, the Count of Artois, who had fled to England.

Supporters of the Revolution were suspicious of all the monarchies in Europe. In the Legislative Assembly, the Girondins, originally a faction of the Jacobins, called for a revolutionary war to rid Europe of monarchies and nobilities. Although the Girondins became known as the "war party," others in the

2.3.   A crowd confronts Louis XVI and Marie Antoinette in the Tuileries Palace, June 20, 1792. (Réunion des Musées Nationaux/Art Resource, New York)

assembly agreed with them. Some believed that a war would serve to unite the country under the new government. The most reactionary hoped for a conflict in which a French defeat would open the way for a restoration of the Old Regime. On April 20 the French declared war on Austria. The reason given was the threat of an Austrian invasion of France from the southern Netherlands. The early stages of the conflict did not go well for the French, as their armies were not well prepared for war. Soon, they were facing not only the Austrians, but also the Prussians, and French defeats were not surprising given these circumstances. At least two-thirds of the officers, mostly nobility, had deserted during the Revolution, and the infantry lacked discipline. Then, on the domestic political front in Paris, the unexpected occurred, when the "second," or radical, revolution began in the summer of 1792.

The war had increased tensions in Paris and exacerbated revolutionary activities to levels not seen since the fall of 1789. The economic situation worsened. Bread prices in the city climbed, in part because food was being requisitioned for the army. There was little gold left in the country, as the émigrés had taken most of it with them. This left the *assignats* as almost the sole currency, and these continued to lose value in the face of an uncertain future. The peasants were not faring well either and regarded the Revolution as having benefited primarily the wealthy. At the same time, they feared the restoration of the Old Regime should France be defeated in war. In Paris, the citizens rallied to the cause of the Revolution, even if they did not have confidence in the new government. Demonstrations occurred across the city, and Jacobins gained control of the section governments.

As the foreign wars went against the French, the Prussian commander issued a statement that served, somewhat ironically, to boost French morale. The Brunswick Manifesto of July 25 declared that if the French king and queen were harmed, the Austro-Prussian forces would severely punish the inhabitants upon their arrival in Paris. Within Paris, as popular discontent intensified, the Jacobins controlling the sections demanded that the king be removed. On the night of August 9 and early morning of August 10, a radical committee ousted the municipal authority and established a revolutionary commune to govern the city. Sans-culottes from the sections, assisted by members of the National Guard and some *fédérés* (members of provincial National Guard units), stormed the Tuileries Palace. While the royal family sought protection in the Legislative Assembly, the invaders killed the king's Swiss Guards and servants. The assembly, under pressure from the new Paris Commune, deposed the monarch, imprisoned the royal family, and ordered the election, by universal male suffrage, of a new constituent body, which came to be called the National Convention. In the interim, a minority consisting mostly of Girondins and dominated by Georges-Jacques Danton was to run the government.

In the following months, tension soared as the events of the war combined with political turmoil to lead to new explosions of popular violence. On September 2, 1792, a Prussian army captured the eastern fortress town of Verdun, thus occupying French territory. The voices of Marat and Danton combined to fuel the sense of outrage, betrayal, and panic within Paris. Many people had already been imprisoned on suspicion of plotting against the Revolution; a large number of them were suspects on the basis of their pre-revolutionary social status as members of the aristocracy and clergy. When rumors began to circulate accusing these prisoners of planning an escape and undermining military efforts, mobs attacked them, helpless in their cells, and slaughtered them. About 1,200 presumed traitors were killed in the September Massacres.

The foreign military advance was effectively stalled near Valmy on September 20, 1792. For the moment, the Revolution had been saved. This occurred on the same day that the newly elected National Convention began its sessions. Although its task was to draft a new constitution, it also became the ruling body of the French nation for the next three years. Delegates to the National Convention included a few artisans, but the majority, as in the previous assemblies, comprised lawyers, professionals, and property owners. However, most were younger, had some revolutionary political experience, and disapproved of the monarchy. They were determined to make a fresh start, abolishing the monarchy and establishing a republic on September 21, 1792. Political agreement beyond this point was difficult to achieve, as the next few months were characterized by factional disputes and power struggles.

The Girondins no longer represented the most revolutionary views in the Jacobin-dominated Convention. A new group, whose members sat in the highest seats in the Assembly, earning the label "the Mountain," was now the more radical. The Girondins, however, still represented mostly provincial interests, whereas the Mountain owed their political strength to the support of popular elements in Paris. The immediate issue was the fate of the deposed king. While the members of the Convention found him guilty of treason, the Girondins were in favor of keeping him alive. The question of penalty was voted upon twice, and the second vote determined the fate of the king. He was condemned to death and executed on January 21, 1793.

Meanwhile, the foreign war raged on as French forces followed up their success at Valmy by pushing across the Rhine and occupying the Austrian Netherlands. On November 19, 1792, the National Convention offered

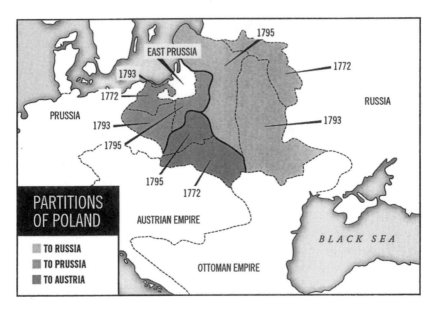

assistance to all people fighting for liberty. In occupied or annexed territories, such as Savoy, Nice, Belgium, and much of the Rhineland, the Convention abolished remaining feudal dues and tithes. French successes were
in part related to developments in the East. From 1787 to 1792, Russia remained at war with the Ottoman Empire, gaining additional territory on the
northern shore of the Black Sea. Russia and Prussia banded together in
the course of suppressing a revolt in Poland to arrange a further partition of
that country. Austria was excluded from the Second Partition of Poland in
January 1793 and, suspicious of its eastern neighbors, did not commit the
bulk of its forces to the West. However, French actions now threatened
the interests of Britain and the Dutch Republic, on which France declared
war on February 1, 1793. When Spain and the kingdoms of Piedmont-
Sardinia and Naples joined this First Coalition, France was at war with all
the major European powers. In March, the French suffered a series of military reverses, and in April, General Dumouriez, who had led the revolutionary forces to victory, defected to Austria. With allied forces on the left
bank of the Rhine, the Revolution was once again threatened from without.
Revolutionaries felt betrayed as prices continued to rise, food became
scarcer, and the value of currency fell further. The Paris Commune, with the
support of the city's *sans-culottes,* put constant pressure on the National
Convention to implement more radical measures to safeguard the nation
and extend reform.

In March 1793, domestic resistance erupted into full-scale insurrection in the western part of France in and around the Vendée. Although aristocratic and clerical interests formed the basis of the resistance, peasants opposed the new draft law passed by the Convention. The insurrection escalated to include major provincial cities, such as Lyon and Marseille, whose inhabitants opposed the centralized authority. The insecurity and vulnerability felt at the political center found expression in the events of May 31 through June 2, 1793, in demonstrations organized by the commune, whose members invaded the Convention and forced the arrest and execution of Girondin leaders. This left the Mountain and its chief spokesman, Maximilien Robespierre, in control of the Convention.

Regardless of who wielded authority in the Convention, the central government did not effectively rule the nation. Regions of France, for instance Brittany, accustomed as they were to regional independence under the Old Regime, repudiated the Convention's authority and found common cause with counterrevolutionaries. In the volatile atmosphere of Paris and other major centers, extreme militants known as *enragés* posed a threat to the Convention. The *enragés* included political leaders and groups who wanted a more direct form of democracy. Among these were the followers and supporters of Jacques René Hébert (1755–1794), who engaged in violent collective action aimed at replacing the Convention with the commune as the governing body. To address these crises at home and simultaneously mobilize the nation to win the war, the Convention gave emergency broad powers to an executive committee called the Committee of Public Safety. From April 1793 to July 1794, first nine and then twelve members were reelected to administer the government of France. Initially dominated by Danton, the committee soon came under the leadership of Robespierre. To meet the foreign crisis, the Committee decreed a national mobilization, which drafted all bachelors and widowers between the ages of eighteen and twenty-five in the *levée en masse* imposed on August 23, 1793. This was a total mobilization of all the resources of France. The forces were democratized so that citizens from the lower classes gained entrance to the officer corps on the basis of merit. In addition, discipline was now maintained, and the morale of the forces improved dramatically. Scientists, including prominent figures such as Lamarck and Lavoisier, were enlisted to work on improvements to armaments and munitions. Married men were called upon to assist in the forging of arms, transportation of supplies, and preparation of food. Women were engaged in the making of clothing, tents, and bandages and in tending to the soldiers. Children were assigned to help wherever possible. In addition, the whole nation was to become involved in the recovery of saltpeter for gunpowder by scraping it from cellars and stables. These efforts resulted in the best-equipped land force seen in Europe up to that time. Some historians regard this effort as integral to the development of modern nationalism, since previous conflicts had focused on dynastic and territorial disputes fought with professional local forces or mercenary troops. The near universal involvement of French citizens in this war effort made it a "people's war" that lacked the restraints of eighteenth-century warfare and in this way appears to have foreshadowed the "total war" of the twentieth century.

The Terror

These measures inspired patriotism, but also generated shortages. There was need for a range of political and economic actions that would address the resulting domestic crisis. The constitution of 1793, which was approved in June and provided for universal male suffrage, was set aside, and the Committee continued to function in a "revolutionary" emergency manner. To assist in conducting the government in the midst of the crises, the Convention's "representatives on mission" in the provinces with the armies were given dictatorial powers to maintain order. They played a key role in government in the outlying regions. Bulletins of Laws were issued to ensure that all citizens were aware of the law and understood the role of local revolutionary committees and tribunals, all of which were staffed by Jacobins. Gradually, local and personal authority were centralized in an administrative network controlled by the Committee.

For military purposes and to address the demands and needs of its supporters among the working class, the Committee instituted a series of economic controls. In an effort to stabilize purchasing power, gold exports were regulated and foreign currency confiscated with reimbursements made using *assignats*. The value of the latter stopped declining. The withholding of goods by producers and hoarding by the general population were forbidden. The distribution of food and supplies for armies and town dwellers was rationed and apportioned. The Law of the Maximum (September 29, 1793) was implemented, which set a limit on wages and prices. In the countryside any remaining feudal levies or compensation payments were abolished, and other reforms made it easier for peasants to purchase land. The measures were not universally popular, and a national administrative machinery that could enforce them did not exist.

This period in the history of the Revolution, known as the Reign of Terror, was marked by the dictatorial characteristics of a regime that enforced decrees and repressed counterrevolutionary activities. The organizational institutions, the Committee of General Security, and the revolutionary tribunals had existed in some form since 1789. In 1793 the police, security, and judicial instruments responsible to the Committee of Public Safety were given sweeping powers to take action against internal enemies. Between August 30 and September 5, 1793, terror was declared to be official policy and became part of the daily agenda, with punishment and coercion constituting the sole policy of the government toward its enemies. On September 17, the Law of Suspects was promulgated, defining crimes against the Revolution in extremely broad terms. As much as rivalries, hostilities, and intrigues had been part of the revolutionary environment since the initial uprisings in 1789, the inception of the Terror brought new fear with *lettres de cachet* and late-night arrests. These resulted in sham trials and the bloodletting of the guillotine.

The revolutionary program consisted of more than destroying the Old Regime and responding to threats, internal and external, to the new order. Some elements of change were of a practical nature and gained acceptance quite readily. A uniform system of weights and measures (metric) was adopted in August of 1793. A series of pamphlets was distributed with the objective of helping farmers improve their agricultural techniques and instructing young people in the trades; also, a military school was established that was open to all social classes. Universal elementary education was one of the intentions of the regime, but this was never implemented.

There were other aspects of the revolutionary initiative that perpetuated controversy and contributed to further resistance. The attempt to create a new order reached an extreme in the policy of de-Christianization. An integral part of this was the adoption of a new republican calendar that eliminated all of the Christian references that had ordered the lives of the French. To emphasize the anti-Christian intent of the new calendar, the names of the months of the year were based in nature and derived from the seasons, seasonal agricultural activities, or prevailing weather patterns. The seven-day week of the Christian calendar, which concluded with a day of rest, was replaced with a ten-day week with one day of rest (*décadie*). This proudly revolutionary calendar, declared retroactive to September 22, 1792, boldly asserted that the Year I was the beginning of a new era, and it remained in place until 1806 (see appendix, Document IX).

The calendar was just the beginning of the break with old habits and the creation of new citizens not bound by the constraints of the old order. By the end of 1793, a Cult of Reason was introduced, and Notre Dame Cathedral in Paris became the Temple of Reason. In November, the Hébertist-controlled Commune devised a ceremony in which an actress impersonated Reason. This was too extreme even for Robespierre, who persuaded the Convention to introduce worship of the Supreme Being. In June 1794, in a festival over which he presided, Robespierre set fire to pasteboard figures of Vice, Folly, and Atheism, and a statue of Wisdom rose from their ashes. The spectators were more derisive than enthusiastic.

On that occasion, as on many others while addressing the Convention or the public, Robespierre emphasized the importance of virtue. Like the philosophes, he spoke of a natural personal integrity and unblemished life. This would find expression in an unselfish dedication to duty and civic responsibility in a "republic of virtue." This democratic republic Robespierre described as embodying "the tranquil enjoyment of liberty and equality" and ensuring the reign of eternal justice, "the laws of which are graven, not in marble or stone, but in the hearts of men."

Revolutionary rhetoric was certainly concretely manifested in the many policies that displaced practices of the Old Regime. Despite the cost in human life, the boundaries of equality were pushed outward to include greater numbers of citizens. Early in 1794 the abolition of slavery was decreed in the French colonies in the Caribbean, where a rebellion had actually achieved this three years earlier. Although the practice of slavery was reestablished under Napoleon Bonaparte, the principle of equality in terms of civil rights was extended for a brief period to blacks within the empire.

Women, despite remarkable participation in major revolutionary events, always stood outside the arena of citizenship. Bread riots had been their traditional method of protest, but as the Revolution advanced, their activities demonstrated a high degree of political understanding, much of which had been gained through the club movement where much political education was passed on. Until 1793 the women continued to make their demands and views known to members of revolutionary clubs, officials of the Paris Commune, and deputies of the National Convention. By October 1793 the women were being perceived as a threat and were denounced in the Convention. On October 30, a decree outlawed women's associations, citing public safety as its justification; however, the words of Jean-Baptiste Amar, a deputy speaking for the Committee of General Security, expressed the traditional prejudices against women. He maintained that women had neither the moral nor physical strength for public office and that they should stay with "the more important cares to which nature calls them." The private sphere was the domain of women.

The Law of Suspects, passed by the National Convention on September 17, 1793, provided the most extreme aspects of revolutionary justice. Apprehension, imprisonment, and execution constituted the fate of those who had shown themselves to be "enemies" of the Revolution. This law greatly enhanced the powers and importance of revolutionary committees and tribunals by widening the definition of a suspect to include "enemies of liberty" and "supporters of tyranny." Such broad terms allowed for the arrest of individuals for a wide variety of activities perceived as hostile to the nation. The popular societies, offshoots of the Jacobin Club, received powers of surveillance and policing, and religious terror was added to political terror. All priests, juring or refractory, were suspect. It became relatively easy to be regarded as a traitor to the country.

The Committee of Public Safety found it increasingly difficult to maintain revolutionary ideals and at the same time control the activities of the most enthusiastic revolutionary supporters. The number and speed of executions increased throughout the autumn of 1793, and by the spring of 1794, members of both the left and right were targeted. On the left, leading *enragés* and Hébertists were arrested and executed in March 1794, thus curbing the power and activities of the Paris Commune. The Terror did not end there but continued at fever pitch as Robespierre grew more and more unstable and became more and more determined to wipe out any opposition to the regime. Those who dared suggest that the Terror was no longer necessary were the next targets. On the right, Georges Danton and Camille Desmoulins and their followers, called the Indulgents, were condemned and guillotined in April 1794. Voices from any position in the political spectrum that questioned the policies of the Committee of Public Safety were effectively and rapidly silenced.

At the same time, the now formidable French forces experienced further military success against the less motivated and ineffectively coordinated coalition forces. In June 1794 the French defeated the Austrians at Fleurus and occupied Belgium. On June 10, the law of the 22 Prairial removed the safeguards of prisoners and in so doing simplified the proceedings of the revolutionary tribunal. During that month alone, there were 2,000 executions in Paris. However, military success served to undermine support for the harsh policies of the Committee of Public Safety. The need for dictatorial rule and economic constraints was questioned, although the moderates in the Convention still feared Robespierre's capacity to act. In July, after Robespierre had threatened his colleagues in the Convention, an anti-Robespierre coalition emerged with enough votes for his condemnation. He was apprehended on July 27 (9 Thermidor) and executed the next day. This resulted in control of the state by moderate elements and the end of the Terror.

2.4. Robespierre and Saint Just are taken to the guillotine, July 28, 1794. (Giraudon/Art Resource, New York)

Estimates of the number of victims of the Terror vary, but it is most commonly thought that about 17,000 executions took place. Approximately 500,000 people were imprisoned, and another 300,000 were placed under house arrest. The terror cut across all classes of French society, and the most commonly used estimates indicate that 2 percent of the victims were clergy,

8 percent were nobility, 25 percent were bourgeoisie, and 60 to 65 percent were peasants and artisans.[1]

The Return of the Moderates

The reorganization of the Committee of Public Safety and its abolition, the dismantling of the Paris Commune, and the closure of the Jacobin clubs by the National Convention took time. These actions were not accompanied by the immediate cessation of violence. In Paris, but particularly in some areas of the South and West, a "white terror," so called after the color that symbolized the Bourbon dynasty, was unleashed by secret groups against the Jacobins. Political order was difficult to restore, and economic stability proved equally elusive. The abolition of the Law of the Maximum in December 1794 marked the end of economic regulation in favor of laissez-faire policies and brought an end to cheap foodstuffs. The prices of basic necessities proceeded to climb steadily, a problem compounded by the further issuance and devaluation of the *assignat,* which many merchants now refused to accept. During the course of a particularly harsh winter, the condition of the poor rapidly deteriorated, and many people around Paris were reduced to scavenging for food. One result was sporadic uprisings in the working-class districts of Paris. In May 1795, the Convention itself felt threatened, and for the first time since 1789, the government called troops into the city to disperse the insurgents.

The people of property, who were now once more wielding political power, also set a new social and cultural tone. In reaction to the idealism associated with Robespierre's republic of virtue, there was a return to high society and a loosening of moral strictures. An era of partying and dancing began with women wearing flowing robes with plunging necklines and young men adopting fancy clothes with square collars and elaborate decorations. The symbols associated with the dominant role of the *sans-culottes* disappeared, as did the familiar republican forms of address, which were replaced by the more formal expressions characteristic of the Old Regime. The celebratory and theatrical events favored by the Jacobins were closed, and noisier, more ostentatious social events marked a change in the style of living. This period, which followed on the heels of the hardships of the Revolution and which was almost frenzied in its gaiety, was known as the Thermidorean Reaction. The Thermidoreans were not about to abandon the Revolution in total. Their quarrel was with the extremes and with the terror perpetrated by the Jacobins. By August 1795 the government had produced France's third constitution since 1791. The constitution of 1793 had been suspended before taking effect, so this was to be France's first formally constituted and functioning republic. While still maintaining the principle of individual legal rights, the constitution of the Year III hoped to ensure stability with a more conservative republicanism.

A bicameral legislative assembly and a five-member executive were designed to build adequate checks and balances into the system, thus ensuring that there would be no repetition of previous mistakes, particularly the episode of the Terror. Active citizens, male taxpayers twenty-one years of age and over, could vote (about two million out of seven million of voting age) in the selection of electors, who, in turn, chose the members of both chambers. The electors had to own or rent property worth at least 100 days' labor. This kept the number of those eligible to vote to 30,000. The lower house, the Council of Five Hundred, initiated legislation, which the Council of Elders (Ancients) with 250 members, could accept or reject. Members of the Upper Chamber, married or widowed forty years of age or over, also selected the executive (the Directory) from a list prepared by the Council of Five Hundred. Continuity from the old order to the new system was to be ensured by requiring that two-thirds of the new assembly be chosen from the ranks of the National Convention. The Directory, by restricting the social base of participation and instituting indirect election, favored the wealthy, a group composed of the prerevolutionary bourgeoisie, former aristocrats, and those who had been able to take advantage of revolutionary and wartime opportunities to obtain property.

Opposition to the new regime came from both the left and the right. The brother of Louis XVI, the Count of Provence, presented himself as Louis XVIII following the death of Louis's son in June 1795. The Count waged a propaganda campaign from Italy, promising an uncompromising restoration of the Old Regime. Although this attitude limited the support for a return to the monarchy, royalists attempted an insurrection in Paris on October 5, 1795. At the request of the Directory, the counterrevolutionaries were dispersed by artillery action under the direction of Napoleon Bonaparte (1769–1821). The young Corsican general had provided the promised "whiff of grapeshot" to defeat the insurgents. This became the first link in the new government's increasing dependence on military support.

On the left, opposition to the regime came not only from the working class, but from all those who continued to favor democratic revolutionary ideals and looked to the government as an instrument to address economic problems. In the spring, a group of radicals led by François-Noel Babeuf (1760–1797), known as Gracchus after the ancient Roman proletarian leader, plotted to overthrow the Directory. The goal was to impose a dictatorial government that would abolish private property and implement economic equality. This "conspiracy of equals" had limited support, and the plot was uncovered. Babeuf and another leader were guillotined a year later, and the occasion was used by the Directory to continue the suppression of suspected Jacobins.

While instability within the Directory was rooted in political and economic domestic circumstances, an additional factor was associated with foreign policy. The constitution of 1795 had been written to apply to Belgium as well as to France; however, neither Austria nor Britain accepted French occupation of the Austrian Netherlands as final. The Directory was thus committed to pursuing a policy of territorial expansion. It was both beneficiary and victim of the success of its own capable military commanders, of whom Napoleon Bonaparte was the most prominent.

NAPOLEON BONAPARTE

Born in Corsica in 1769, shortly after the island's annexation to France, Napoleon Bonaparte had studied in French military schools, been commissioned during the Old Regime, and risen to the rank of brigadier-general under the Convention. The Directory, acknowledging his military contributions and talents, had given him command of an army. In March 1796, he married Josephine de Beauharnais, whose husband, Alexander, had been executed during the Terror. As a result of his brilliant military campaigns against the Austrians in northern Italy and the inability of the Directory to control him, Napoleon pursued his own foreign policy. The Austrians negotiated with Napoleon, and his ideas formed the basis of the Treaty of Campo Formio, which was approved by the Directory in October 1797. Through this treaty, Austria retained most of Venetia, but the majority of the Italian peninsula was reorganized as a series of republics dependent on France. In Switzerland, republicans cooperated with the French to create a new Helvetic republic, and the treaty also recognized French control of Belgium and the left bank of the Rhine.

Peace prevailed between France and her neighbors as Prussia also recognized French hegemony on the Rhine. The Third Partition of Poland had occurred in 1795 when Russia had suppressed an uprising and then arranged with Prussia and Austria to complete the final territorial division of independent Poland. Although Britain and France remained at war, neither was in a position to pursue the conflict. Britain was contending with inflation, poor crops, civil unrest, and rebellion in Ireland. France, too, was exhausted and in need of economic reforms. Tax collection was deteriorating, inflation was rising, and the *assignats* were rendered worthless. The Directory cancelled a portion of the national debt in 1797, antagonizing many of the bourgeoisie, who lost money as a result.

Coup d'Etat of 18 Brumaire

The Directory's leadership was not willing to maintain peace at all costs, and this precipitated another political crisis. In the elections of 1797, the first fully free elections held under the republican constitution, a large number of royalists won seats in the Council of Five Hundred. Since they were the party of peace who would likely surrender republican conquests and restore the monarchy, the Directory annulled the election results. This was accomplished with assistance from Napoleon and the army, and this event is known as the *coup d'état* of 18 Fructidor (September 4, 1797). The result was that the wealthy republicans retained power but did not restore political order. Over the next two years, more elections were quashed, uprisings were suppressed, and retaliations against political opponents on the left and on the right became common. At the same time, speculators and carpetbaggers took advantage of political uncertainty and continuing monetary problems to make fortunes in property and government contracts. Corruption and graft compounded economic stagnation and widened the circle of the government's unpopularity.

It was not surprising that the Directory continued to pursue an aggressive foreign policy to deflect, at least in part, popular discontent. Meanwhile, Napoleon was nursing his ambitions and awaiting an opportunity to act politically. France was involved with plans to provide aid to rebels in Ireland and one unsuccessful attempt had been made in the spring to land troops at Bantry Bay on Ireland's southwest coast. A direct invasion of England by the French was under discussion, but in May 1798, Napoleon, having opposed such an invasion, sailed with an army to Egypt with the intention of encountering the English there and threatening their interests in the East. In this way the blow would be indirect, but potentially more successful and certainly just as damaging.

Russia became extremely alarmed by the French presence in the Near East, and Austria objected to the terms imposed on the German territories of the Holy Roman Empire. These two major powers found common cause with Britain and a number of lesser states, so that France was once again involved in a general conflict with the members of this Second Coalition (1799–1802). Although French forces landed successfully at the mouth of the Nile and defeated the Egyptians at the Battle of the Pyramids, these land forces were subsequently isolated by the British destruction of the French fleet. Meanwhile, in Europe the French army was encountering Russian forces as far west as Switzerland.

In the midst of these pressures, Siéyès, a member of the Directory since 1797, plotted to overthrow the government. Talleyrand, now foreign minister, provided the communication link with Napoleon, who was summoned back to Paris, arriving in October 1799. On November 9, 1799 (18 Brumaire), Siéyès, Napoleon, and their supporters used troops to drive opposing deputies from the legislative chambers and then proclaimed a new republic to be called the Consulate.

The Napoleonic Reforms

A new constitution (Year VIII) was quickly prepared. It provided for democratic government structures, yet it concentrated political power in a collective executive consisting of three consuls. Under the Consulate the most powerful position, that of first consul, was held by Napoleon. As first consul he controlled the executive directly, guided the legislative authority, and determined bureaucratic appointments in addition to maintaining military leadership and conducting foreign affairs. This new system of administration was a dictatorship but one draped in a parliamentary and even democratic disguise. Universal male suffrage, through indirect elections, created a political body of notables, a national list of about 6,000 men from which members of the Council of State, the Tribunate, the Legislative Body, and the Senate were selected. All of these bodies held legislative functions, but none had the power to take the initiative in government. Only bills that had been drafted by the first consul could be discussed or voted upon. The consuls chose members of the Senate, which, in turn, determined the membership of the Tribunate. It was the responsibility of the Tribunate to discuss bills, and the Legislative Body voted on them. The Council of State, charged with the task of drafting legislation, was chosen by the first consul. Napoleon, as first consul, also appointed prefects (heads of *départements*), subprefects, and

2.5. Napoleon Bonaparte (Courtesy of Bruce Peel Special Collections, University of Alberta Libraries)

mayors for all of France. After implementing the new system, Napoleon submitted it to voters in a plebiscite, and in this way he presented it as rule by the will of the people. In this plebiscite, more than 99 percent of the all-male electorate registered its approval, supposedly. In reality, less than half the eligible voters actually cast votes, with Napoleon subsequently falsifying the results, supposedly including the votes of the army. In fact, the soldiers had not voted at all.

French citizens, it seems, were prepared to accept strong executive authority as the price for political stability at home and peace abroad, which was also promised by Napoleon (see appendix, Document X). The political machinery quickly became a façade, with the first consul making all the decisions and effectively running the state. He initiated two further constitutional revisions: the first in 1802 (Year X) extended his term as first consul from ten years to life; the second in 1804 "entrusted" the republic to an emperor. Due to the latter revision, France became once again a monarchy with Napoleon as Emperor Napoleon I. In both cases the results of the plebiscites appeared to be overwhelmingly favorable. In the first case, it has been recorded that one general assembled his troops and announced that they were free to hold their own opinions, but the first man not to vote for Napoleon would be shot in front of the regiment. He won easily with 3.6 million votes in favor and only 8,374 opposed!

The press had been suppressed, and certainly pressure had been exerted on the electorate, but support for Napoleon undoubtedly rested on a broad political base from which he staffed his highly centralized administration. The primary criterion for appointment was ability rather than factional loyalty, and, thus, his regime incorporated former émigrés as well as ex-Jacobins. In addition, his military triumphs encouraged nationalism, and the establishment of empire was accompanied by rewards in the form of opportunities, titles, and appointments for the leaders of the middle class. Acceptance of and support for Napoleon's rule was not universal by any means, but expressions of dissent were ruthlessly suppressed and calculated to allow a view of Napoleon as a just preserver of political and social order. In 1800 an assassination attempt was misrepresented as a Jacobin conspiracy and used as an excuse to round up and deport about 100 old republicans, an act thoroughly approved of by the right. On the other hand, in 1804 Napoleon exaggerated a possible royalist plot and ordered the invasion of the independent state of Baden to apprehend the Duke of Enghien, a Bourbon relative. Despite the lack of any evidence to inculpate the duke, Napoleon ordered his execution, thereby reassuring old Jacobins that they had nothing to fear from their association with the death of the king in 1793.

It should be noted that Napoleon was creating a new political system that retained something of the old while adding elements of the new and continued much that the Revolution had attained, while supporting elements that represented a return to the Old Regime. This regime once again vested supreme power in the person of one man and, in this way, resembled the absolute rule of Louis XVI. In 1804 Napoleon transformed his title to that of emperor of the French and made his rule hereditary. He had the pope conduct an elaborate coronation ceremony, but he insisted upon crowning himself, indicating that he owed his power not to God or to the church, but to his own abilities. This act characterized one of the basic tenets of his regime, the idea of career open to talent.

Napoleon's regime, dictatorial from the start, became more autocratic as time passed. In 1799 the three consuls asserted that "the revolution is established on the principles with which it began. It is complete." Subsequently, Napoleon maintained that his actions had ensured the French people that the "gains of the revolution had been preserved." Historical assessment has ranged from support for this position to condemnation of Napoleon. It is obvious, however, that his basic policies revealed him to be a man of the Enlightenment, rather than one of the Old Regime, and he embodied the attributes of an enlightened despot. He was authoritarian, but it must be admitted that he attempted to establish a set of institutions that would enable him to rule France in a rational and efficient manner. His new, highly centralized administration serves as an example. He retained the eighty-three *départements* of the Revolution and put each under the charge of a miniature despot, called a prefect, who ruled within his own region in Napoleon's name. Policies were made in Paris by the first consul and his ministers. This centralized and bureaucratic administration was a remarkably improved and more efficient system. It streamlined tax collection and permitted the government to perform that function efficiently. In addition, an equitable system of property taxation was implemented. At the same time, however, the hated salt tax was revived, together with other indirect taxes. Another of his first moves was directed toward the improvement of commerce within the country with the establishment of a national bank, the Bank of France, and he succeeded in stabilizing the currency, with the franc retaining its value for a century thereafter. In this way, Napoleon won the support of the bourgeoisie, and he succeeded in finding favor with the aristocracy by allowing the émigrés to return to France. He brought the former Jacobins to his side by offering them positions in his new administration.

In 1801 Napoleon made peace with the Catholic Church, which had been for over a decade an implacable enemy of the Revolution. Napoleon regarded religion as a matter of convenience, stating that he could be a Muslim in Egypt, a Catholic in France, or a freethinker if circumstances required it. But he also viewed religion pragmatically, seeing in the institution a way of encouraging public morality and acceptance of life's circumstances. Some normalization of church and state would also have the political benefit of undermining support for monarchists wishing for a Bourbon restoration to reestablish the church in its official capacity. Negotiations with Pope Pius VII resulted in the Concordat of 1801.

Although both parties gained from the settlement, the French state made limited concessions. The pope could once more appoint bishops, but only upon the recommendation of the first consul. The church was permitted to hold public processions and reopen seminaries, but the pope agreed to abandon all claims to former church lands, papal bulls (decrees) could not be read in churches without the government's permission, and government decrees were to be read from the pulpits. Catholicism was recognized as the faith of the majority of the French people, but not as the state religion. The clergy would receive salaries from the state in compensation for losses of both property and the tithe. However, Protestant clergy were extended the same privileges, thus dispelling the notion of any special status for a particular religion. A subsequent imperial decree (1808) provided for property concessions to Judaism in France, but rabbis were not to be paid by the state. The Concordat ensured that the church was no longer the enemy of the French government. Some of Napoleon's supporters on the left felt betrayed by the agreement, while those on the right viewed the outcome as the church capitulating to state supervision.

Many of the *cahiers* submitted to the Estates General had requested that the laws be made uniform. In addition to the hundreds of regional legal codes under the Old Regime, the revolutionary governments had added thousands of laws, many of which were contradictory or rarely implemented. The process of codification had begun during the time of the National Convention, but Napoleon completed the mammoth task. The work was, of course, done by lawyers and administrators, although Napoleon personally participated in the discussions on critical issues. The outcome was several law codes of which the Civil Code, or Code Napoleon, is the best known. From St. Helena, during the last years of his life, Napoleon stated, "My real glory is not my having won forty battles. . . . What will never be effaced, what will endure forever, is the Civil Code." Some principles of the Enlightenment and revolutionary initiatives were affirmed, but in other respects the code reflected traditional attitudes. It was a moderate document that attempted to reconcile the interests of opposing groups in the population. The Civil Code recognized the principle of equality. Career was now open to talent with no regard for social origins, and French citizens could practice the religion of their choice. The right to own property, freedom of speech, and freedom of conscience were ensured. The comprehensiveness and uniformity of the new legal system reflected the ideals of the Enlightenment and the aspirations of the revolutionaries. The rights of some people, however, were still restricted. Property rights and economic freedom favored employers over employees, and prohibitions on associations outlawed organized trade unions and the right to strike. Freedom of speech was compromised by Napoleon's manipulation and control of information. He reduced the number of newspapers in Paris and attempted to make theater a vehicle for shaping public opinion. One of the strongest deviations from the radical changes of the revolutionary period pertained to marriage and family. Civil marriage and divorce were retained, but the control of families was restored to the patriarch. Fathers had despotic control over their children, and women were of inferior status with almost no claim over common property. They remained subject to their fathers until they became subject to their husbands. Another major change introduced by Napoleon was the introduction of a highly centralized system of education. Revolutionary governments had planned such a system, but never implemented it; under Napoleon's regime, the new Imperial University was established, although in reality it was not so much a university but a department of secondary education. His main goal was to educate bureaucrats to run his new administrative machine, and in so doing he set up a system of secular, state education, but left primary schooling in the hands of the church.

In brief, it can be said that Napoleon set up a personal dictatorship, but one that cannot be regarded as a return to absolute monarchy or military dictatorship. As a former revolutionary, he constructed a system that certainly had the appearances of parliamentary self-government and even of democracy. In substance, it was neither. As for the ideals of the Revolution, Napoleon did retain a great deal of the principle of legal and civil equality, but he had no use for the ideal of liberty. This was certainly illustrated by the fact that he shaped a type of police state that allowed for no political opposition and no freedom of the press or opinion. At the same time, it was neither a violent nor a brutal state. Napoleon believed in the rule of law, and certainly he did attempt to give France efficient, rational, enlightened government.

The Napoleonic Wars

France had been continually at war since 1792, and the French had generally benefited from the activity in terms of both land and money. Napoleon's domestic reforms served to make his country even stronger, and at the end of 1804, Napoleon began a series of campaigns designed to show that France was invincible and that he was a remarkable military leader. Until the Russian campaign ended in defeat, he proved himself an outstanding commander. In 1803 and 1804 he prepared to invade Great Britain, but the French

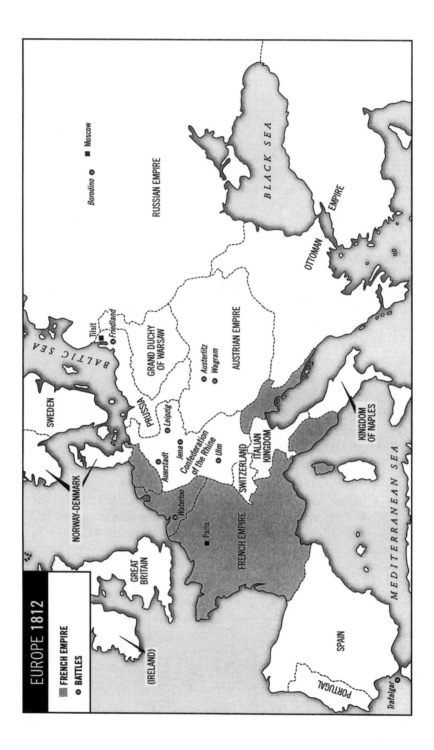

EUROPE 1812

FRENCH EMPIRE
⊗ BATTLES

GREAT
BRITAIN

(IRELAND)

NORWAY-DENMARK

SWEDEN

BALTIC SEA

Tilsit ⊗
⊗ Friedland

PRUSSIA

GRAND DUCHY
OF WARSAW

⊗ Leipzig

Jena ⊗
Auerstadt ⊗
Confederation
of the Rhine
⊗ Ulm

Waterloo ⊗

Paris ■

FRENCH EMPIRE

SWITZERLAND
ITALIAN
KINGDOM

AUSTRIAN EMPIRE

Austerlitz ⊗
⊗ Wagram

Borodino ⊗

■ Moscow

RUSSIAN EMPIRE

BLACK SEA

OTTOMAN

EMPIRE

KINGDOM
OF NAPLES

MEDITERRANEAN SEA

SPAIN

PORTUGAL

Trafalgar ⊗

navy could never win control of the Channel. In addition, Napoleon was forced to march eastward with his army after the formation of the Third Coalition in 1805. This alliance, consisting of Great Britain, Russia, Austria, and Sweden, followed upon the First Coalition of 1792 (initially Austria, and Prussia) and the Second Coalition of 1799 (Britain, Austria, Russia, Naples, and the Ottoman Empire). In the ensuing battles, Napoleon's armies were victorious at Ulm in October 1805 and at Austerlitz in December. Meanwhile, also in October, Admiral Nelson and the British destroyed the French-Spanish fleet in the Battle of Trafalgar.

In October 1806 Napoleon's soldiers beat the Prussians in the battles of Jena and Auerstadt. His troops occupied Berlin, and he established the Continental System, which served to blockade the continent in an effort to deprive Britain of trade with the rest of Europe. In June 1807, he defeated the Russians at the Battle of Friedland, and Tsar Alexander I signed the Treaty of Tilsit on a raft in the middle of the Niemen River. This treaty brought the Russians and the French together to make common cause against Great Britain. At the beginning of 1808, Napoleon stood at the height of power in Europe; the French were in a position of dominance on the continent surpassing anything previously achieved. Napoleon placed three of his brothers and his brother-in-law on various European thrones.

The profound impact of Napoleon's conquest of Europe manifested itself in a series of smaller revolutions. Britain, in response to the continental blockade industrialized at a rate that put her miles ahead of the continent by 1815. Ideologies and reforms born of the French Revolution were carried far and wide during the Napoleonic campaigns. The demise of privilege, feudalism, and general repression accompanied the spread of the French ideas of liberty, equality, and fraternity in the wake of Napoleon's destruction of the social and governmental institutions of the Old Regime in his march across Europe. The presence of the French in these areas of conquest did not pass without reaction. Many Europeans believed that Napoleon was an imperialist who had simply given a new face to the existing despotism. The responses varied from resigned passivity in the case of the Poles to rebellion in Spain and Portugal and a wave of passionate nationalism in Germany. The determination of the Spanish and Portuguese to rout the French in the Peninsular War served to drain the French treasury, trigger uprisings in the colonies, and tie down an enormous number of French troops for more than five years. Despite his best efforts, Napoleon never was able to quell this rebellion.

In Germany, the changes triggered by the Napoleonic conquests were equally profound. He destroyed the old Holy Roman Empire and got rid of

112 states as well as 44 of 50 free cities. He reduced the number of German political units from 300 to only 39 and, in making his drastic changes, succeeded in creating a wave of nationalism that was to pave the way for liberation. Prussia rose with particular determination to meet the challenge of throwing off the Napoleonic yoke, and many German nationalists began to look to Berlin for leadership. Reform politicians Baron Heinrich von Stein and Karl August von Hardenberg began a program of social change that initiated the abolition of serfdom, gave some self-government to the cities, and emancipated the Jews. Napoleon had placed a limit of 42,000 troops on the Prussian army, but this was successfully circumvented by a system that trained one army and immediately put it on reserve, with a new army being called up for training. In this way, Prussia was able to build a force of 270,000 men. In addition, Prussian intellectuals used education as a means to spread nationalistic propaganda, with the University of Berlin as the center of this effort.

In both Austria and Russia, opposition to Napoleon was steadily increasing. After defeat at the Battle of Wagram in 1809, the Austrians became more docile, but were not reconciled to their fate. Although by now Napoleon had married Marie Louise (r. 1801–1814), the daughter of Francis II (r. 1792–1835) of Austria, the tie was at best a tenuous one. The Russians hated the Treaty of Tilsit, and the Continental System was a constant thorn in their side. Furthermore, Napoleon held out the hope of independence to the people of Poland. This was a grave threat to Tsar Alexander I (r. 1810–1825), who held the greater part of Poland and had no intention of letting it go. Any alliance between the French and the Russians under the circumstances could only be temporary, and by 1810 the two countries were preparing for war against each other. In 1812, Napoleon launched a massive invasion of Russia. A military alliance with Austria allowed him to move an international army of more than 600,000 soldiers across the Russian frontier. On September 7, 1812, at Borodino, about sixty miles west of Moscow, Napoleon's Grand Army suffered high casualties, but defeated the Russians and pressed on to Moscow, only to find it deserted. For five weeks Napoleon and his army waited, expecting overtures of peace from Alexander. These never came, but fires leveled three-quarters of the city and provisions ran dangerously low. Disorder spread through the ranks, and on October 18 Napoleon gave the order to withdraw. The horror and starvation of the retreat has become legendary. The ragged, half-starved soldiers struggled against the encroaching cold and attempted to fight off the Cossacks who rode out of the blizzards to finish off the stragglers. Napoleon left his army and made it back to Paris in thirteen days, while fewer than 50,000 men of his decimated soldiery survived the struggle to get home.

In 1813, Napoleon faced combined forces from Russia, Prussia, and Austria in central Europe. At Leipzig, from October 16 to 19, 1813, the Battle of the Nations took place, and the Grand Army was decisively defeated and forced to retreat across the Rhine. Meanwhile, British forces crossed over the Pyrenees and entered France. The Napoleonic empire collapsed, and the opening months of 1814 saw Napoleon on the defensive in France against armies that totaled over 400,000 men. Britain, Prussia, Russia, and Austria set aside their differences and in signing the Treaty of Chaumont formed the Quadruple Alliance. They committed themselves to the defeat of Napoleon and to the preservation of the peace settlements that would soon be hammered out. On March 31, 1814, the allies entered Paris, and Napoleon, at Fontainebleau, agreed to abdicate. He was granted a pension of two million francs per year and sovereignty over the little island of Elba, near his native Corsica in the Mediterranean. The Bourbon line was restored to the throne of France, and the first Treaty of Paris signed with the allies. This was a fairly generous settlement, with French boundaries returned to those of 1792, but without the imposition of an indemnity. The powers then prepared to gather at an international congress in Vienna to shape the future of Europe in the aftermath of Napoleon's activities.

THE CONGRESS OF VIENNA AND THE HUNDRED DAYS

The Congress of Vienna opened in September 1814, and its deliberations were not to conclude until November 1815. A division of the spoils would prove to be one aspect of the agenda. The diplomats also saw as their primary duty the construction of a stable order after the period of confusion and devastating war that had been unleashed in 1792. The Congress has been viewed as one big party, but eventually it did accomplish its objectives, despite the hunting and sleighing parties, military parades, spectacles, and fireworks. Endless receptions were held at Schönnbrun, and it seemed that there was endless dancing; it has often been said that the Congress danced, period! It was as if an almost mad gaiety was manifesting itself in reaction to the turbulent times just past, as Europe emerged from under the shadow of war.

It is estimated that 207 states, which included extinct principalities as well as one global empire (Britain), sent one or more delegates to Vienna. Most of these could do little more than lobby the representatives of the victorious

2.6. Compositions by Beethoven were performed during the Congress of Vienna. (Erich Lessing/Art Resource, New York)

powers, who decided all important matters and worked out the details of a new Europe. The host country, Austria, was represented by Prince Klemens von Metternich, Great Britain by Lord Castlereagh and later by the Duke of Wellington, and Prussia by Prince von Hardenberg. Alexander I of Russia was present with his adviser, Count Nesselrode, who later became foreign minister. Other heads of state, in addition to the tsar, were in attendance; however, these leading statesmen of the triumphant powers dominated the decision making. Talleyrand led the French delegation. The diplomatic skills of this survivor of the Old Regime, who took advantage of some of the dissension that arose among the four Great Powers, provided a stronger voice for France at the conference table than was anticipated.

In the view of the victors, the major problem confronting the leaders at Vienna was keeping France from again running rampant all over Europe, and with this in mind, a system of buffer states was devised. Belgium (the Austrian Netherlands) was joined to the Dutch Netherlands, and Prussia received extensive territories along the left bank of the Rhine. Switzerland was enlarged and its neutrality guaranteed. In the Italian peninsula, Nice and Genoa were added to a restored Piedmont-Sardinia. Away from the borders of France, Lombardy and Venetia were transferred to Austria as compensation for its loss of the Austrian Netherlands. In other smaller duchies, such as Parma and Modena, former rulers were restored, and the papal states were returned to the pope. For a brief period the Bourbons were not restored to the throne of the Kingdom of Naples (the Kingdom of the Two Sicilies), where Joachim Murat, Napoleon's brother-in-law, continued to rule.

The quarantine of France and the promotion of a balance of power were not always compatible with restoring prerevolutionary conditions. In the center of Europe, this meant choosing not to reconstruct the old Holy Roman Empire. Rather, a simplified Germany consisted of thirty-nine states called the Germanic Confederation, which included Prussia and Austria. Within the confederation every state retained its sovereignty. However, in the diet of the confederation, composed of representatives from the member states, Austria was to dominate. Metternich, fearing a strong and united Germany, was particularly anxious for this arrangement. There were other territorial changes as well. Finland was annexed by Russia, and Sweden was compensated for this loss by union with Norway. Great Britain retained small, but strategic, territories seized during the conflicts. These included Malta, Ceylon, Cape Colony, and Heligoland. Some possessions that had been taken by the British were returned to France and the Netherlands.

An explosive issue erupted in early 1815, demonstrating that national interests and ambitions were ever present at the congress. Tsar Alexander wanted to re-create a Polish kingdom with himself as the constitutional monarch. Austria and Prussia would be required to relinquish the portions of Poland they had acquired through earlier partitions. Prussia was willing to accept the arrangement in return for all of Saxony. Such an expansion for those two countries was an alarming prospect for Austria. The Polish-Saxon question divided the powers, and the threat of conflict loomed. After months of negotiation in which Talleyrand assumed a key role, a compromise was devised. It provided for a reduced "congress" Poland linked to Russia, while Prussia was to receive two-thirds of Saxony. As this question was resolved and final drafts of the overall agreement were prepared, another crisis arose.

Napoleon made an attempt to recover the throne of France. With an army of 1,100 men, he left Elba and landed at Fréjus near Cannes on March 1, 1815, and gained many supporters as the French, already disenchanted with Bourbon rule, rushed to his aid. Even Marshal Ney, who had vowed to arrest Napoleon and bring him back to Paris in a cage, joined with him instead. On March 20, Louis XVIII (r. 1814–1815 and 1815–1824) fled the Tuileries just hours before Napoleon took up residence there. With the Great Powers aligned against him, Napoleon hastily organized an army, knowing that he must face battle immediately and that the Great Powers had agreed to never

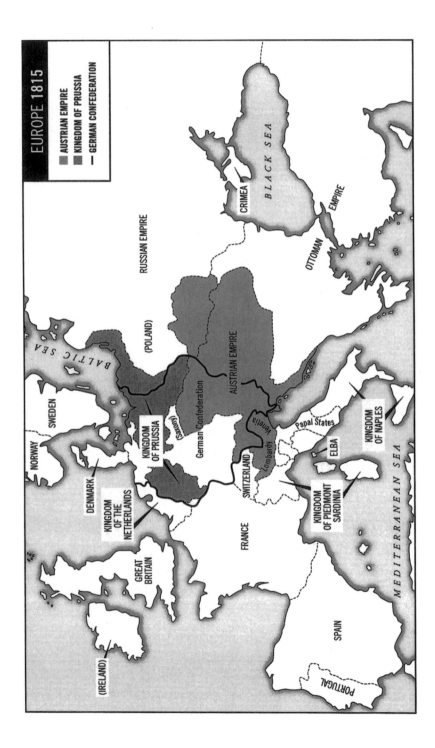

EUROPE 1815

■ AUSTRIAN EMPIRE
■ KINGDOM OF PRUSSIA
— GERMAN CONFEDERATION

BLACK SEA

CRIMEA

OTTOMAN EMPIRE

RUSSIAN EMPIRE

(POLAND)

AUSTRIAN EMPIRE

BALTIC SEA

KINGDOM OF PRUSSIA

(Saxony)

German Confederation

Venetia

Papal States

Lombardy

KINGDOM OF NAPLES

ELBA

NORWAY

SWEDEN

DENMARK

KINGDOM OF THE NETHERLANDS

SWITZERLAND

KINGDOM OF PIEDMONT SARDINIA

GREAT BRITAIN

FRANCE

(IRELAND)

SPAIN

PORTUGAL

MEDITERRANEAN SEA

stop fighting until he had been defeated. On June 16 his troops repulsed a
Prussian force that was advancing through Belgium and then faced the army
of the Duke of Wellington near Brussels. Two days later, Wellington's army
stood solidly against the assaults of Napoleon's troops. Blücher, the Prussian
general, returned in time to come to Wellington's aid, and by nightfall it was
all over. This was the Battle of Waterloo, the final scene of the Napoleonic
drama.

The time Napoleon abdicated, surrendering to the English, and was exiled to the lonely island of St. Helena in the southern Atlantic for the remainder of his life. One hundred days after fleeing Paris, Louis XVIII was
once more restored to the throne of France. By the terms of a second Treaty
of Paris, the French were to pay an indemnity of 700 million francs and to return the art treasures that had been removed by Napoleon from foreign museums and galleries, in addition to having their boundaries further reduced.
An allied army was to occupy the northern provinces of the country for five
years. The only congress decision changed by the Hundred Days episode
was the restoration of the Bourbon monarchy in Naples. Murat, who had
supported Napoleon, was captured and executed.

The leaders, having worked to achieve a settlement among the nations,
were determined that it should endure, despite all assaults against it. Tsar
Alexander I, often under the shadow of religious mysticism, proposed a document that pledged the rulers to act together in harmony within the precepts
of Christianity. "Christian justice, charity, and peace" were to be the founding precepts of this new Holy Alliance. All the leaders signed, except the
pope, the British regent, and the Ottoman sultan, who was spared the indig-
nity of being asked. The document was called "a piece of sublime mysticism
and nonsense" by Castlereagh and dismissed by Metternich as "a loud-
sounding nothing." The Holy Alliance seems not to have had the slightest effect on anything ever and was forgotten immediately upon the death of the
tsar.

The Quadruple Alliance, however, was quite another matter. The commitments made at Chaumont were reaffirmed as a solid diplomatic fact, and the
Great Powers signed the agreement in November 1815. By this treaty, Austria,
Prussia, Russia, and Great Britain bound themselves to maintain the settlements of Vienna and Paris for a period of twenty years. Their objectives were
the preservation of the territorial boundaries and the perpetual exclusion of the
Napoleonic dynasty from the French throne. In addition, their aim was to
combat the principles of the French Revolution and to prevent any further revolutionary uprisings. This agreement outlined a new system for administering

the affairs of Europe, and this new congress system, as it was called, determined that the powers would meet at fixed intervals "for the purpose of consulting upon common interests." Between 1818 and 1822, a series of congresses was held that dealt with problems arising from the dissatisfaction of various European peoples with the restraints of the Vienna settlement. The delegates to the Congress of Vienna may have danced, but they also fashioned a new European order and new methods of preserving that which they had made.

It would be another century before Europe was again embroiled in a massive series of wars involving all of the Great Powers. Despite the fact that there were no international wars for a time, the impulses of liberty, equality, and fraternity unleashed by the French Revolution were only temporarily defeated and certainly were not dead. Many of the issues raised by the Revolution and Napoleon Bonaparte would re-emerge before long and would form much of the fabric of the nineteenth century in Europe, as well as in other parts of the world.

NOTE

1. See analyses in Donald Greer, *The Incidence of the Terror during the French Revolution; A Statistical Interpretation* (Gloucester, Mass.: Harvard University Press, 1966).

Chapter 3

INDUSTRIALIZATION
SHAPES THE
NATION-STATE

REVOLUTION IN INDUSTRY AND LABOR

Just as the events of the French Revolution and Napoleonic era changed the political landscape of Europe and had repercussions beyond the continent, so did the Industrial Revolution initiate a transformation in European life that had much broader implications. Human and animal power were gradually replaced by new sources of energy that resulted in new ways of organizing human labor to maximize the use of new machinery. It was a long slow process that witnessed the movement of people from their traditional rural world to the developing urban centers in search of work and opportunity. Changes in transportation made it possible to use raw materials and reach markets far beyond the borders of one's own country. Economic and social relations among people were altered, and relations between the countries of Europe and the rest of the world were transformed as well. The Industrial Revolution had its beginnings in Great Britain during the second half of the eighteenth century, but its impact on the continent was not felt until after 1815. For a time in the middle of the nineteenth century, Great Britain was the industrial powerhouse of the globe, but by 1900 this had changed with Germany and the United States taking the lead in industrial production.

Industrial Revolution in Great Britain

A variety of factors and circumstances combined to give Great Britain the initial advantage. Commercialized agriculture, which incorporated improved farming methods, contributed earlier than elsewhere to a substantial increase in the food supply. The resulting lower prices for some foods made it possible for families to use a portion of their income for other things, thus contributing to a potential demand for manufactured goods. In addition, the need for less labor in food production combined with population growth provided a pool of workers for the new emerging factories. The important mineral resources of coal and iron, essential to the manufacturing process, were abundant in Great Britain. The small size of the country and the absence of significant topographical barriers made the movement of resources and finished products relatively easy. Navigable rivers enhanced by canals and road construction linked the major centers and the coast by the 1780s, facilitating domestic and foreign trade.

Financial instruments conducive to industrial development were also present in Great Britain. The capital required for investment came from the growing cottage industry and extensive colonial trade. Textiles, in particular, generated a lucrative transatlantic trade in cotton for spinning and weaving and in slaves for work on the plantations. Other profitable colonial commodities such as tobacco, sugar, and tea similarly funded rising industrial enterprises. Commercial transactions were aided by an effective banking system. Paper notes, which had come into increasing use during the Napoleonic Wars as the supply of coins dwindled, were placed under the control of the Bank of England. This ensured the reliability of paper currency. The British government played a significant role in economic expansion in other respects as well. The stability of government, evolving parliamentary institutions, and the protection of private property contributed to a favorable business climate. Minimal restrictions placed on entrepreneurs, provisions for limited liability, enactment of protective tariffs on foreign goods, and funding for transportation were all means by which the British government encouraged economic expansion.

Economic development in Great Britain was also furthered by the changes that had occurred in social structures and attitudes. Social barriers did not deter the land-owning nobility and rural gentry with entrepreneurial interests from associating with merchant capitalists. Industry had access to a supply of markets for manufactured goods. Domestic circumstances were favorable, as British citizens enjoyed the highest standard of living with more discretionary income than consumers on the continent. Also critical were Great Britain's colonial empire and merchant marine, which provided access to markets in the Americas, Africa, and Asia. In the early stages of industrialization, British machine-produced textiles delivered durable and inexpensive clothing both at home and abroad. The demands from these markets strained the capacity of the cottage industry and led entrepreneurs to seek and adopt new methods of manufacturing.

These factors, in conjunction with their complex interrelationships, contributed to Great Britain's leading role. Debates about what actually precipitated an eighteenth-century economic take-off have been replaced by a consensus that the process entailed a gradual transformation. In seeking to identify crucial elements in the industrialization process, some interpretations give prominence to the problem of energy. Until the eighteenth century, there was a reliance on the conversion of energy derived mainly from plant products and animal and human muscle to provide power. Increased efficiency in the use of water and wind helped with such tasks as pumping, milling, or sailing. However, by the eighteenth century, Great Britain in particular was experiencing an energy shortage. Wood, the primary source of heat for homes and industries and also used in the iron industry as processed charcoal, was diminishing in supply. Great Britain had large amounts of coal; however, there were not yet efficient means by which to produce mechanical energy or to power machinery. This was to occur with progress in the development of the steam engine.

In the 1760s James Watt (1736–1819) carefully examined a version of Thomas Newcomen's engine, which had been initially designed in 1705 for use in pumping water from mines. Watt slowly obtained the financing, skilled assistance, and precision parts to implement improvements that over the next twenty years made the steam engine mechanically more efficient and commercially viable. It was soon applied to a variety of industrial uses as it became cheaper to use. The engine helped solve the problem of draining mines and increased the production of coal needed to power steam engines elsewhere. A rotary engine attached to the steam engine enabled shafts to be turned and machines to be driven, resulting in mills using steam power to spin and weave cotton. Since the steam engine was fired by coal, the large mills did not need to be located by rivers, as had water-driven machines. The shift to increased mechanization in cotton production is apparent in the import of raw cotton and sale of cotton goods. Between 1760 and 1850, the amount of raw cotton imported increased 230 times. At the same time, yarn decreased in price so that spinners and weavers elsewhere in the world could not compete with either the quality or quantity of British cotton goods. Production increased sixtyfold, and cotton cloth was Great Britain's most important product and accounted for about one-half of all exports. The success of the steam engine increased the demand for coal, and the consequent increase in coal production was made possible as the steam-powered pumps drained water from the ever-deeper coal seams found below the water table. The availability of steam power and the demands for new machines facilitated the transformation of the iron industry. Charcoal, made from wood and thus in limited supply, was replaced with coal-derived coke as steam-driven bellows came into use in the smelting of pig iron. Impurities were burnt away with the use of coke, producing a high-quality refined iron. Reduced cost was also instrumental in developing steam-powered rolling mills capable of varying the shape and size of finished iron. The resulting boom in the iron industry expanded the annual output by more than 170 times between 1740 and 1840, and by the 1850s Great Britain was producing more tons of iron than the rest of the world combined. The developments in the iron industry were in part a response to the demand for more machines and the ever-widening use of higher-quality iron in other industries.

Steam power and iron combined to produce a revolution in transportation. Improvements in road construction and sailing had occurred, but the shipment of heavy freight over land remained expensive, even with the use of rivers and canals wherever possible. Parallel wooden rails had long been used in mining operations to allow horses and humans to move bigger loads. Cast-iron rails reduced friction even more and came into increasing use by the early 1800s. Although these rails were also used for surface transportation, horses were still the source of power. The arrival of the steam engine initiated a complete transformation in rail transportation. The early work of Richard Trevithick (1771–1833) with a steam-powered locomotive on a rail line yielded impressive, but slow-moving, results. Ten tons of ore could be moved at five miles per hour. George Stephenson (1781–1848) developed an effective locomotive by 1825, and his "Rocket" traveling at sixteen miles per hour was used in the first public railway line in 1830. Within twenty years, locomotives reached speeds of fifty miles an hour and featured a much larger carrying capacity. Private companies quickly formed and obtained government approval for rights of way. By 1850, 6,000 miles of railway track had been laid in Great Britain.

The railway entrenched and expanded the Industrial Revolution. The immediate demand for more coal and iron stimulated those industries. However, as transportation improved, distant and larger markets within the nation could be reached, thereby encouraging the development of larger factories to keep pace with increasing sales. Greater productivity and rising demands provided entrepreneurs with profits that could be reinvested to take advantage of new technologies to further expand capacity or seek alternative investment opportunities. Dynamic self-sustaining growth was replacing the comparatively static traditional economy. The availability of jobs in railway construction attracted many rural laborers accustomed to seasonal and temporary employment. When the work was completed, many moved to other construction jobs or to factory work in cities and towns. In the growing urban centers, they became part of an expanding working class that fuelled further demands. Workers entering the factory found that such work placed significantly different demands on them than had the farm, peasant cottage, or artisan's workshop. In contrast to the irregular hours and hectic work followed by periods of inactivity, factory labor required new discipline and work formats. Laborers were required to put in regular hours and shifts to maximize the output from machines. Tasks were simplified and performed repetitively and as efficiently as possible. Factory owners imposed stringent regulations involving severe fines or even dismissal for a variety of infractions. Child laborers were often subject to beatings since they were less likely to be responsive to the consequences of fines and dismissal. The working conditions could be appalling, yet as industrialization progressed, the concepts of regular daily hours of work and a defined workweek became the norm.

3.1. Interior of London's Crystal Palace during the International Exhibition of 1851 (Tate Gallery, London/Art Resource, New York)

In 1851 London was host to the first industrial exposition. The Crystal Palace, a pavilion designed to house the exhibits, was an architectural feat of the new industrial era. This large-scale prefabricated glass and iron structure was erected in London's Hyde Park and covered almost twenty acres. It contained over 100,000 exhibits from participating countries in Europe and North America. Approximately six million visitors came to view the displays over a period of six months. They marveled at the wide range of goods and materials, but the variety and quantity of British machines were most impressive, and the Great Exhibition of 1851 was a showcase of British industrial achievement.

Industrialization on the Continent

During the first half of the nineteenth-century, industrialization spread throughout the continent at varying rates, with Belgium, France, and the German states being the first to move in new economic directions. Once again several factors account for the variations in rates and forms of industrialization. Elements that contributed to a lag on the continent in comparison to Great Britain included the lack of good roads, the continuation of guild regulations, and a less enterprising and risk-taking business attitude. In addition, the French revolutionary wars and those of the Napoleonic era not only caused destruction and interrupted trade, but produced political instability. The disruption of communication between the continent and Great Britain meant that the flow of information and technology to the former also suffered. As a result, the gap in the development of industrial machinery had widened. On the other hand, continental countries were able to obtain both advanced British machinery and skilled technicians, although Great Britain attempted to restrict the movement of both of these beyond its borders.

A significant difference between British and continental industrialization, which assisted economic growth in continental countries, was the important role played by governments. In contrast to the relatively laissez-faire orientation that prevailed in Great Britain, continental governments continued to intervene in economic affairs to a greater extent. Important elements of this approach included the establishment of technical schools, the systematic application of protective tariffs, subsidies for technical innovations, and extensive financing for transportation.

Continental industrialization varied from region to region. As in Great Britain, cotton manufacturing was instrumental in the early stages of industrialization on the continent; however, the coal and iron industries gained early significance as well. In Belgium, banks obtained government permission to establish themselves as limited-liability corporations, thus attracting a large number of stockholders. This development placed these industrial banks in the prominent role of financing and encouraging industrial development. France retained more rural industry, and a larger proportion of the population remained engaged in agriculture. Workshop production of traditional luxury items was not displaced by mass production in factories as rapidly as it was in Great Britain or Belgium. The German states, facing the challenges of political division, formed a customs union (*Zollverein*) in 1834, thereby expanding the strongly protected domestic markets.

In other European regions, such as the Italian states and Spain, industrialization tended to occur in localized pockets. One important inhibiting factor was limited access to essential natural resources. Eastern and southern Europe, also lacking natural resources and investment capital, remained largely agrarian with the exception of localized areas of industrial development, such as Bohemia. Russia possessed a wide range of natural resources, but was hampered by serfdom in the first half of the nineteenth century and then by its aftermath following the Emancipation of 1861. Further obstacles arose from opposition to industrial change on the part of the political and economic elite and a general hostility toward the West supported by the Russian Orthodox Church.

Demographic and Social Changes

The slow process of industrialization was accompanied by a rise in the European population that became more and more dramatic as the nineteenth century progressed. Between 1750 and 1850 the total European population almost doubled to over 265 million. Industrialization did not initially cause this population growth, but the two developments combined to produce significant social consequences. A decline in death rates was the primary factor accounting for the population increase. In the early stages, it was attributable to a decline in the number of major epidemics and a general increase in the food supply, which began with the agricultural revolution of the eighteenth century.

Since the need for industrial workers was not uniform across Great Britain or the continent, some rural areas experienced population pressures. Industrial growth attracted and absorbed large numbers of economic refugees, but many emigrated. From the 1820s to the 1850s, more than 100,000 left Europe each year, mainly for destinations in the Americas, but during times of agrarian crisis, such as the bad harvests of 1846–1847, these numbers were greatly expanded. Over an eight-year period ending in 1855, more than 1.5 million left Ireland, and just under one million emigrated from the southern German states. While this "safety valve" of emigration relieved the strain on rural areas, it was the movement of people to towns and cities within Europe that had the greatest impact on the continent.

This urbanization was directly related to burgeoning industry. Towns and cities, which had always functioned as combination of market, commercial, administrative, and religious centers, now grew in size, as manufacturing and industry supported and demanded a higher population. In 1800 Great Britain had only seven cities with a population of over 50,000. Fifty years later there were over twenty-five such cities, and almost 50 percent of the population lived in urban areas. Urbanization, like industrialization, proceeded at a slower rate on the continent. By midcentury only about 25 percent of the French population lived in towns and cities. Statistics for Belgium and the German states indicate a higher rate; however, further to the South and East and on the Iberian Peninsula, populations remained predominantly rural.

The changing economic and demographic conditions affected social groupings and social relations. Particularly significant was the rise of two new economic and social groups composed of industrial capitalists and industrial workers, who were also frequently labeled capital and labor, respectively. These two groups transformed the middle and working classes. The orders, or estates, of the previous centuries were fading or, as in France, had been abolished by the Revolution; however, rural-based social classes did not disappear, and continuity with the past was as noteworthy as the novelty of new social divisions. The aristocracy continued to possess much of the wealth, retained political influence, and in some cases wielded considerable political power; at the same time, the privileges of the nobility had been undermined as wealth based on industry grew in comparison to the traditional forms based on land and commerce. On the continent, the majority of the population at the beginning of the nineteenth century was still comprised of peasants. In addition to the uncertain forces of nature, they were subjected to pressures arising from the commercialization of agriculture, population growth, and industrialization. Frequently regarded as bound by tradition, peasants, generally living at subsistence levels, carefully and cautiously judged the impact of the possibilities and opportunities that presented themselves. It is not surprising that they tended to be skeptical of the comprehensive reform proposals of urban outsiders and continued to maintain traditional patterns.

Urban areas directly and dramatically experienced the shifting social composition that accompanied industrialization and urbanization. The middle class, or bourgeoisie, was transformed as industrial entrepreneurs joined its ranks. In the early stages of industrialization, these men had diverse social origins, as no particular social segment could monopolize or dominate the new activities of building factories, obtaining machines, securing resources, and reaching markets. Initiative, determination, resourcefulness, and motivation were more critical to success than the advantages of birth, inheritance, or social status. Many came from humble backgrounds, having started as artisans, skilled workers, or social minorities, and were able to take advantage of opportunities, but well-established commercial and landowning families were also represented. As industries developed and required greater capital investment, fewer opportunities presented themselves for those without wealth to become factory owners. Those who survived the intensely competitive climate were able to pass on established enterprises to the next generation. Along with this, there developed a sense of belonging to a distinct social group with common interests. In the broadest terms, members of the middle class opposed privilege derived from tradition and supported change that rewarded hard work and self-reliance.

In the early stages of industrialization, the working class remained a mixture of diverse groups; factory workers did not become the majority until the second half of the nineteenth century. These groups included domestic servants, skilled workers, and the more independent artisans. The numbers of domestic servants increased as the middle class expanded. Artisans continued to supply traditional goods and services through small workshops and industries. As the growth of factories threatened to displace craft production with cheaper mass-produced goods, artisans tended to oppose industrialization. Nevertheless, as guild regulations had been eliminated or severely restricted, skilled craftsmen found some common cause with the slowly growing number of factory workers. Among these was the increasing lack of control over the nature and conditions of their work. The experience of the factory workers was unique with regard to their working and living conditions. Laborers faced twelve- to sixteen-hour shifts, six days a week, with no security of employment or of wage levels adequate to sustain a family. Women and children continued to remain a part of the workplace out of necessity and to the advantage of employers, who were able to pay them even less than they paid the men. Whether the unhealthy and horrific conditions occurred in the heat and dust of cotton mills or the damp danger of the coal mines, the places of work were appalling.

3.2. A mid–nineteenth century London street scene by Gustave Doré (SEF/Art Re-source, New York)

The few hours of the day that could be spent away from the work site promised no relief. Industrial workers lived in a state of urban poverty. The largest portion of their incomes was spent on food that was inadequate for a healthy diet and consisted primarily of bread. The remainder of the wages had to be spent on clothing and housing. The crowded, hastily built tene-ment structures in which many lived provided barely adequate shelter amidst exposure to garbage and raw sewage. These conditions, compounded by heavy industrial pollution, contributed to frequent eruptions of disease, which could spread rapidly. The diverse changes wrought by industrialization were in many cases detrimental to the well-being of the individuals involved, and the cost to society was extremely high (see appendix, Document XI).

POLITICS IN THE AGE OF METTERNICH

The peace settlements of 1815 seemingly calmed the upheaval that had been engendered by the French Revolution and the conquests of Napoleon. The traditional wealth and power of throne, land, altar, and bureaucracy were for the most part reestablished. On the international scene, the forces of conservatism attempted to maintain the new (restored) arrangement, but the fact of the matter was that the European world had undergone a radical change and its peoples would not readily revert to the ways of the old system. New ideologies of change had made an appearance and paramount among these were liberalism and nationalism. These ideologies were the result of forces that had led to revolution in France, and their impact was far too powerful and too widespread to be contained for very long. Waves of revolution swept Europe during the 1820s and 1830s, and by midcentury it was apparent that the constraints imposed by the Vienna settlement were not strong enough to triumph over the new forces shaking the continent. Unleashed by the Industrial and French Revolutions, these forces made a return to the old order unthinkable.

Conservatism and Intellectual Responses

The archconservatism inherent in the Vienna settlement as personified by Metternich and determination to preserve the status quo came into direct conflict with these new and powerful forces. What was the basis of the ideology of conservatism, which held the leaders at Vienna in its grip? It dated from 1790 when Edmund Burke wrote his *Reflections on the Revolution in France* as a reaction to the radical ideals that the Revolution espoused. Burke maintained that society was indeed a contract, but it was not simply a pact between the state and the living. It was a contract between the state and the dead, the living, and those yet to be born. One generation could not take it upon itself to destroy the partnership; rather, it was the duty of each successive generation to preserve it and transmit it to the next. Gradual evolutionary change was acceptable, but sudden change was not. The conservatism of Joseph de Maistre (1753–1821) went far beyond that of Burke. Whereas Burke regarded the monarchy as the cement that would hold society together, de Maistre saw it as a divinely sanctioned institution. In his view, only the divine right of kings could ensure order in society and avoid the type of chaos engendered by the French Revolution. Although there existed these differences among conservatives, most held a common body of beliefs. They believed in political obedience and organized religion as a means to a well-ordered society. They hated revolution and would accept neither liberal demands for civil liberties and representational government nor the nationalism that had arisen in the wake of the French Revolution. The well-being of the community took precedence over that of the individual, society must be ordered and organized, and tradition was the best guide to order. After 1815, political conservatism was supported by hereditary monarchs, government bureaucracies, landowning aristocrats, and churches, all of which appeared to be the dominant forces in the era from 1815 to 1848 that came to be known as the Age of Metternich.

Steeped as he was in conservative belief, it was Metternich's contention that he was guided by the principle of legitimacy at Vienna. He believed that the reimposition of peace and order would come from the restoration of legitimate monarchs who would guard traditional institutions. Although this did occur in France, elsewhere it seems that legitimacy as a guiding principle was largely ignored and practical considerations dominated. Foremost among these were territorial arrangements aimed at maintaining a balance of power or an equilibrium among the Great Powers, which now included France. This meant that a balance of political and military forces must be maintained on the continent so that no one power could achieve dominance over the others. These considerations superseded all others, with the result that territories and peoples were transferred between the Great Powers with very little or no regard at all for the wishes of those involved. This orientation was illustrated in the treatment accorded Poland and the compensation granted Austria for the loss of the Austrian Netherlands at the Congress of Vienna. It also resulted in a tension between the forces dedicated to the preservation of the status quo and those determined to bring about change.

Working against the traditional order of political conservatives, monarchs, monarchists, and churches, powerful forces for change manifested themselves in internal upheavals and revolutions directed against the guardians of the status quo within the various regions and countries of Europe. There developed as well responses of an intellectual nature. Liberalism, nationalism, and radicalism were three of these responses. They constituted self-conscious movements in political and social arenas that took deliberate aim at the established order. Liberalism was both political and economic in nature. Politically, it stood for the principles of the French Revolution, especially those of liberty and civic equality. Characteristic of liberalism were written constitutions and parliamentary governments, both revolutionary innovations for that time. Liberals came to hold a basic set of beliefs that included equality before the law, freedom of the press and of speech, and the right to free assembly, as well as freedom from arbitrary arrest. Ideally, for all citizens of all countries, these rights and freedoms should be guaranteed in writing, as in the French Declaration of the Rights of Man and Citizen. Religious toleration, separation of church and state, the right of peaceful opposition to government, and the making of laws by a representative assembly elected by qualified voters were all basic to liberal belief.

Many liberals also advocated a form of ministerial responsibility in which ministers were responsible to the elected assembly rather than to the king, thus giving the legislative branch a check on the power of the executive branch. Liberals of the early nineteenth century believed in a limited suffrage only. They did not believe that all people should be entitled to vote, although they felt that all should have equal civil rights. In their minds, the right to vote and to hold office should be restricted to men who met certain property qualifications. Liberals, as middle-class industrialists for the most part, were hostile to absolute monarchy, aristocracy, and the power of the churches, but they did wish to share in the power of the landed classes. They had no desire to extend that power to those below them in the social hierarchy, since liberalism was in no way synonymous with democracy; rather, it was middle class or bourgeois in its orientation.

Economic liberalism embraced the theories of the classical economists and their ideas of laissez-faire. Their ideals of freedom and property rights reflected the interests of the bourgeoisie with little regard for the needs and interests of the growing numbers of workers in society.

Nationalism, another force for change, involved the belief that each nation should govern itself and thus be self-determined. It can be defined as a state of mind arising out of an awareness of being part of a community with common institutions, traditions, language, and customs. The community is regarded as the nation, and the primary loyalty of individuals should be to the nation, rather than to a dynasty, city-state, or other institution. During the eighteenth century, people began to examine their language, history, literature, art, and folklore to understand the essence of their nations, and this cultural nationalism is thought to have undergone an evolution into a political awareness of nationality. This, in turn, resulted in a search for nation-states wherein subject peoples and minorities sought self-determination and political and cultural autonomy. Since most European states were not organized on a national basis and political boundaries and national boundaries were not the same, nationalism usually constituted a revolutionary force. It was extremely upsetting to the conservatives of the nineteenth century since its goals were totally incompatible with the attempts on the part of the Great Power leaders to maintain the status quo so painstakingly established in 1815. Independence for Hungary, for example, would mean the end of the Austrian Empire. But nationalism was not abhorrent to liberalism; to the contrary, it was often allied with the other most powerful force of the period. Most liberals were in favor of self-determination of nationalities and self-rule, and they believed, therefore, that boundaries of nations and states should be coterminous, with no nation in a position of dominance over another.

The democratic movement, or radicalism, was associated with the forces of nationalism and liberalism, but it was far weaker and differed from them in several important features. Liberalism advocated government by the middle classes, whereas nationalism was strongly concerned with government of the whole nation, with leadership in the hands, usually, of the middle classes, whose goal was a liberal, national state. Democrats, however, wanted all adult males to participate in politics, and in this way they went beyond liberalism in that their goals encompassed those of the liberals and even more. They were often nationalists as well, believing in power and participation for the masses rather than being solely the domain of the middle classes. It is understandable that they were regarded as a great danger, not only by kings and aristocrats, but by liberals as well. Furthermore, the democratic, or radical, movement was sometimes, but not always, republican in nature. It was possible to find democrats who were not republicans and, certainly, republicans who were not democrats. As for those who were both, republican democrats wanted no absolute king and no constitutional king, but advocated a democratic republic; for this reason, they were often referred to as radicals.

The Concert of Europe and National Uprisings

The delegates to the Congress of Vienna may have danced, but they also fashioned a new European order and new methods of preserving their achievements. It was not long before the congress system was called upon to deal with dissatisfied groups in various regions and countries of Europe.

The first congress was to be held was at Aix-la-Chapelle in September 1818. It was agreed at this conference that the occupying armies would be withdrawn from French soil, and with the decision that the French would be allowed to participate in the Concert of Europe, the Quadruple Alliance became the Quintuple Alliance. A project was proposed at this congress that would mean a union of the five powers against any country rising against the status quo. Great Britain refused to be part of such a plan, but otherwise things went smoothly, prompting Metternich to proclaim that he "had never seen a prettier little Congress."

Early in 1820 a revolt against the reactionary government in Spain caused the European powers major concern. The throne of Ferdinand VII, a Bourbon, had been restored after Napoleon's downfall. He immediately stamped out all representative institutions, the liberal constitution was abolished, decrees were declared null and void if they had been issued during his exile, the Inquisition was reestablished, and freedom of the press was curtailed. In brief, Ferdinand imposed upon his subjects restrictions much harsher than any known in the eighteenth century. With secret societies working against him and after several aborted attempts at rebellion, the army rose against him in January 1820. Two months later, Ferdinand took the oath of allegiance to the constitution. The powers stood by, anxious, but not intervening. In July 1820 a similar uprising occurred in Naples, where another Bourbon, Ferdinand I (r. 1816–1825), was forced to introduce the very liberal Spanish constitution formulated in 1812. Metternich called a congress to meet at Troppau in October 1820. This one went less smoothly than the previous one had, and the first cracks in the arrangement appeared. Metternich proposed intervention as a remedy to the unrest in Italy and the threat it posed to Austrian domination there. He brought forward a protocol proclaiming the right of intervention by members of the congress in the domestic affairs of other countries. This meant that the Great Powers could send armies into countries where revolution was taking place to restore legitimate monarchs. Great Britain refused to agree to such blatant interference, but Austria, Prussia, and Russia met again at a third congress, this one in Laibach in January 1821. This meeting resulted in Austrian troops being sent to Naples, extinguishing the revolt there, and restoring Ferdinand to the throne. Then, the troops moved northward into Piedmont-Sardinia (also commonly called Piedmont) to suppress the revolt taking place there.

In October 1822, a fourth congress was held, this time at Verona. The same powers authorized France to invade Spain and put down another revolt against Ferdinand VII. This was carried out in the spring of 1823. By this time, the split between Britain and the more conservative powers had become irreparable in that revolutionary upheavals had been quelled and Britain had adamantly refused to participate in such activity. The Quintuple Alliance no longer existed. In December 1823, a congress of the powers was called to discuss the difficulties Spain and Portugal were having with revolutions in their colonies in the New World. The British refused flatly to participate, after which the Concert of Europe no longer existed. In its place stood an alliance of Austria, Prussia, and Russia for the purpose of defending autocracy.

The uprisings dealt with by the congresses were not the only ones to take place in the period after 1815. Uprisings occurred that were directed not so much against international provisions of the Vienna settlement, but as internal movements within regions and countries of Europe that reflected a growing nationalism and awareness of the peoples in those areas. One such expression of discontent was the revolt that occurred in 1821 when the Greeks rose against their Ottoman rulers. The principle of intervention, which could either quell rebellion or support it, proved very useful. Even Great Britain made common cause with France and Russia regarding the situation in the Ottoman Empire, an area of increasing interest. Since the early nineteenth century, the Ottoman Empire had been in decline and the "Eastern Question" was to become more and more important as the century progressed. Religious bonds between the Russian people and the Greek Orthodox Christians in the Ottoman regions of southeastern Europe caused the other powers to fear Russian influence there. While the Russians wished control of the area and the Dardanelles to ensure their access to the Mediterranean, other powers had their own agendas. France and Britain were interested in commerce and naval bases, and Austria strongly desired more territory in the Balkans.

When the Greeks revolted against Ottoman rule in 1821, European powers saw it as an opportunity to realize some of their own ambitions. Although they had initially viewed the outbreak as just one more challenge to order and stability, they soon endowed it with noble characteristics and supported it; liberals were touting it, in fact, as a rebirth of democracy in Greece. There was no intervention, however, until 1827 when a combined British and French fleet went to Greece. Once there, they defeated a huge Ottoman fleet. The next year, Russia declared war on the Ottoman Empire and invaded the European provinces of Moldavia and Wallachia. In 1829 the Treaty of Adrianople ended the war between Russia and the Ottoman Empire, with Moldavia and Wallachia becoming Russian protectorates. By this same treaty, the

Turks agreed that Russia, France, and Britain should decide the fate of Greece. Greece was declared to be an independent kingdom in 1830, and two years later a new royal dynasty was established in the hands of the son of the king of Bavaria (see appendix, Document XII).

This Greek revolt was important for a variety of reasons. It was the first successful revolt against the established powers, and it was without a doubt a victory for the liberal and national sentiments that the Great Powers were devoted to suppressing. The Great Powers, however, did not see it quite this way. They felt that they had made inroads into southeastern Europe by giving the new Greece a German king. Furthermore, the revolt had succeeded because it had received support from the European powers. Up until 1830, the Greek revolt was the only successful one and, in general terms, conservatism still gripped most of Europe.

In France, the restoration of the Bourbon line had taken place in 1814 and again, after the Hundred Days, in 1815. Under the new king, Louis XVIII, the concordat with the pope was maintained, as was the Napoleonic Civil Code, according to which all citizens enjoyed equality before the law. The property rights of those who had purchased confiscated property during the Revolution were maintained. The system of government that had come into being with the Charter of 1814 provided for a bicameral legislature with a Chamber of Peers chosen by the king and a Chamber of Deputies, which was elected; the electorate was restricted to about 100,000 wealthy people. The moderation of this government was undermined on all sides by liberals and ultraroyalists alike. In 1824 Charles X (r. 1824–1830) succeeded Louis XVIII, and in 1827 he had to accept the principle of ministerial responsibility, with ministers being responsible to the legislature. By 1829 his discontent was obvious when he announced that he "would rather saw wood than be a king of the English type." Elections produced a further victory for the liberal forces in France, and the king decided that he had to make a decisive stand. On July 26, 1830, he issued the July Ordinances, a set of edicts that censored the press, dissolved the Chamber of Deputies, and placed restrictions on who was eligible to vote in the upcoming election. The result was the July Revolution. Barricades constructed from overturned carts, tables, and paving stones were thrown up all over Paris as liberals, radicals, and journalists took to the streets in an immediate response to these decrees. For three days, the protestors fought the army in the streets of Paris. Charles X fled to England, and a provisional government composed of moderate liberals was formed. Louis-Philippe, a cousin of the Bourbons who belonged to the House of Orléans, was asked to take the throne as constitutional king of France. A new constitutional monarchy had been born.

Liberals across the continent came under the influence of events in Paris, but only in Belgium was there any lasting result. The Congress of Vienna had placed the Belgians under the Dutch crown, but such a settlement did not take into account the vast cultural, economic, religious, and linguistic differences between the two peoples. The people of Belgium were for the most part French-speaking Catholic farmers and workers, while the people of Holland were Dutch-speaking Protestant seafarers and traders. The union was doomed from the start. William of Orange, the Dutch king, refused the request of Belgian liberals to grant them their own administration in August 1830. The rioting that erupted resulted in the expulsion of Dutch troops from Belgium and in the Belgian declaration of independence from the Dutch, as well as the formulation of a liberal constitution for Belgium. William requested help from Tsar Nicholas I (r. 1825–1855) and was ignored, signaling with finality the end of the principle of legitimacy. Nothing ensued until the summer of 1831, when the Belgian National Assembly met in Brussels and Prince Leopold of Saxe-Cobourg-Gotha was chosen as king of Belgium. In 1839 the international status of the new state was settled, and Belgium was recognized as "a perpetually neutral state," a status that was to prove important in the twentieth century.

The upheaval in France had an impact in Poland, where in Warsaw the people rose up in the name of liberal and national principles. Since the set-

3.3. *Episodes from September Days, 1830, on the Place de l'Hôtel de Ville in Brussels* by Gustaf Wappers (Royal Museum of Fine Arts, Belgium, Brussels)

tlement at Vienna, the area around the city had a special status as a grand duchy. As the Russian tsar became more and more repressive, discontent increased, until in the winter of 1830–1831 the Poles broke into open rebellion. In December, the Polish diet declared the revolution a nationalist movement and in January 1831 voted to depose Nicholas as ruler of Poland. Instrumental to the revolt were the students and young army officers fed up with the repressive regime of the tsar. Nicholas lost no time in sending in troops and succeeded in suppressing the revolt over the course of the next few months. The landed aristocracy had become involved on the side of the revolution, but the peasantry remained for the most part aloof, with the result that the revolutionaries did not have the necessary strength to stand up to the Russian army. In February, Nicholas issued the Organic Statute, which stated that Poland was an integral part of the Russian Empire. The guarantee of certain Polish liberties contained within it was ignored. Other governments refused to intervene, despite the requests of liberals within those countries. Once the revolt was crushed, a Russian military dictatorship took over government in Poland, and Russia became the *gendarme* of Europe after this fright. The only real accomplishment of the Poles was that they successfully tied down Russian troops so they could not be used in Belgium, thus possibly saving the Belgian revolution.

In the Italian states, revolts in Modena, Parma, and the papal states, also inspired by the July Revolution in France, hoped for support from Louis-Philippe in standing up against the Austrians. When this support was not forthcoming, Metternich sent troops and crushed the insurrections. He then restored the deposed rulers. In summary, it is obvious that the revolutions in Poland and Italy were not nearly so successful as the one in Belgium, which had seen the formation of an independent, neutral country guaranteed by the Great Powers.

The forces of reaction reigned most successfully in central Europe in the years following 1815. Metternich's spies were everywhere, determined to sniff out any signs of liberalism and nationalism. Initially, these forces were so weak as to pose little threat. Until the 1830s and 1840s when the Industrial Revolution emerged, there was no viable industrial middle class to take up the liberal cause. After 1815, central Europe was divided into more easily governable political units, and it had benefited during the Napoleonic era from a different type of government from the traditional. At the Vienna congress, Metternich had ensured that Austria would be the dominant partner in the Germanic Confederation. Nationalism and liberalism increased as it found many adherents among the young who were exposed to such ideas through the works of the German poets and philosophers and in classrooms where they heard lectures on new intellectual and political currents. Metternich moved harshly against the students in the liberal societies (*Burschenschaften*) working toward a free and united Germany. An assembly at Wartburg Castle in 1817 marked the tricentenary of Luther's *95 Theses*, and the students used this occasion to burn books written by conservative authors. When one of the students, Karl Sand, assassinated a reactionary playwright, Metternich used this as the excuse he had been waiting for to push through the Carlsbad Decrees (1819). These decrees dissolved student societies, censored the press, and restricted academic freedom. However, they failed to contain the forces of liberalism and nationalism, which underwent steady growth over the next twenty years.

The collection of peoples living in the Habsburg lands under one emperor was diverse. The population was composed of eleven nationalities, with the Germans being the most powerful both numerically and economically and playing the leading role in governing the empire. The landed nobility constituted the most important class as the country was mainly agricultural, and this segment held most of the important positions as army officers, diplomats, ministers, and civil servants. The national groups, especially the Hungarians, who resented their position within the empire worked as a powerful impetus for breaking apart the old system.

Metternich's insistence on the preservation of the status quo was grounded in his fear of the potential for destabilization within the Austrian Empire. The liberal belief that each nationality should determine its own system of government was frightening in the extreme in an empire containing such a diversity of peoples. The emperor, Francis II (r. 1792–1835), refused any slight reforms that Metternich suggested, and so the government trusted in inertia, while the forces of liberalism and nationalism continued to grow.

At the beginning of the nineteenth century, Russia was also primarily an agricultural country. Most of the land was controlled by wealthy nobles, who dominated the civil service and the army officer corps. The land was tilled by serfs, who endured the worst conditions of any class in all Europe. Alexander I gave the appearance of a liberal monarch, but his type of liberalism was strongly influenced by the autocratic tradition of his predecessors, and the nobility resisted any reform. As a result, the serfs were not freed, nor was a constitution formulated, and Alexander, exhibiting strong tendencies toward mysticism and engaged in his struggle with Napoleon, became increasingly removed from ideas of reform. The government reverted to rigid censorship, and soon opposition expressed itself in the form of secret societies. One such society was the Northern Union. Its members were young men who had been outside Russia with the military campaigns and who, along with a group of Russian intellectuals, saw the need for reform. They advocated a constitutional monarchy and the abolition of serfdom. When Alexander died unexpectedly in 1825, the members of the Northern Union saw their opportunity and revolted, favoring Alexander's brother Constantine over Nicholas, the third brother, who was less liberal. This uprising, known as the Decembrist Revolt (1825), was crushed and the leaders exiled to Siberia or executed. But the revolt so traumatized Nicholas that he was determined to entrench the old order by means of political police to whom he accorded sweeping powers over the people. He became known as the "policeman of Europe" and was famous for his determination that there should be no revolution in either Russia or the rest of Europe.

REFORM AND REVOLUTION

Despite the fact that there had occurred several successful revolutions in 1820 and 1830 and that by the latter date the forces of change were making inroads, the conservative order remained dominant in most of Europe in the period preceding 1848. On the continent, by 1830 revolution had succeeded in France, Belgium, and Greece, but in Germany, Italy, Russia, Poland, and Spain, it had failed. The forces of liberalism and nationalism, at first involving junior army officers, writers, students, professors and liberal-minded nobles, continued to gain in strength. The other great revolution of those years, the one occurring in industry, brought together other groups of people who were also in the mood for change.

Early Socialism

The problems resulting from industrialization produced a rapid expansion of a fledgling political theory that had appeared early in the nineteenth century. This theory, called socialism, reflected a certain optimism that there could be an improvement in living and working conditions for members of the expanding industrial working class. This early socialist theory supposed that cooperation was superior to competition and more natural to humans. Such idealism later earned for them the title, bestowed by Karl Marx, of "utopian" socialists. They believed that man was not fundamentally evil, but ultimately perfectible and that most of the misery suffered by humankind was the result of an economic system that made some rich and many poor. They were against private property and the competition inherent in early industrial capitalism, and they looked for ways to change the existing system so that a better human environment could be achieved.

In France, Henri Saint Simon (1760–1825) was one of these early utopian socialists. His goal was to organize all of society into a cooperative community where industrial and scientific technology would be utilized to coordinate society for the benefit of all, and in the final analysis all government would be eradicated. Saint Simon's fellow countryman Charles Fourier (1772–1838) advocated the formation of voluntary associations for the purpose of cooperative living. His detailed plan called for the organization of "phalansteries," in which all aspects of daily work would be shared among the inhabitants, but his plan was never tested. Although he waited patiently everyday at noon in his favorite Parisian cafe for many years, a benefactor willing to finance his experiment never did appear. Again in France, Louis Blanc had another vision for a better world, and his belief that governments should bear some responsibility for a better society required government assistance as essential to the resolution of social problems. He felt that competition was responsible for many of the economic evils of the time, and he called for cooperation in utilizing workshops to produce goods. The money for these could be provided by the state, but they would be owned by the workers who would operate them, and in this way cooperation, rather than competition, would be the basis for the new economic system.

Robert Owen (1771–1858), a British industrialist, also believed that the best in human nature would mature within a cooperative environment. Beginning in 1800, at New Lanark in Scotland, he implemented this vision, and the result was a flourishing, healthy community. In New Harmony, Indiana (1825), however, the same dream was to wither and die. The inability of individuals to subordinate self-interest and to look to the welfare of the whole community buried Owen's hopes for a new and better world.

The utopian socialists all recognized the need to change the situation of women within society and brought forth a variety of suggestions for realizing this goal. The Saint-Simonians favored equality in both the workplace and at home. Fourier's plan gave men and women equal job and educational opportunities; men would participate in household tasks and in the rearing of children. Flora Tristan, also in France, envisioned the liberation of both women and workers. In a crusade to bring these two oppressed segments of society together for the benefit of both, she traveled and wrote extensively on

3.4. New Lanark Mills where Robert Owen developed his model community (Image Select/Art Resource, New York)

the topic, but with little result. However laudatory their vision, the utopian socialists were largely ignored by their contemporaries.

In 1848 Karl Marx (1818–1883) and Friedrich Engels (1820–1895) published *The Communist Manifesto,* which laid the foundation for subsequent socialist thought. Marx and Engels believed that human history was the record of mankind's confrontation with physical nature in an effort to produce the goods necessary for the human race to survive. The process leading to this production defines the structures, values, and ideals of a society. According to Marx and Engels, conflict has been a constant between the class that owned and controlled the means of production and those who worked for them. The only way to alleviate the social and economic ills would be through revolution, which is the inevitable outcome of the growth and development of capitalism. This theory was certainly based on an extremely pessimistic view of society as it existed and of the likelihood for change within it. It embraced the idea of controlled violence as a means to societal change. Marx predicted that the workers would eventually rise up and overthrow those who controlled the means of production. With the ringing words of *The Communist Manifesto,* Marx exhorted the workers to rise against those who enslaved them. "The proletarians have nothing to lose but their chains. They have a world to win. Working men of all countries, unite!"

(see appendix, Document XIII). As we know, this did not actually happen; instead, as the nineteenth century wore on, more and more people benefited from the growing industry in European countries. Nonetheless, Marxism did capture the imagination of many people, some already adherents of other socialist doctrines, utopian or anarchistic, as well as that of large numbers of workers. Since Marx's theory posited that material forces determined the course of history and because it emphasized the necessity of revolution rather than reform, it actually excluded the utopians. It should be noted that at the time of the revolutions of 1848, socialism was vague; it was not utopian, and it was certainly not Marxian but, rather, it was a movement in favor of workers, led by theoretical socialists and by the workers themselves.

Reform in Great Britain

In Great Britain change came ultimately as the result of reform rather than revolution. In December 1816, popular agitation for parliamentary reform resulted in a mass gathering at Spa Fields near London. This disturbance served as an excuse to pass the Coercion Acts of March 1817, which temporarily suspended habeas corpus and extended existing laws against seditious gatherings. A gathering at St. Peter's Fields near Manchester in August 1819 erupted into violence when the militia moved against the crowd. The result was eleven dead and many injured. This became known as the Peterloo Massacre, so named as a parody of Waterloo. Shortly thereafter, Parliament passed the Six Acts (1819), which outlawed large gatherings and clamped down on political agitators. Then came the Cato Street Conspiracy (1820), which involved a plot to blow up the entire British cabinet and ultimately resulted in arrests and executions. This whole business has been termed a half-baked plot, but it did provide further provocation for government repression and served to further discredit the movement for parliamentary reform.

However, there had developed by 1830 a group of industrial leaders who wanted a place in the country's government. Their intention was to put an end to the system that excluded them from the political life of the nation, and the Whigs, who had come to power in 1830, could see that reform was preferable to revolution. They introduced, after much parliamentary debate and dissension, the Reform Bill of 1832, which gave voice to the industrial urban communities and recognized changes brought about by the Industrial Revolution, disenfranchising many rotten boroughs, recognizing new towns and cities that had sprung up, and reorganizing others. A property qualification was maintained so that the number of actual voters could not increase too much. The electorate was amazingly small to begin with and with the new stipulations, it grew by a very small proportion from 478,000 to 814,000 out of 16 million, or by 2.1 percent. The Reform Bill benefited mainly the upper middle class, leaving the lower middle class, the artisans, and the industrial workers with no vote. The basic composition of the House of Commons remained the same. At the same time, this bill did represent a significant change, as it joined the landed aristocracy to the new money of the industrial era. In addition, it established a basis for the extension of the franchise through electoral reform bills later in the century.

In the 1830s and 1840s, the landed aristocracy usually provided the force behind changes to end the worst abuses resulting from industrialization. At the same time, however, much of their activity was based on self-interest, as demonstrated by the Corn Laws, which had been designed to protect British agriculture. The changes came in the form of regulations governing working conditions in factories and mines. The industrialists and manufacturers were, of course, for the most part opposed to such regulation due to their belief in economic liberalism. The Poor Law of 1834 was designed to punish the poor and to make their lives so wretched that they would prefer employment, striving to get out of the poor houses and to find employment, albeit at subsistence wages, as quickly as possible. The Corn Laws, which had been in effect since the fourteenth century, were intended to regulate the import and export of grain. These laws forbade export unless the domestic price was low and forbade import unless the domestic price was high. The purpose of the laws was to ensure stability and sufficiency of supply for domestic use and from domestic sources, but allowed for import in times of shortages. The Law of 1815 was passed to keep prices high and to avoid an agricultural depression after the Napoleonic Wars. Industrialists, consumers, and laborers objected to the high price of food and an Anti–Corn Law League was formed. The objectives of this organization were directly opposed to those of the gentry, whose argument was based on the need to maintain the traditional aristocracy of the country. Horrific famine struck Ireland in the 1840s as the result of potato blight, and out of a population of 8.5 million, an estimated one million died of starvation and disease in the years between 1846 and 1851. This horrendous event served to exacerbate the demands of the Anti–Corn Law sector, and in 1846 the Tory government of Sir Robert Peel repealed the Corn Laws.

In 1848, when revolutionary forces came to the fore in the countries of continental Europe, crises in Britain were not such that they threatened

20

political stability. The middle class had been satisfied by the Reform Bill of 1832 and the repeal of the Corn Laws in 1846, and it was not until the last half of the century that measures were taken to alleviate the miserable lot of the workers. A movement of some importance began in Britain during the late 1840s as the working class mobilized politically in response to the misery of its economic position. In 1838 the London Workingmen's Association issued a charter that made six specific demands: (1) universal manhood suffrage, (2) annual election of House of Commons, (3) secret ballot, (4) equal electoral districts, (5) abolition of property qualifications for Members of Parliament, and (6) payment of Members of Parliament.

This movement, known as Chartism, grew, and the Chartists presented their demands to Parliament three times during the next decade. Their charter was never passed. Mass petitions and strikes were used in an effort to obtain recognition. A newspaper, the *Northern Star,* was published, and the eloquent Fergus O'Connor made speeches throughout the country. However, nothing succeeded in moving Parliament to act on these demands, and the Chartists themselves split over the issue of violent versus nonviolent means. In March 1848, the Chartists put forth their greatest effort with a planned march and demonstration at which they intended to present Parliament with a petition of two million names. When met with a force of 150,000 special constables, backed up by soldiers and artillery, the demonstrators peacefully dispersed after making a few speeches. They sent their petition to Parliament in a taxi (see appendix, Document XIV). Chartism had been born of poverty, and it died as prosperity increased. But it is necessary to recognize that Chartism does represent the first large-scale working-class political movement. Its existence taught the ruling class that the workers were a force to be reckoned with; eventually all but one of the six points were enacted into law. The movement also served as an example to workers on the continent; they realized that a mass movement of this type was necessary for their goals to receive recognition.

Revolution in France

In France the reign of Louis-Philippe (r. 1830–1848) has been referred to as the "bourgeois monarchy" since his political support was strongest among upper-class liberals. In return, the new monarch was an enthusiastic supporter of the interests of the wealthy. He cultivated the image of the "bourgeois king." He replaced the white flag of the Bourbons with the revolutionary tricolor, which had not been seen in France for many years, and wore a

business suit and a top hat. His rule consistently favored the upper bourgeoisie and landed gentry and shut the workers and lower middle classes out
of the political arena. His government was a compromise between the republicans and the relatively liberal-minded supporters of the House of Orléans. The Charter of 1814, revoked by Charles X with his ordinances, was
restored. Qualifications for voting were reduced, but remained high enough
that the number of those eligible to vote only increased from about 100,000
to 200,000 out of a population of 32 million. This guaranteed that only the
wealthiest people could vote.

The lesser bourgeoisie and the working class were disappointed with the
results of their effort to overthrow Charles X, and an increasing discontent
among the steadily growing population of workers simmered just below the
surface. They had no part in the political life of the nation, economic crises
led to high levels of unemployment, and they endured horrific living conditions. This situation led to unrest and outbreaks of violence in 1831 and again
in 1834 when government troops were brought in to crush uprisings of the
silk workers in Lyon. These revolts were the result of an alliance developing
between workers and republicans, who were growing in number in response
to their perception of an increasingly alienated monarchy completely out of
touch with French society and the rapidly emerging class of workers. However, the response to the insurrections, which took the form of repression and
censorship of the press, did seem to calm the situation superficially.

By 1848 France was facing a serious crisis, and the country erupted into
revolution. In the aftermath, most of Europe experienced a great wave of
revolution the like of which had not been seen before. Two years earlier an
industrial and agricultural depression had occurred in France. It was responsible for extreme hardship within the lower middle class and among the
workers and the peasants. Unemployment was rampant by the end of 1847
with one-third of workers affected. The government was plagued with scandal and corruption, and those within the middle class who were disenfranchised were angry and restless. Even the members of the upper middle class
were angry with the so-called citizen king.

Opposition to the government of Louis-Philippe grew as the government
refused to address these problems and make changes. Radical republicans
and socialists were joined by members of the upper middle class. Forbidden
by law to stage political rallies, the protesters used the political banquet as
a tool to press for electoral reforms. During the winter of 1847–1848, about
seventy of these banquets were held in France. A grand culminating banquet planned for Paris on February 22, 1848, was cancelled by government

order. Despite the prohibition, protesters gathered and proceeded to parade through the streets. Students and workers threw up barricades in Paris. When Louis-Philippe called out the National Guard, many of its members joined with the protesters. The king, too late, accepted electoral reform. He was unable to form a new ministry and abdicated on February 24, fleeing to England. The triumphant insurgents created a provisional government, which proclaimed France a republic once again. Under the leadership of the poet Alphonse Lamartine (1790–1869), this new government combined moderate and radical republicans and even included the socialist Louis Blanc. In April, a National Assembly was elected by universal manhood suffrage, whose purpose would be the formulatation of a republican constitution.

The assembly replaced the provisional government with an Executive Commission, began to draw up a new constitution, and established national workshops in an effort to provide work and relief from economic hardship for the mass of unemployed (see appendix, Document XV). The workshops, however, became unemployment or public-works corps, providing little in the way of meaningful work. Rather than a means of production, they simply became an increasingly costly welfare program. Those in the workshops saw the dream of a social republic slipping away. Clashes between unemployed workers and artisans and government troops were frequent, and on May 15 the insurgents temporarily set up a new provisional government. But the National Guard soon restored the Executive Commission. Lamartine, as head of government, planned to transfer the unemployed from the national workshops to a railway-building project. The National Assembly, determined to put an end to socialism, rejected this proposal, and the workshops were closed on June 24. In response, the workers poured into the streets of the capital and erected barricades in much of the city. Martial law was declared, and all powers were given to General Cavaignac and the regular army. There followed the bloodiest insurrection that Paris had yet endured. Several thousand were killed and 11,000 prisoners were taken, some of whom were later deported to Algeria. These days are remembered as the June Days, and they marked a failed social revolution.

A new constitution was adopted in early November providing for a unicameral legislature of 750 elected representatives, to serve three-year terms, and a president elected for a term of four years. Both were elected by universal manhood suffrage. The elections for the presidency were held in December 1848 with four republicans in the running, of whom General Cavaignac was most favored to win. All four candidates had been associated with the early months of the Second Republic. They were defeated by Charles Louis Napoleon Bonaparte (1808–1873), a nephew of the original, who had recently returned to France from England. His landslide victory could not have been predicted given his background of bumbling and failure and his awkwardness that so alienated him from the lively debates of the French politicians. Five months later in the legislative election, the monarchist right triumphed. France had become a republic with a Bonaparte for a president and a legislature where monarchists predominated. Disaster was just around the corner.

Louis Napoleon proved masterful at using liberal and nationalistic means to further his authoritarian ambitions. While he appeared to be bumbling and unsophisticated, in reality he was crafty and calculating. He spent the first three years after his election gaining the confidence of the people while securing the loyalty of the army and the Catholic Church. The National Assembly with its conservative-monarchist majority presented considerable opposition, but when it voted to take away the vote of three million men, Louis Napoleon overruled it, thereby gaining favor by appearing to save universal manhood suffrage. When the assembly refused to revise the constitution or to allow him to stand for another term as president, he organized a successful *coup d'état*, involving the army and leading to the deaths of 150 people. Initially, he established a dictatorship, and on December 2, 1852, Louis Napoleon Bonaparte took the title of Emperor Napoleon III (r. 1852–1870). France's Second Republic had been replaced by the Second Empire.

The Revolution Spreads

The news of the February Revolution in France had crossed the Rhine, and in many German states there were uprisings against authoritarian regimes. In Bavaria a student demonstration escalated into a full-scale protest against the rule of Ludwig I and culminated in his abdication. Some states, including Hanover, Saxony, and Baden, appointed liberals to cabinets forming the so-called March governments. On March 15, when the subjects of Frederick William IV (r. 1840–1861) of Prussia erected barricades in Berlin, the king decided that reform was the answer and made concessions designed to avoid further violence. He ordered the army out of the city and promised a parliament, a constitution, and a united Germany. When word of this development in Prussia reached the leaders of the other German states, they decided it was time to establish constitutions and guarantee basic civil rights.

In addition, a cry for unification went forth from assemblies of patriotic liberals. The Frankfurt Assembly, which was to be known as the "parliament of professors," opened in mid-May with more than 500 delegates in attendance. These came from the various German states and from Austria and Bohemia. The representatives were largely middle class and were mainly lawyers (200), professors (100), doctors, and judges. The assembly excelled at theoretical debate, and the discussion of what was necessary for a unified Germany centered on whether or not to include Austria, with its large non-German population, in the new unified Germany. Meanwhile, the conservatives were recovering their force and power and rejoiced as the "parliament of professors" kept on with their debates with no liberal solution to political problems in sight. In Prussia, the king recovered his confidence and was able to regain control, largely because the army remained loyal and the large peasant population showed no interest in politics.

Despite the strength of the revived antiliberal forces, the assembly was able to formulate and approve a Declaration of the Rights of the German People, which articulated the political and social ideals of 1848. In April 1849, the assembly approved a constitution for a united Germany, and this made provision for an emperor advised by a ministry and for a legislature elected by a secret ballot. Austria refused to join, and when the crown of the new German nation was offered to Frederick William, he refused it on the grounds that he would not accept "a crown from the gutter." After this, most of the assembly's members returned home, leaving only a rump parliament in Frankfurt, which was later dispersed by the army. Any further outbreaks against conservative domination were met with arms, and thousands of prominent, middle-class liberals fled, many emigrating to North America.

The situation in the Habsburg lands was also unstable, and in 1848 the regime faced rebellions in Prague, Hungary, and Italy. It was also involved in disturbances in Germany. The rulers confronted an expanding middle class that desired civil liberties and laissez-faire economic policies. At the same time, the workers and artisans demanded social reform. The government was certain that the empire was rife with revolutionary causes and refused to heed any demands for liberal institutions. It ignored the principle of nationalism, and serfdom persisted. Even Metternich recognized that reform was necessary, but it was not forthcoming.

The troubles in the Austrian Empire actually began in Hungary. On March 3, 1848, Lajos Kossuth, a Magyar nationalist, attacked the Austrian domination of Hungary. His call was for Hungarian independence and a responsible ministry under the Habsburg crown. Ten days later on March 13, inspired by Kossuth, a group of liberals and radicals, mainly students and artisans, demonstrated in Vienna. Several were killed and the army was unable to restore order. Metternich resigned and subsequently fled to England. A people's militia was formed and workshops for the unemployed were established. The emperor, Ferdinand (r. 1835–1848), promised a relatively liberal constitution, but the radical students were unsatisfied. They felt that nothing of value had actually been accomplished, although there had been promises of expanded suffrage, freedom of the press, and the abolition of serfdom. On May 17, the emperor and his court fled to Innsbruck, leaving the government in Vienna in the hands of a committee of some 200 people whose main concern was eliminating the poverty of the Viennese workers. Democratic clubs were formed in the city for the purpose of pushing the revolution further, but by far the most serious potential threat to peace in the empire came from the serfs. The Habsburgs feared an uprising in the countryside more than they feared urban rebellion. A short time after the Vienna uprising, the imperial government freed the serfs throughout much of Austria. The Hungarian diet also abolished serfdom in March 1848. Together, these emancipations quelled the largest, potentially disruptive force in the empire. The serfs now had little reason to support the urban revolutionary movement.

The Hungarians (Magyars) had hoped to establish a separate Hungarian state within the empire. They wished to annex Transylvania, Croatia, and other eastern territories of the Habsburg lands. Rumanians, Croatians, and Serbs would then be under Magyar rule. These nationalities resisted the Magyar drive for hegemony, believing that they were better off under the Habsburgs. In a desperate attempt to protect their interests and identities, these groups turned against Hungary and rebelled against the already rebelling Hungarians. The government in Vienna, alarmed by the threat of mayhem, appointed Baron Joseph Jellachich, a Croatian, commander of the border troops, which he led in action against the Hungarian forces. The final suppression came with the aid of over 100,000 Russian troops sent by Tsar Nicholas I at the request of the new Habsburg emperor, Franz-Josef I (r. 1848–1916), who had assumed the throne following the abdication of his uncle in December 1848.

Czech nationalists had also risen up in March 1848, voicing demands for an autonomous Slavic state within the empire. This state would be comprised of Bohemia, Moravia, and Silesia. The Czechs organized the Congress of Slavs, which met in Prague during early June; then, on June 12 an insurrection by radicals began. General Windischgrätz moved with his troops to put it down, and the Germans in the area supported this

3.5. The Austrian minister of war, hanged by revolutionaries in Vienna on October 6, 1848 (Erich Lessing/Art Resource, New York)

suppression wholeheartedly, thus cementing the animosity between the Czechs and Germans. Autocratic government was restored, the emperor and the propertied classes were in control, and the numerous nationalities of the empire were subject to the government of Austria. Revolution had failed in the lands of the Habsburgs.

A cultural and political resurgence in Italy known as the *risorgimento* was generated during the eighteenth century. After 1830 the leadership of these forces passed into the hands of Giuseppe Mazzini (1805–1872). In

1831 he founded the Young Italy movement, and its goal was the formation of a united Italian republic to follow upon the expulsion of the Austrians. Lombardy and Venetia were part of the Austrian Empire and Tuscany, although supposedly independent, was governed by an Austrian archduke. The Kingdom of Naples, or of the Two Sicilies, comprising all of Italy south of Rome, was a protectorate of Vienna. The papal states also looked to Vienna for political leadership. In 1846 the College of Cardinals elected a liberal pope, Pius IX (1792–1878), who became less and less liberal and more and more conservative as the revolution unfolded. In November 1848, revolution erupted in the papal states, and the pope was forced to appoint a radical ministry. He soon thereafter made good his escape to Naples. A constitutional assembly was called for by the revolutionaries, and in February 1849 a Roman republic was proclaimed. Leaders such as Mazzini and Guiseppe Garibaldi (1807–1882) went immediately to Rome in the hope that the city could become a base for those wishing to unite the country. Rebellions spread northward through the Italian states, and ruler after ruler granted a constitution to his people. Lombardy and Venetia both declared independence from their Austrian overlords. Venetians revolted and declared a republic, and in Piedmont in March 1849 King Charles Albert (r. 1831–1849) declared a war of liberation from Austrian domination.

It was soon evident, however, that the forces of counterrevolution would triumph. Charles Albert's defeat was almost immediate. At the battle of Custozza and then at Novara, his forces were routed, and he abdicated in favor of his son, Victor Emmanuel II (r. 1849–1878). Ferdinand II (r. 1830–1859) was restored in Sicily, and the Venetians refused a suggested union with the House of Savoy. The Roman republic, headed by Mazzini, was left standing alone in its defense of liberalism and declared itself to be the nucleus of a united Italy, but it was to fall to the French army in July, and Pius IX regained control of Rome due to this intervention. The French did not want a strong, unified Italy on their southern border, and once victorious in Rome, French troops remained there in support of the now-archconservative pope until 1870. The forces of counterrevolution prevailed throughout Italy, and in the end only Piedmont kept its liberal constitution. In the final tally, Piedmont had emerged as the only possible leader among the Italian states, and the experience of 1848 and 1849 showed that Italy would never throw off Austrian rule without foreign help.

The successes of the early months of the 1848 revolutions turned quickly to failure and, in some instances, to outright disaster. Socialists, nationalists, and liberals had all tried and failed. One obvious reason for this was the division within the ranks of the revolutionaries. The middle classes used the workers to support them in their attempts, and then, with the exception of France, suffrage was not extended to the masses. The propertied classes pulled closer to the traditional ruling classes in their desire for peace and prosperity and their outright panic at the thought of the working class rising up against them. Those who had shored up the middle-class liberals were forsaken in favor of order and due to fear of social revolution. Divisions among nationalities were also instrumental in bringing the revolutions to a halt. Those who had won concessions, at least temporarily, refused to pass them on to those under their rule. Universal manhood suffrage was usually at issue. A case in point is Hungary, where the Slovenes, Croats, and Serbs were not to be considered for the same autonomy that the Hungarian leaders had demanded for themselves of the Austrians. Obviously, these rebellious minorities could be used to Austria's benefit in the battle with Hungary. Once the Austrians pitted the rebellious minorities of the Hungarian provinces against the Hungarians, they were able to begin the successful recovery of those parts of the empire.

The time of liberal revolution ended with the uncertainties and general turmoil from 1848 to 1850 in Europe. Liberals and nationalists had come to see the ineffectiveness of small insurrections and rational argument. Nationalists and workers both saw the need for new tactics against the dominant conservative forces. After 1848 the middle class ceased for the most part to be revolutionary and worried mainly about the protection of its property.

INDUSTRY TRANSFORMS SOCIETY

Industrialization and advances in science and technology during the nineteenth century led Europeans to believe that they stood on the brink of a whole new age, an era in which they would experience dramatic advances over preceding years in all areas. The doctrine of progress had at this time become an article of great faith in Europe. A mass society had emerged in which the lower classes benefited from some extension of voting rights, as well as a better standard of living and improvements in public education. In addition, new forms of transportation, such as railways and streetcars transported the masses to increased recreational opportunities in their new leisure time.

Second Industrial Revolution

Western and central Europe experienced rapid technological and economic development during the second half of the nineteenth century. Whereas the first Industrial Revolution had been associated with textiles, steam, and iron, the second was based on steel, chemicals, electricity, and oil. It was during this second revolution that Europe witnessed a shift in the economic balance of power. Britain in the 1870s produced twice as much steel as Germany, but by 1910 Germany was not only leading the European countries in output, it was producing twice as much steel as Britain. Britain also fell behind in the paper, soap, and textile industries because of new chemical processes in the making of soda that put France and Germany in the lead. In addition, German scientists overtook the British in the development of new organic chemical compounds for artificial dyes, giving Germany the edge in the marketing of dye materials. This resulted in the development of photographic plates and film. Electricity as a new form of energy brought great changes to the lives of Europeans and was responsible for many new inventions, among them further developments in transportation and communication, and it was due to electricity that countries without adequate supplies of coal were able to enter into the industrial age. The development of the internal combustion engine was basic to the invention of the automobile and the airplane.

After 1870, foreign markets were saturated with European goods, and it became necessary for governments to look more closely at domestic markets. Population increases, the lower costs of transporting goods, and the rise in national incomes made these markets distinct possibilities for increased consumerism, a demand that was met with the idea of large department stores that featured a great variety of consumer goods under one roof. These could cater efficiently to the new consumer mentality. As for foreign markets, free trade came under scrutiny as many industrialists and politicians advocated protective tariffs to guarantee domestic markets for their products. Of the European countries, only Britain, Denmark, and the Netherlands did not return to protective tariffs between 1874 and 1892.

In the field of European agriculture, advances in science and technology brought about changes in farming methods, and as more grain was produced and transportation costs were lowered, the price of farm produce fell drastically. Protective tariffs were implemented in some areas, and machines were introduced to replace scarce and expensive farm laborers. Countries were forced to shift their attention to other commodities in the wake of the slump in grain prices. In order to adjust and compete, small farmers were forced to form cooperatives, which enabled them to survive.

3.6. Steam trains and workers in the London underground (1872) (Image Select/Art Resource, New York)

Social Structure

The new patterns that had begun to emerge in the social structure of Europe during the early stages of industrialization became more pronounced toward the end of the nineteenth century. A new industrial elite formed as families from the traditional landed aristocracy allied with the growing wealthy upper middle class engaged in banking, industry, and large-scale commerce. The diverse middle-class groupings arrayed below this elite, all of which reflected the impact of industrialization, were engaged in various occupations. Traditional professionals such as lawyers, doctors, bureaucrats, and successful merchants were joined by business managers and new professionals arising from industrial specialization, including engineers and accountants. Below them in status and income were small-scale entrepreneurs, shopkeepers, and the growing ranks of white-collar workers. The latter included bookkeepers, tellers, secretaries, and salesmen. These people, like teachers and nurses, whose numbers increased as public education and health services expanded, did not own property, but nonetheless viewed themselves as distinct from laborers.

Landholding peasants and agricultural workers together made up a good portion of the lower class, while the industrial working class, distinct because the livelihood of its members depended on physical labor, contained a variety of groups. In the skilled-labor category, a shift was occurring from the traditional trades and crafts to the specialized types of work developing metal, machine tooling, and some construction. The remainder consisted of various semiskilled workers employed in factories and unskilled laborers whose employment depended primarily on daily opportunities.

Responses of the Working Class

As industrialization continued, workers faced the challenges of developing the means to improve their lot. Many were motivated to form political parties and labor unions, and strong ties emerged between the two. Factory owners remained free to hire labor on their own terms in response to the requirements of the market. The workers organized to fight for better working conditions and higher wages. Bourgeois liberals naturally regarded such organizations as detrimental to their interests, or even as criminal agencies, viewed as a threat to private property because of their use of strikes and pickets to obtain their objectives.

The formation of trade unions took place gradually despite such opposition, and their organization even obtained sanction from conservatives who hoped to supersede the liberals by gaining the support of the workers. But the trade unions did not have as their membership all the workers, nor were all workers socialists, although the theories of socialism did form a major part of ongoing discussion and debate within the union movement. In 1864 the Workingmen's Association, which was formed by British and French trade unionists and known as the First International, provided a forum for the discussion of socialist ideas in the context of workers' goals. Its inaugural address was written and delivered by Karl Marx. As Marxian socialism and unionism became increasingly intertwined, working-class political parties emerged. One of the most important of these socialist parties was formed in Germany in 1875. Its leaders were Wilhelm Liebnecht and August Bebel, both Marxists, who organized the German Social Democratic Party (SPD) (see appendix, Document XVI). Once elected to the Reichstag, SPD members worked to improve the condition of the working class, and the party, as the representative of this segment of society, continued to grow. Other countries also had socialist parties: Jean Jaurès led the French socialists, looking to the ideals of the French Revolution for his inspiration, and in other European countries social democratic parties were founded, most of which followed the German model. By 1898, Russia had a Marxist Social Democratic Labor Party.

Despite the expansion of the unionism and the workers' parties, the First International disintegrated due primarily to the events in France in 1871 (see the Second Empire and Prussia). In 1889, the Second International was formed in response to the socialist call for cooperation to combat the exploitation of workers worldwide. As the advocates of true Marxian socialism awaited the revolution they believed to be imminent, a severe challenge arose to their position in the form of revisionism. The leader of the revisionist school was Eduard Bernstein, a member of the German SPD who had been in exile in Britain. While there, he had been strongly influenced by moderate English socialism and the British parliamentary system. As a result, he pointed out that Marx's ideas were not always correct and that some of them, in fact, had turned out to be quite wrong. In *Evolutionary Socialism,* Bernstein pointed out that the disintegration of the capitalist system had not yet occurred, nor did it appear imminent. Furthermore, the middle class was actually expanding and not declining in the way Marx had predicted. The proletariat was not sinking, but rather enjoying an increasing standard of living. Nationalism was another divisive issue for international socialism, although Marx and Engels believed that class divisions would supersede divisions based on nationality. This belief proved erroneous; socialist parties varied in their aims from country to country and remained linked to national concerns and issues, as the events of World War I were to demonstrate.

In the last two decades of the nineteenth century, attempts were made to unionize the workers. Strikes proved a necessary element in the arsenal of the unions, and the last years of the century witnessed several walkouts. In 1888, female workers in a London match factory walked off the job, and in 1889 London dock workers did the same. Trade unions were organized the next year for both groups, and by 1900, two million workers were enrolled in British trade unions. By 1914 this number had risen to between three and four million; however, this was still less than one-fifth of the total workforce. On the continent, trade unions developed much more slowly than they had in Britain. In France, the union movement was very closely tied to the socialist parties, and since there were several of these, the movement was badly fragmented. Not until 1895 did the French trade unions organize in the Confédération Générale de Travail, which was decentralized and failed to include some of the major unions and, therefore, never really gained much strength. In Germany, the unions were also tied closely to political parties. First formed in the 1860s, there were liberal unions and unions comprised of Christians, but the largest were those with socialist members. Strikes and collective bargaining were the tools used to gain wages and improve conditions. Increasingly, the success of these tactics served to convince the German workers to forego revolution in favor of these gradual improvements.

This is not to say, however, that progress for the working class was constant. Between 1873 and 1896 Europe experienced a series of economic crises collectively called the Long Depression. It was sparked by the fall in grain prices, and it affected industry and trade. Rising costs, increased competition, and shrinking access to markets resulted in reduced profit and brought about stock and bank panics. All of this led to periods of high unemployment, with the jobless rate in Britain rising among unionized workers from 1 percent in 1872 to 11 percent in 1879, from 2 percent in 1882 to 10 percent in 1886, and again from 2 percent in 1890 to 7.5 percent in 1893. These periods caused much suffering among working-class families and increased support for labor unions. Despite the fact that wage fluctuations were a fact of life in times of crisis, there was an overall improvement in wages between 1870 and 1900. Real wages rose by 37 percent, increasing by a third in France and Germany and by more than half in Britain.

In general, conditions improved for urban workers as the century progressed. Health improved as diets became more varied with the decline in prices and increase in purchasing power, while sewage systems, clean water supplies, and advances in the control of disease contributed to improved health in the cities. Workers were better dressed and better housed than ever before, although rent was a major drain on income. Despite the increase in wages and advances in quality of life for workers, the overall expansion and increase in productivity widened the gap between the workers and the middle classes. Overall, the European population increased dramatically from 270 million in 1850 to over 460 million by 1910. Increases during the first half of this period were due to rising birth rates; later, medical discoveries and improved environmental conditions served to further increase population by reducing the death rate. The smallpox vaccine represented a giant step forward in public health. Infectious diseases such as dysentery, typhoid fever, and cholera, which had long been spread through contaminated water and improper disposal of sewage, were slowed by new knowledge and environmental improvements. The pasteurization of milk contributed to a lower infant-mortality rate.

It was soon evident that despite the improvements that accompanied advances in science and technology, it was improbable that the European continent would be able to support the increased population. This was especially true of rural areas where little industrialization had occurred and overpopulation was a problem. As a result, the excess labor from the underdeveloped areas migrated to the industrialized zones. When it became obvious around the turn of the century that the industrialized zones could not possibly support the influx of labor from the agricultural areas (southern Italy, Spain, Hungary, Rumania), a mass emigration to America took place. The economic motive for emigration loomed large, but there were others. For instance, some emigrants from Austria and Hungary belonged to oppressed minority groups, such as Poles, Slovaks, Serbs, Croats, and Jews. Proportionately fewer Germans or Magyars left the area.

Popular Culture

Just as the Industrial Revolution altered social structures and social relations, it also dramatically affected gender roles and family life. The diversity of and range within the emerging urban classes ensured that experiences would vary widely. In preindustrial Europe, excluding the aristocracy, there had been a tendency for husbands and wives to work alongside one another, whether in trade, commerce, or agriculture. Industrialization brought with it an increased separation of home and work, with an accompanying emphasis on a gendered division of labor. Stereotypes developed that came to be regarded as universal truths. As men were more able to earn a family wage, particularly if they remained hardworking and competitive, the role of women shifted to running a household and rearing children. These tasks came to be viewed as more suitable to their delicate and sensitive natures. Women were to be valued for domesticity and motherhood, while men were to be the breadwinners.

Women, particularly those of the middle classes, appeared to hold a position of great authority in the home; this perception, however, was to some extent misleading. The marriage laws of the day left a woman with few rights and entailed the virtual loss of her legal identity when she married. In addition, the idealized role of women was a social construct that rarely coincided with reality. Women were not only expected to provide an island of comfort for the family and run the household, they also engaged in the strenuous work of preparing food, maintaining the dwelling, sewing clothing, and rearing children, all with very little assistance, since only a small fraction of middle-class families could actually afford significant domestic services. This view of women as nurturers and caregivers extended into the world of work as women sought employment outside the home. They were excluded from the realm of business and commerce, but welcomed into nursing and teaching. Challenges to this bourgeois ideal were discouraged and could cause scandal. The popular English novelist Elizabeth Gaskell (1810–1865) was known simply as Mrs. Gaskell, and in France Aurore Dupin (1804–1876) wrote as George Sand and scandalized society with her independent life and association with the composer-pianist Frédéric Chopin (1810–1849).

Although economic considerations remained an important factor in marriage, there were also indications that emotional attachment was a stronger influence in family life. More mothers, even those from the less affluent middle-class families, gave more direct attention to babies. The use of wet nurses declined, and the publishing and purchasing of books on child rearing increased. The extended dependency of middle-class children on parents as more time was spent in formal schooling served to reinforce the role of the mother in the home. In addition, a decline in the birth rate contributed to increased parental concern for the children in each family. Among the working classes, marriage for women remained mainly an economic consideration. Hard work remained the norm both before and after marriage, with one of the most common employment possibilities being that of domestic servant. There were very few opportunities for work that would lead to personal independence. When a woman became a working-class wife and mother with her own domestic responsibilities, economic circumstances usually required her to take on work that would supplement a husband's income. Women often did piecework at home or in crowded quarters for small-scale manufacturers in arrangements comparable to those of the preindustrial cottage industries. In contrast with their middle-class counterparts, working-class boys and girls frequently began earning their own wages in adolescence, thus becoming less directly dependent on parents. As time went on and living standards improved, working-class families also began to have few children and to rely more strongly on the husband's income.

Literacy rates rose dramatically in the final decades of the nineteenth century, but many traditional differentiations persisted. More men, urban residents, and people from the upper classes were able to read and write than were women, rural residents, and lower-class individuals. In addition, the literacy rates in southern and eastern Europe were generally lower than those in the western part of the continent. In large part the increases can be attributed to educational reforms such as those passed in Great Britain and France. These countries made school attendance obligatory for all children until the ages of twelve and thirteen, respectively. Other reforms encouraged a more uniform curricular experience through the use of a common language and monitored instruction. However, some distinctions among social groups were actually reinforced. Only a few children from the lower classes entered secondary-level schools, and the schooling received by girls stressed their future roles as wives and mothers rather than providing employment skills.

The growth of an increasingly literate population, combined with technological advances, contributed to an expansion of the press. The number, quality, and circulation of newspapers rose. Technical improvements in paper making and printing reduced costs, making newspapers more accessible to larger numbers. The content both diversified and specialized to include articles about business and culture, as well as politics. Many readers were drawn to newspapers by the serialization of novels by Elizabeth Gaskell and Charles Dickens (1812–1870) in Great Britain or by Honoré de Balzac (1799–1850) and Alexandre Dumas (1802–1870) in France. The existence of this more literate public with more money and leisure time contributed to a transformation of high and popular culture in the nineteenth century. One interpretation of these developments views high culture as becoming the popular culture of the middle class. Some derisively labeled the new phenomenon as "bourgeois," perceiving a decline in standards in the appeal to the masses. Although anyone with more than a modest income could influence cultural directions, it is still useful to distinguish between the predominantly popular-cultural themes and the more formal expressions identifiable in retrospect as noteworthy trends or as movements.

By the mid–nineteenth century, there were many indications that high culture was no longer the preserve of a small elite. Public concert halls erected with public funds became the venue for a wide range of entertainment offerings. These included music hall presentations, symphonies, and opera, a particular nineteenth-century favorite. Museums, galleries, and lending libraries attracted the increasingly educated and curious middle class. The popularity of brutal sports declined and was replaced by participatory and mass-spectator sports. The popularity of team sports such as soccer and rugby, which were initially played in Great Britain, spread quickly to other countries. The invention and development of the bicycle not only provided a means of transportation affordable to many, but it also made cycling a leisure activity, available to women as well as men, although generally frowned upon for women since it required clothing considered inappropriate. Cycling competitions gained a significant following, as did autoracing before the end of the century.

The context for these changes was shifting, along with the population, away from the countryside and transforming the urban environment. Between 1871 and 1911, the urban population of England rose from 62 to 78 percent of the whole, and in France it increased from 33 to 44 percent. In Germany the increase was spectacular, from 36 to 60 percent. Western Europe now exhibited a predominantly urban culture, and Baron Haussmann's redevelopment of Paris during the Second Empire serves as an example of a government's attempts to meet the changing times. A civic official and city planner hired to change the face of the city, Haussmann did so without hesitation in a series of bold alterations to the existing plan. He broadened the existing streets and cut new ones to facilitate the circulation of traffic, relocated the railway stations in a circle around the outskirts of the city, thus ensuring wide, easy access; he placed monuments in wide spaces, as evidenced by the Place de l'Opera, Place de la Nation, and Place d'Etoile, all of which were central points for the wide avenues that radiated outward from them. One of the greatest accomplishments of Napoleon III and Haussmann was the transformation of the Bois de Boulogne into a city park popular with all classes of society that provided Parisians with a beautiful spot to enjoy. For residents of the east end of the city, the Bois de Vincennes was also developed into a popular park. This redevelopment of Paris provided a model for modernization in Vienna, where the Ringstrasse was modeled on Haussmann's boulevards. During the 1870s, London and Berlin followed suit with

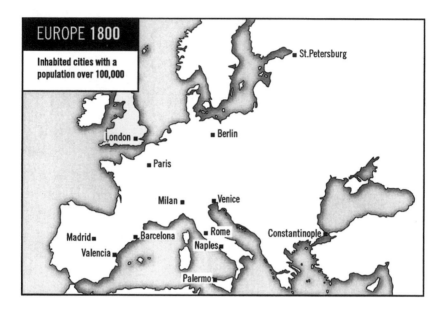

EUROPE 1800

Inhabited cities with a
population over 100,000

St.Petersburg

London

Berlin

Paris

Milan

Venice

Madrid

Barcelona

Rome

Constantinople

Valencia

Naples

Palermo

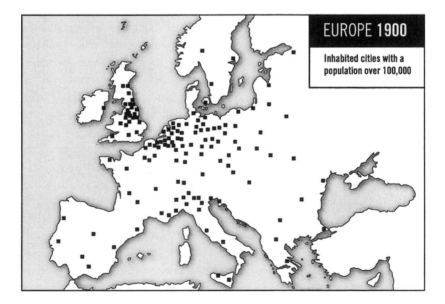

EUROPE 1900

Inhabited cities with a
population over 100,000

the reconstruction of their inner-city areas, and by the end of the century, advances in engineering, building materials, and construction techniques began to change the appearance of cities. The Eiffel Tower, constructed in 1889, was unique to Paris, but symbolic of the new city in general. Sewers, sidewalks, and electric lights transformed the urban landscape, and the cities became much more pleasant places to live and work.

For most of the nineteenth century, architectural design was primarily a matter of stylistic revival; classicism drew inspiration from Greece and Rome, while Gothic elements were given impetus by the romantic movement's interest in the medieval. These revivalist styles utilized modern building techniques, but it was also in the second half of the nineteenth century that an exploration of the potential of iron and glass as building materials heralded a new era in style and construction. Large glass-covered galleries were built in Paris and other major cities, making use of wrought iron and steel, and occupied by independent shops and cafes. The first major department store the world had seen was the Bon Marché, which opened in Paris in the 1860s. In addition, tenements, which had traditionally housed the urban working classes, were replaced with apartment complexes in France, and the British added to this idea with the invention of garden apartments. With improved transportation, more and more of the population went to live on the outskirts of the cities in the suburbs. The European cities adopted each other's ideas, with parks and suburbs styled after those found in London and with wide boulevards, cafes, and apartments like those in French cities. All the cities constructed grand public buildings and centers of culture; opera houses, museums, concert halls, and public libraries proliferated. In addition, they developed the same problems with pollution, noise, and overcrowding characteristic of the urban landscape. By 1900, the cities of Europe and the rest of the world had begun to assume their modern appearance.

Formal Culture and Modern Science

Scientific knowledge, technological advances, and social change in the nineteenth century influenced formal intellectual developments as well. This is evident in the shift from romanticism to realism, as emphasis on the inner world gave way to interest in the material world and individual well-being. The materialistic outlook was increasingly influential, and after 1850 it contributed to a new literary and artistic movement labeled realism. Previous literature and art had not, of course, excluded all elements of real life. The

3.7. Electric lights outline the Bon Marché at night in this 1902 photograph. (CORBIS/MAGMA)

nineteenth-century movement is characterized by its rejection of romanticism and its connection to a positivist and materialist view of the world. Realist writing and painting tended toward the ordinary, that is, people in typical and commonplace settings. It eschewed the romantic heroes and exotic places.

In France, Honoré de Balzac wrote a series of books called *The Human Comedy* in which hundreds of characters people novels that present the many dynamic sectors of the changing urban society. Gustave Flaubert (1821–1880) in *Madame Bovary* portrayed the middle class as cold and hypocritical, while Emile Zola (1840–1902) is well known for his depiction of working-class life as revealed in *Germinal*, set in the northern French coal-mining region.

In Great Britain the novels of Mary Ann Evans, writing under the pseudonym George Eliot, examined the interplay of social influence and personal character; her novel *Middlemarch: A Study in Provincial Life* was a great success. Charles Dickens, in such works as *Hard Times*, brought the poverty and brutality that accompanied industrialization and urbanization to the attention of the public. Russia also produced well-known realist writers.

Count Leo Tolstoy's (1828–1910) immense novel *War and Peace* is set during the Napoleonic invasion of Russia and is the best-known work of Russian realist fiction. The numerous fictional characters interact with historical figures, allowing Tolstoy to weave into the story a theory of history that strongly questions the ability of individuals to influence the course of events.

Realist painters also sought to base their work on careful observation and to examine significant social issues. Gustave Courbet (1819–1877), perhaps the most famous of the realist painters, chose ordinary rural and urban workers as his subjects. His *Stonebreakers* presents heavy, daily labor without romantic illusions. He incurred the wrath of middle-class critics, who demanded that art ennoble the individual and have social purpose. Jean François Millet (1814–1875) was similarly criticized for portraying French peasants in *The Gleaners* and *The Sowers* as having a dignity not befitting their social class.

While it can be argued that high culture by the end of the nineteenth century had been transformed into a mass culture with a middle-class base, there still developed various distinct artistic and literary movements that existed in a state of tension with popular culture. There was a belief among artists and writers that the uniformity of urban culture and the materialism of middle-class society were destroying high culture, or "art for art's sake." The proliferation of artists, the diversity of audiences, and variety of aims and ambitions led to frequent shifts in style as comments on popular culture combined with reaction against competing styles. The concept of artists and their works forming an *avant-garde* that rejected established tastes became a dominant theme. Artists, while embracing innovation and originality and the unique and novel, were dependent for their livelihood on the bourgeois society against which they were rebelling. The complexity of this relationship and the status of the arts are further demonstrated by the fact that a larger and more sophisticated audience resulted in increased prestige for individual artists and writers.

In painting, the process of breaking with the past began with the Impressionist movement. These painters attempted to capture what they saw before them at first glance or impression. They used small dabs of paint of lighter colors to depict the visual impact of light falling on the scene before them. Claude Monet (1840–1926) painted certain subjects, such as the cathedral at Rouen, repeatedly, conveying the variations in light on its surfaces at different times. Postimpressionism, which followed, focused more on what the painter felt about the subjects rather than what was seen. Georges Seurat (1859–1891) evoked emotions using a technique called pointillism, whereby thousands of dots of color form the figures and landscapes. Painting was moving closer to subjectivity and abstraction. Paul Cézanne (1839–1906) stressed the geometric shapes underlying the structure of the subject matter he painted. Vincent Van Gogh (1853–1890) applied brilliant colors in thick swirls to express his emotional reaction on canvas. This expressionist style was, in turn, succeeded by the beginning of abstract painting in the early twentieth century. In Paris, Spanish painter Pablo Picasso (1881–1973) and Georges Braque (1882–1963) rejected the traditional mode of perspective by dismantling their subjects to present them on canvas as flat, simplified, and distorted geometric designs in a new style called cubism.

Analogous developments occurred in the other arts. In literature, for example, character, plot, and narrative began to recede from their central roles as novels explored alternative approaches. The works of Henry James (1842–1916) frequently present visual glimpses and impressions of sound and touch that connect to create atmosphere and mood. In *Remembrance of the Things Past (In Search of Time Lost),* Marcel Proust (1871–1922) re-traced a life along the circuitous path of memories. A group of writers known as the symbolists regarded the reality that the individual perceives as symbolic of a deeper inner reality. Writing reflected the working of the writer's mind and became an expression of his personal language. The poetry of Arthur Rimbaud (1854–1891) and Rainer Maria Rilke (1875–1926) provides examples of symbolism.

Music also felt the impact of the impressionist movement. Claude Debussy (1862–1918) in *Prelude to the Afternoon of a Faun* attempted to recreate the emotions evoked in a poem written by the symbolist poet Stephane Mallarmé (1842–1898). Another composer who broke with traditional harmonies to the delightful approval of some listeners and disdain of others was Erik Satie (1866–1925) in compositions with such titles as *Gymnopedie* and *Gnossienne.* The artistic breaks with the past and the controversies that resulted are well exemplified by the events accompanying the first performance of Serge Diaghilov's (1872–1929) ballet *The Rite of Spring* (May 1913), for which Igor Stravinsky (1882–1971) composed the music. At its first performance, the unconventional choreography and music shocked one segment of the audience, which clashed in a near riot with cheering avant-garde supporters.

These rebellions against traditional artistic and literary styles, frequently called modernism, were not only reactions to the past, but products of the contemporary culture. As science pressed against the boundaries of classical physics and analysts of human behavior explored the irrational, the arts sought to probe and express what was explicit and implicit in the new discoveries and developments. Basic scientific research was expanding and was more rapidly applied to technology in the nineteenth century than in any earlier period. Examples include the laws of thermodynamics, Louis Pasteur's (1822–1895) formulation of germ theory, and Dmitri Mendeleev's (1834–1907) work in chemistry, which culminated in the foundation of the periodic table. The work of Michael Faraday (1791–1867) produced the groundwork for electricity with his discovery of electromagnetic induction. However, the intellectual developments of this period were also calling into question basic tenets that had been preeminent since the scientific revolution and the Enlightenment. In the physical sciences, discoveries that gave rise to the "new physics" challenged the fundamental assumptions about the universe as synthesized by Isaac Newton. In 1896 Marie Curie (1867–1934) discovered radioactivity, which suggested the presence of subatomic particles that did not behave in a mechanical manner. Max Planck (1858–1947), building on this and other work, furthered knowledge in the physical sciences by determining that matter, energy, and electronic waves were quantized, being radiated in particles rather in a steady stream. This raised further questions about Newtonian physics. In 1905, Albert Einstein (1879–1955) published a paper promulgating his general theory of relativity, which held that space and time are relative to the observer and not absolute and independent of human experience. These discoveries and theories were grounded in new hard science and undermined the comfortable assumption that new knowledge would simply be an elaboration of the established fundamentals.

This growth in scientific knowledge and interest was accompanied by an increasing secularization as more and more people turned toward a more worldly orientation. One factor that contributed to the increasing emphasis on materialism was the work of Charles Darwin (1809–1882). His theory of organic evolution, as it resulted from natural selection, was one of the most important scientific events of the nineteenth century. Darwin's theory, which he brought forward in 1859, was not new, but most people still believed that the world and its life were the work of a divine power. Others, however, began to question the biblical version of events. Jean-Baptiste Lamarck (1744–1829), a forerunner of Darwin, presented in 1809 a theory of evolution. His argument was unacceptable because he believed that changes brought about by events in the environment could be passed on immediately to offspring. In *Principles of Geology*, Charles Lyell (1797–1875) vividly described the struggle for existence between species and the forces that led to extinction. Darwin was greatly influenced by this work and by Steven Henslow, a botanist with whom he often discussed science. Henslow was responsible for Darwin's post as naturalist on the *Beagle,* a naval vessel that the British government was sending around the world to make nautical observations. During the voyage, Darwin was able to study plant and animal life on islands virtually untouched by external forces. As a result of his observations, Darwin was eventually convinced that animals evolved over time and that this evolution took place in response to conditions of environment. In his famous book entitled *On the Origin of Species by Means of Natural Selection,* he explained the struggle for survival in which all species in the natural world are forced to participate. He explained how those that survived did so due to a superior ability to adapt made possible by the appearance of "variants." Darwin called this process natural selection and theorized that it enabled the fit to survive and to pass their successful variations on to offspring. The unfit became extinct.

Needless to say, Darwin's theory was highly controversial in his time and brought forth a firestorm of indignation and rage from religious circles. Darwin, a devout Christian himself, was greatly troubled by his findings, and his theory was judged to be the "monkey damnification of mankind." It also had its supporters, however, including Herbert Spencer and Thomas Henry Huxley. It was through Darwin's theory of evolution that the idea of nature as a static system fixed in time at the point of creation changed to the concept of a dynamic ongoing process. An unfortunate offshoot of Darwin's work was the attempt to apply ideas developed through his study of the natural world to society itself, resulting in the phenomenon of Social Darwinism, which posited that some races were naturally superior to others. During the nineteenth century this argument was used as justification for the conquest of peoples in non-European regions. The phrase "survival of the fittest," coined by Herbert Spencer, put forth the idea that nations, like living things, must struggle to survive and that weaker nations succumb to the more powerful; thus, imperialism was part of the natural order (see appendix, Document XVII).

Rigorous attempts at systematic application of the methods of science are evident in the work of Karl Marx and Auguste Comte (1798–1857). In his *System of Positive Philosophy,* Comte argued that a science of human society could discover the general laws of human relations. This new science, called sociology, would provide the means for achieving social progress. A scientifically based "religion of humanity" could replace older theological and metaphysical belief systems with a positivist approach. However, a challenge to the fundamental values of reason and progress came from philosophy, particularly the writings of Friedrich Nietzsche (1844–1900), who argued that bourgeois society and culture had stifled the emotions and instincts that were the very basis of human creativity. The Western emphasis on the rational and the adherence to Christianity had crushed spontaneity and the potential of the human will. Nietzsche held that within society there were intellects that could free themselves from these constraints. These were the individuals who would create their own values and lead the masses.

Additional attacks came from other theorists who also cast doubt on the value of reason. The philosopher Henri Bergson (1859–1941) and the political theorist Georges Sorel (1847–1922) were among the most prominent. Bergson held that reality was not divisible in a Cartesian fashion and that its wholeness could be grasped intuitively. Sorel took the irrational and intuitive into the political arena with his argument that revolutionary aims could only be achieved through violent means. He doubted the ability of the masses to participate in governing and believed that decision making should be placed in the hands of a capable elite. Further intellectual challenges to dominant assumptions came from psychology. In the newly developed scientific study of human behavior, Sigmund Freud (1856–1939), a Viennese physician, concluded that the emotional disturbances he had been treating in some of his patients originated from repressed experiences and inner drives. His investigations led him to explore the unconscious and irrational aspects of human behavior. Freud came to stress the interpretation of dreams as a key to understanding the human psyche and the irrational unconscious. He asserted that individual human behavior is a product of instinctive drives rather than the constraints exerted by rational thought alone or even primarily.

Other analysts turned their attention to the array of social and personal problems that seemed to accompany industrialization and urbanization. The increasing maintenance of reliable records and statistics made it possible to note that hysteria, hypochondria, neurasthenia, alcoholism, opium use, and violent crime were all on the rise. In France, Emile Durkheim (1858–1917), adhering to systematic and positivist (objective) approaches, investigated suicide rates, and his early work led him to conclude that the dislocating impact on the individual of the anonymous urban and industrial world was leading to personal disorganization (anomie). It should be noted, however, that these intellectual developments of the late nineteenth century remained isolated and did not have much impact beyond small communities of colleagues and interested academics. It was only after the Great War that they gained a broader audience.

Organized religion was not exempt from the effects of modernization. In the early part of the nineteenth century, it experienced revival. The Roman Catholic Church benefited from its alliance with the restored monarchies and nobility following the Congress of Vienna. Some romantics were attracted to the expression of emotion and the glories of the Middle Ages and returned or converted to the Catholic faith, particularly in the German states. Among Protestant denominations, increased attention was paid to the revival that had begun in the eighteenth century. However, as the impact of industrialization and urbanization strengthened, a variety of factors combined to reduce the influence of the established churches. The mass migration of people from rural to urban areas disrupted the traditional community in which the local church had been a strong cohesive force. The continued secularization of political life, state control of education, and general loss of faith undermined organized religion. In some of the more liberal nation-states such as republican France, hostility to the churches was expressed in the form of anticlericalism. The expanding influence of scientific thinking and intellectual curiosity, in particular Darwinian theory, challenged and appeared to contradict the doctrine of divine creation. Christian responses were not uniform. Fundamentalists opposed any deviation from literal interpretations of the Bible. In 1864, Pope Pius IX (r. 1846–1878) issued an encyclical called the *Syllabus of Errors* condemning modern scientific and political thought. Within Protestantism some efforts were made to reinterpret the Bible in the light of contemporary developments.

A moderate response was evident in the Catholic Church during the pontificate of Leo XIII (r. 1878–1893). In 1891 his encyclical entitled *Rerum Novarum* criticized the worst abuses of laissez-faire capitalism, which had left the working class in poverty. It defended private property and condemned Marxian socialism because it was irreligious and materialistic. Catholics were encouraged to form and support Christian socialist political parties and other organizations approved by the church. This more modern attitude encouraged social activism and social reform. In addition, outside the traditional churches, new organizations were established to address new needs. In 1844 the Young Men's Christian Association was founded, and in 1878 William Booth (1829–1912) initiated the more evangelical Salvation Army. The latter took direct action providing food and shelter programs for the poor.

Although traditional churches experienced a decline in support during the latter part of the nineteenth century, the shift in religious practice did not occur uniformly. More women than men remained churchgoers, and in the more Catholic countries, a number of miracles were reported, giving rise to pilgrimages by many people to those sites. Judaism also experienced crises, but in addition to the pressures felt by Christianity, Jews were subjected to a rise in anti-Semitism. Some Christians blamed Jews for the social ills and secularism of the changing world. Responses in the Jewish community were varied. Some abandoned their religion in order to be less conspicuous, and others became Christian converts. The anti-Semitism also gave impetus to the Zionist movement for the establishment of a Jewish homeland in Palestine of which Theodor Herzl (1860–1909) was founder.

THE CHALLENGES OF NATION BUILDING

Although it seemed by 1850 that the forces of conservatism were firmly reentrenched across Europe, scarcely thirty years later many of the goals of the liberals and nationalists had been realized. National unity had been achieved in Germany and Italy, and many European states were governed by constitutional monarchies, although the constitutional-parliamentary features of government were often nothing more than façades. It is interesting that these goals were not achieved by liberals and nationalists, but by a new generation of conservatives who practiced *realpolitik,* or the "politics of reality." The ruling conservatives prided themselves on their "toughness of mind" and on their ability to handle power. Armies and power politics carried the day in foreign policy, and after 1850 the new generation of European statesmen presented an attitude markedly different from that which had prevailed in the years following the Vienna settlement in 1815. Although conservative in outlook, they were deeply aware of the strengths inherent in liberal and nationalistic platforms, and they realized that these could be engaged to advance their own authoritarian objectives. On the other hand, the defeated revolutionaries of 1848 had exposed the precarious position of a system based on privilege and the inherent weaknesses of a society whose institutions and authority had no popular basis. By 1880 almost every state on the continent, with the exception of Russia, was governed under a written constitution.

The Crimean War

Despite the relative calm prevalent in the countries of Europe after 1848, the first challenge to the apparent stability of Europe arose as the result of an international dispute. War in the Crimea (1854–1856) pitted Russia against France and Great Britain. The origins of the conflict reached far back in history and

3.8. British nurse Florence Nightingale administered to soldiers during the Crimean War. (Courtesy of Bruce Peel Special Collections, University of Alberta Libraries)

were rooted in the longstanding animosity and rivalry between Russia and the Ottoman Empire. Russia wished to control Wallachia and Moldavia, and the Tzar used the pretence of wishing to protect Orthodox Russian Christians living in those areas. Russia moved in and occupied the areas during the summer of 1853, and the other Great Powers were soon involved as well. Since both France and Britain were against Russian expansion in the region, it was not long before these powers declared war on Russia, while Austria and Prussia chose to remain neutral.

The waging of the war was a masterpiece of ineptitude from the outset with the armies soon stalemated along the Crimean coast of the Black Sea. The Russian fortress of Sevastopol fell in September 1855 after a prolonged siege, and in March 1856 a peace was concluded in Paris. With the signing of the treaty, the image of a strong and powerful Russia disappeared, as she was required to surrender territory near the mouth of the Danube, to recognize the neutrality of the Black Sea, and to renounce all claims of protection over Christians in the Ottoman Empire. Prior to the conference, Austria had forced the Russians to withdraw from Moldavia and Wallachia. The Concert of Europe had been destroyed as a means of keeping peace among the powers on the continent.

The Unification of Italy

The disruption of the European status quo that resulted from the Crimean War was followed by an upsurge in the expression of nationalist aspirations. Once again, the voices of individual nations were heard as each revealed its own ambitions. In France, Napoleon III needed success in foreign affairs. The Italians wanted a unified Italy. Prussia wished to enhance its reputation on the international scene. Each stood to benefit from change, and the first test was to come in Italy.

The goal of Italian nationalists had for a long time been the unification of the small Italian principalities into a single state. There were, however, major differences in opinion as to how this should be accomplished. Romantic republicans working toward unification formed secret societies, the best known of which was the Carbonari. Guiseppe Mazzini became the leader of the romantic republicans and the most important nationalist leader in Europe. He believed nationality to be a divine concept, its ultimate objective to realize God's plan for the world. Mazzini's Young Italy Society, which he founded in 1831, had as its goal the removal of Austrian power from the Italian peninsula and the establishment of an Italian republic. Throughout the 1830s and 1840s, Mazzini and Guiseppe Garibaldi, a soldier and patriot, led insurrections toward this purpose, and in the 1850s they continued to conduct guerrilla warfare to this end. As a result of their efforts, both men spent much time in exile with unification eventually being achieved through the moderate efforts of Camillo Cavour (1810–1857). Cavour was prime minister of Piedmont from 1852 to 1861, and far from being a romantic nationalist, he was conservative in his attitudes and politics and was the active force behind King Victor Emmanuel II. How did the unification come about?

Since the Congress of Vienna, Piedmont had served as a buffer between Italian and Austrian ambitions on the Italian peninsula. King Charles Albert had in 1848 and 1849 fought the Austrians and been defeated, leading to his abdication in favor of his son, Victor Emmanuel, who appointed Cavour prime minister. Cavour was a strong monarchist, and he believed in economic and material progress rather than romantic ideals as the path to a united Italian state, working with the Nationalist Society, which had branches in other Italian states and whose main objective was unification under the leadership of Piedmont. Cavour believed that the support and aid of France was necessary to bring this about, and the recent accession of Louis Napoleon as emperor seemed fortuitous. When an Italian nationalist, Orsini, attempted to assassinate him in January 1858, Louis Napoleon became convinced that he should continue in his uncle's footsteps and work for the liberation of the peninsula. He and Cavour decided that the best way to do this was to provoke a war in Italy that would permit Piedmont and France to intervene against Austria. A formal treaty was drawn up in December 1858 between the two countries, and France was to receive Nice and Savoy in return for its aid.

During the winter and spring of 1859, Piedmont mobilized its army. In April the Piedmontese received an ultimatum from Austria demanding that they cease mobilization immediately. This act provided grounds for an accusation of provoking war, which Victor Emmanuel then leveled against the Austrians, with France coming to the assistance of its ally. The Austrians suffered defeat on June 4 and June 24 at Magenta and Solferino, respectively. In addition, revolutions had broken out in many of the Italian states with Tuscany, Modena, Parma, and Romagna all experiencing rebellion. Napoleon III began to view the extent of upheaval with trepidation since the Austrians were in retreat, and the Italian states in revolt were calling for union with Piedmont. He feared too broad a Piedmontese victory, and as a result he independently concluded a peace with Austria on July 11 at Villafranca. Piedmont received Lombardy while Venetia remained with Austria and a federal union of existing Italian governments presided over by the pope was proposed. Austria had successfully been removed from most of northern Italy, but this did not lessen Cavour's feeling that the French had betrayed the Italian people. The patriots were dissatisfied with the arrangement and revolution continued to spread. Toward summer's end, Parma, Modena, Tuscany, and Romagna got rid of their old rulers and voted to join with Piedmont.

The spirit of romantic republicanism now joined the upheaval, and the goal became the complete unification of the North and South. When Garibaldi landed in Sicily in May 1860 with more than 1,000 soldiers and

3.9.   Garibaldi hails Victor Emmanuel as king of a united Italy at the bridge of Teano in the fall of 1860. (Scala/Art Resource, New York)

began the advance northward, taking control of Naples, Cavour realized that it was necessary to take action against Garibaldi and his dream of an Italian republic. Cavour sent Piedmontese troops south for a confrontation, and Garibaldi accepted domination by the government of Piedmont, thereby allowing his nationalism to take precedence over his republicanism. In late 1860 the southern states joined the northern union under the leadership of Piedmont. Venetia and Rome still remained outside the new union. In 1866, Austria was forced to relinquish the former during conflict with Prussia. Unification was completed in 1870 when France, due to war with Prussia, withdrew from Rome the garrisons that had been supporting papal rule. In March 1871, Victor Emmanuel became king of the united Italian state, which was by no means free of problems (see appendix, Document XVIII). Corruption became endemic, as bribery and favors formed the underpinnings of the new Italy in a system known as *trasformismo*. In addition, there existed other territories that many felt should have been part of the Italian state. Trent and Trieste were smaller areas with a largely Italian population that remained under Austrian rule. These areas were regarded as *italia irredenta* ("unredeemed Italy") and continued to be rallying points for discontent within the newly unified nation.

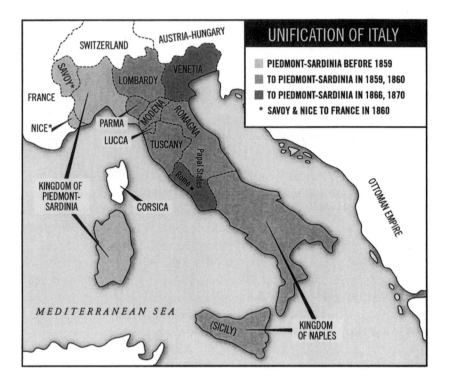

Prussia and Austria: German Unification Begins

The unification of Germany is regarded as the single most important event in European politics between 1848 and 1914. The driving force for this accomplishment came not from Austria, as might have been expected, but from Prussia, which had taken the first step toward unification with the formation of the *Zollverein,* or customs union, in January 1834. This union brought together most of Germany outside of Austria in a single commercial entity. Thus, most of Germany had been unified for trade and commercial purposes long before political unity was achieved.

After Wilhelm I (r. 1861–1888) became king of Prussia, he engaged in an ongoing battle with liberals in the lower house. He felt the need for a strong army to support him in his rule, while the liberals saw this army as a means of keeping them in subjection. The liberals believed that by adopting democratic principles of government, Prussia would gain support from the smaller German states. When the army reform bill was presented, reorganizing and enlarging the Prussian army, it was passed in the upper house, but rejected in the Chamber of Deputies. The king dissolved the assembly, but the next election brought an even larger number of liberals to the lower house. It was at this point that Otto von Bismarck (1815–1898) was called into service. He had studied law and political science and had been renowned for his ability to drink large quantities of beer and engage in duels. After an interesting career in public life, which included service as representative to the Frankfurt diet and a stint in Russia as ambassador, he was appointed in September 1862 to the post of chancellor. This appointment was a direct challenge to the liberals in the assembly, as Bismarck was well-known as a reactionary. He began his twenty-eight years in office by declaring that he would not let the constitution stand in the way of military reforms and in his keynote address of September 30 declared that "the great questions of the time cannot be solved by speeches and parliamentary majorities—that was the mistake of 1848–1849—but by blood and iron."

At the same time as he was ensuring the prowess of the Prussian army, Bismarck was seeking to isolate Austria so that in the event of a war between the two powers, Austria would be defeated and Bismarck would be free to pursue his aims. He only needed a pretext for war and found one readily available in the Schleswig-Holstein question. He had to make war appear to be inevitable and that Prussia was being forced into hostilities, since Wilhelm I was very much against war. The question of Schleswig-Holstein was an intricate one, a Gordian knot that, as Lord Palmerston, a British diplomat, stated, had only ever been understood by three people. One was dead, the other was insane, and the third, which happened to be himself, had forgotten everything he had ever known about it. Schleswig was adjacent to Denmark and Holstein to Prussia, and each country was anxious to annex both areas. When in March 1863 the Danish king, Frederick VII, incorporated Schleswig and voted in a joint constitution, Bismarck convinced Austria to join Prussia in occupying both Schleswig and Holstein. The Danes, despite a desperate fight, had to cede the territory (1864).

Now the victors had to decide who was to rule Schleswig-Holstein; by the Convention of Gastein, Prussia assumed control of Schleswig and Austria of Holstein. Just as Bismarck had calculated, relations soon became strained, and because Austria had supported the claim of the Duke of Augustenburg to the duchies, its conduct was deemed by Bismarck to be an "alliance with revolution." This, according to Bismarck, justified the occupation of Holstein, and his attitude resulted in the entry of Prussian forces into Holstein, forcing the Austrians to withdraw. They complained to the Diet of the Germanic Confederation for aid, which led to the mobilization of Prussian troops. In the ensuing war, known as the Seven Weeks' War, Austria was supported by most of the states in the Germanic Confederation, and Prussia depended on Italy as its only ally. On July 3, 1866, at Sadowa (Königgrätz), the Austrian army was completely routed. Crafty as always, and hoping to gain the Austrians as allies, Bismarck did not annex any territory, but called for a lenient peace settlement that would not arouse desire for vengeance. Austria paid a small indemnity, relinquished rights to Holstein, and agreed to a new German organization in which Austria would not be included. This was to be the North German Confederation, which preserved the independence of the princes, but at the same time established the king of Prussia as the supreme head. Hanover, Hesse, Nassau, and the city of Frankfurt had supported Austria during the war, and they were now incorporated into Prussia. After the addition of Schleswig and Holstein, this new arrangement marked the beginning of a strong federal German state with an army organized on the Prussian model and under the direction of Prussia. A federal council and a diet elected by the people as a whole were to be responsible for legislation. Bismarck's actions made him a hero almost overnight, and even the liberals became his supporters with the result that in the diet he no longer had to force his will. He made his wishes known, they were deferred to, and in this way Prussian liberalism died. The monarchy and the army were now the most popular institutions in the country.

Within the Austrian Empire, the government continued to search for institutions and policies that would bind the diverse nationalities and regions into a stable political unit. Emperor Franz Josef, although described as conscientious and hardworking, is also viewed as a slave to routine and roundly lacking in imagination. The army was to some extent a unifying force, but political reform was required to ensure domestic order. Hungarians within the empire were harboring feelings of having been deeply wronged by the suppression that followed the revolution of 1848, and they were sullen and resentful subjects. These problems between the Austrians and the Hungarians contributed to Austrian defeats at Magenta and Solferino in 1859 and 1860. Due to the discontent in Hungary, the Austrians were unable to withdraw their troops for use in Italy. Hungarians even joined with the enemy to fight the Austrians. It became clear to Franz Josef at this time that he would have to pacify public discontent by constitutional means. In October 1860 he issued the October Diploma (or Decree), which announced the arrival of constitutional government. Measures to be introduced included granting some authority to regional diets. This suggested a move toward federalism, while retaining strong central control and making no significant liberal provisions. The diploma pleased few and when the constitution was promulgated as the February Patent of 1861, the direction of change had been reversed. Each region had its own diet and sent representatives to an imperial parliament in Vienna. The new constitution, although more liberal, still failed to satisfy the demands for representative government.

The Magyars would only accept full recognition of their historic rights. At Sadowa in 1866, when Austria was for all practical purposes expelled from Germany, the Austrians became dependent on the good will of the non-Germans in the empire. As a result, Austria's drive to centralize was abandoned, and in 1867 *Ausgleich* ("compromise") was reached. This arrangement, while essentially a bargain between the Germans and the Magyars, was of definite disadvantage to the Slavs, who received little consideration. The Dual Monarchy, which the Ausgleich created, included the Empire of Austria and the Kingdom of Hungary. Each had its own constitution and its own parliament, and neither state was to interfere in the affairs of the other. Austria's administrative language would be German and Hungary's would be Magyar. All nationalities were to have equal rights. Local languages in schools, administrations, and public life were guaranteed. The realms would be united in the person of the emperor and king, who would always be the Habsburg ruler. The two areas would share a common ministry for finance, foreign affairs, and war. In form, both Austria and Hungary were constitutional, parliamentary states, but in reality the principles of responsible government were not always carried out, and universal manhood suffrage did not occur in Austria until 1907. By 1914 only one-quarter of the adult male population of Hungary was allowed to vote. The new state contained within it many dissatisfied nationalities, and the Magyars fuelled their rebelliousness by refusing to accord to the other nationalities the same rights that they had demanded and received for themselves in the realms of education, language, and culture.

The union with Austria was not a happy one, but the Hungarians knew that in the event of war with Russia, they would not stand a chance alone. Franz Josef, on the other hand, needed the support of the Hungarians in dealing with the Prussians. In this respect, the Dual Monarchy was held together by external pressures. Within the new arrangement, territory and population were fairly evenly divided. The population in the Austrian domain numbered about 24 million, while in the Hungarian lands it numbered about 17.5 million. The area of Austria covered 115,903 square miles and Hungary covered 125,039; within these small areas many nationalities battled for recognition. As much as Franz Josef I tried to pacify the national groups, there seemed to be no way to soothe the dissension and mend the rifts. He refused to use force to end the strife, but failed in his efforts to use constitutional means. Meanwhile, the ministers played one group off against another, and eventually the imperial parliament was deadlocked.

The Second Empire and Prussia: German Unification Completed

The Second Empire of Napoleon III in France has in some ways been an enigma to historians. It was the first authoritarian regime to interrupt the succession of parliamentary governments that had existed since 1815, and it consisted of two quite distinct periods, the first constituting the authoritarian phase from 1851 until 1859, and the second being a more liberal period up to 1870. After the coup of 1851, support for the regime came from the traditional right, that is, from the businessmen, the property owners, and the Catholic Church. Louis Napoleon controlled both the legislature and the press and allowed little room for political dissent. The victory of the French in the Crimean War served to increase the popularity of the emperor.

During the late 1850s, he began to loosen his grip, making some liberal concessions domestically to compensate for a failing foreign policy. For example, in 1860 he began to relax his hold on the legislature and allowed the members freer discussion. He concluded a free-trade agreement with Britain, relaxed the press laws during the 1860s, and in 1870 he allowed moderates in the legislature to form a ministry. In addition, he agreed to a liberal constitution that made ministers responsible to the legislature. Externally, Louis Napoleon had lost control of Italian unification, had supported a failed military expedition into Mexico, and watched from the sidelines as Bismarck and Prussian officials had begun to reorganize German affairs.

The south German states still had to be drawn into an enlarged confederation, and to this end Bismarck took the peoples of the North German Confederation to war. A question of succession in Spain provided the opportunity he was seeking. The Spanish people were searching for a new monarch after 1868, when a revolution led by conservatives had succeeded in deposing the Bourbon queen. Prince Leopold of Hohenzollern-Sigmaringen, a cousin to Wilhelm I of Prussia, was chosen. This choice greatly disturbed Napoleon III, who, strangely enough, was a closer blood relative to the candidate than was Wilhelm. Louis Napoleon did not wish to see Hohenzollerns on two sides of his empire. Leopold refused the crown twice and then accepted in June 1870. The French government sent Count Vincent Benedetti to consult with Wilhelm I, who was vacationing at Bad Ems. On

July 12, Wilhelm I persuaded Leopold to withdraw. The matter might have been settled had the French been less demanding, but Benedetti sought assurances that at no time in the future would the candidacy of a Hohenzollern be renewed. Wilhelm refused to broker such an agreement and stated that from that time on Benedetti would have to discuss the matter with his ministers. When Wilhelm sent Bismarck a telegram informing him of this exchange, the chancellor was greatly disturbed. It now appeared that there were no reasons for precipitating a war. He decided to deal with this by editing the telegram and having it published in the evening newspaper. His editing produced the impression that the German people had been insulted by the French ambassador, which greatly disturbed the Germans. On the other hand, the French read it and saw it as insolence on the part of the German ambassador. In Paris, the people demanded retaliation, and although Napoleon III hesitated, war was declared on July 19, 1870 (see appendix, Document XIX).

The French army was generally inferior to the Prussians', and when Napoleon looked around him for allies, he found them wanting. The Austrians could not accommodate him because they feared Russia, which was firmly tied to Prussia. The Italians on whom Louis Napoleon had been counting did not come to his aid, but rather used the situation to occupy Rome and complete its unification as soon as the French garrison was withdrawn. Victory for Prussia under these circumstances was inevitable and not long in coming. A series of Prussian successes during the month of August softened up the French forces, and on September 1, 1870, at the Battle of the Sedan, the French army surrendered. The emperor was captured and allowed to go to England, where he died two years later.

On September 4, 1870, the Second Empire came to an end. A republic was proclaimed in France and a provisional government established. The Parisian masses, determined to keep on fighting despite the defeat that had occurred, were optimistic that the city could hold out against the advancing German armies. By September 19, the Germans surrounded the city and isolated it almost completely to the point where communication with the provinces was conducted with balloons and carrier pigeons. On October 8, Leon Gambetta, minister of the Interior, having done all that he felt was possible in preparing the population of Paris for the upcoming siege, escaped the city in a balloon. Over the next few weeks, operating from Bordeaux, he equipped a force of some 600,000 men. These soldiers fought well, despite their lack of training and equipment, with the result that the war continued. However, by the end of October, the situation in Paris was critical. Hunger

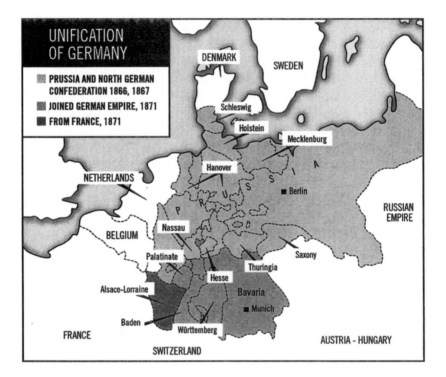

UNIFICATION OF GERMANY

- PRUSSIA AND NORTH GERMAN CONFEDERATION 1866, 1867
- JOINED GERMAN EMPIRE, 1871
- FROM FRANCE, 1871

DENMARK, SWEDEN, Schleswig, Holstein, Mecklenburg, NETHERLANDS, Hanover, Berlin, RUSSIAN EMPIRE, BELGIUM, Nassau, Palatinate, Saxony, Thuringia, Hesse, Alsace-Lorraine, Bavaria, Munich, Baden, FRANCE, Württemberg, SWITZERLAND, AUSTRIA - HUNGARY

and disease had claimed over 60,000 lives, and on January 28, 1871, the city of Paris finally capitulated and Jules Favre, vice president of the provisional government, signed an armistice with the Germans. A few days earlier, the new German Empire had been proclaimed in the Hall of Mirrors at Versailles, with Wilhelm I as *kaiser* ("emperor"). This did not, however, end the misfortunes of France, where civil war erupted almost immediately.

Because Bismarck refused to make peace with the provisional government, elections were called for February 8, 1871. When the new assembly met at Bordeaux five days later, with Adolphe Thiers (1797–1877) as president, it became obvious that only 200 of the 600 deputies were republican in sentiment. The others were strongly monarchist, but fortunately for the republicans, the monarchists were split between those who supported the Bourbons and those who supported the House of Orléans, and both preferred a republican government to one headed by the rival monarchist faction. The people of Paris were for the most part republican and feared domination by the monarchists. They resented the way the siege of Paris had been handled by the provisional government and the fact that the new government had chosen to sit at Versailles rather than Paris. To be superseded by Versailles was regarded as a direct insult because of the valiant stand taken by Parisians against the enemy. Furthermore, they resented the negotiated settlement with the Prussian government, which agreed to French payment of a large indemnity, the presence of an occupying force on French soil, and the surrender of the provinces of Alsace and Lorraine. The Parisians, who had suffered much and held out the longest, experienced a deep sense of betrayal and felt that they had been sold down the river by the National Assembly, now sitting at Versailles. When Thiers ordered the disarmament of the Parisian National Guard on March 17, the people of the city regarded the new government as its outright enemy.

A new government, called the Paris Commune, was elected in Paris nine days later; it provided an administration for the city of Paris, which would be separate from that of the rest of the country. The national government moved rapidly against the commune and, by early April, Paris was once more under siege, surrounded this time by an army of her fellow countrymen. On May 8 the bombardment of the city began and continued for three weeks. On May 21, the forces of the National Assembly broke through into the city and the days that followed are known as Bloody Week, during which the national troops suppressed the uprising. An estimated 20,000 Parisians were killed, and many more of the communards were exiled after the dust had settled. The last of the communards were lined up against the wall of Père Lachaise cemetery and shot. With the defeat of the Paris Commune, the nation had proven itself triumphant over the centrifugal forces of dissent and parochialism.

Many of the political aims of nationalists and nation builders in the decades prior to 1871 had been realized, mainly through a succession of wars. The forty years of relative peace that had followed upon the settlement at Vienna had come to an abrupt end at midcentury with the conflict in the Crimea. This was followed by an era in which the wars of unification resulted in the formation of new nation-states. On the economic front, the developments in industry and technology would result in further alterations in relationships within Europe and would facilitate greater interaction with foreign peoples.

Chapter 4

WAR, REVOLUTION, AND THE NATION-STATE

Industrialization and nationalism continued to reshape European society as the nineteenth century unfolded and the nation-state increasingly became the focus of people's lives. National loyalty was deliberately fostered, and young men were conscripted into the military with the goal of building strong national armies. State functions were extended as governments assumed increased responsibility for public health and housing. In western Europe and Great Britain after 1871, the right to vote was extended to all adult males, and with the new political democracy, a new mass politics and press developed. The introduction of liberal and democratic practices was not always peaceful, as violent clashes of interest erupted. Some countries used their industrial power to extend or gain empires, and in a surge of new imperialism, European influence was extended around the world. The technological and organizational dominance unleashed by the Europeans upon other parts of the world led to a global imbalance in power, and the new imperialism resulted in increased tension among European states. These domestic and international gains and shifts were accompanied by other forces, some old and others new, which would coalesce to precipitate a catastrophic upheaval in European civilization with global repercussions.

THE POLITICAL LANDSCAPE: 1870-1914

We should be aware by now that France had been the strongest power in Europe since the fall of Rome. Although it was sometimes weakened by

domestic divisions or external factors, it possessed human and natural resources that outstripped any other European nation. These resources were
managed by a highly developed government, one of the most advanced and
sophisticated in Europe. But by the end of the nineteenth century, and for
some time before, this situation underwent quite dramatic change. Industrialization doubled and redoubled British strength, and the unification of
Germany resulted in the creation of a state that was larger and more populous than France. Between 1871 and the turn of the century, governments
were dealing with social problems resulting from industrialization and
with political problems that stemmed from the growth of an increasingly
aware working class. They were as well confronting one another in an international scene that had been transformed and was vaguely defined at
best. It was a scene in which tradition had little value, and under these new
circumstances, the strength of other nations, be they allies or opponents,
could only be estimated.

Britain at this time was in search of raw materials and markets to service an industrial economy, while France, defeated in the Franco-Prussian
War, had been torn asunder by the experience of the Paris Commune and
civil war. Engaged in another republican experiment within, the French
government felt an extreme threat to security from the direction of the
newly unified Germany. Meanwhile, Italy and Germany, being new states
in Europe, had to find means of national development. Austria was struggling to maintain stability in the face of ongoing nationalistic discontent
in its multinational empire. It faced hostility from Germany, from which it
was now excluded, and from Italy, whose people coveted some of the
Habsburg lands. Russia, having been defeated and isolated after the
Crimean War, needed to define her place on the international scene, to
look to the development of her Asian territories, and to achieve an industrial basis for a modern economy. This period in history is often presented
as dominated by the giant of imperialist ambition, which seemingly
loomed over every action and every event. In reality, this was a time when
there also existed domestic questions that were paramount in importance
and whose solutions, or attempted solutions, had grave consequences for
the twentieth century.

Great Britain and France

In Britain, government was dominated during the 1870s and 1880s by
William Gladstone (Liberal) and Benjamin Disraeli (Conservative). During

this time, due to the growth of a prosperous and increasingly socially acceptable working class, the need arose for a broadened franchise, one that would give the vote to more of the workers. In 1867, the second Reform Bill was adopted by Parliament, increasing the number of voters from 1.43 million to 2.7 million. It was a modest gain for democracy in Britain and was followed by a further extension of the franchise in 1884; however, 25 percent of males were still disenfranchised. It was not until the closing months of World War I that all men got the vote, and suffrage was won for women thirty years of age and over. Other democratic gains during this period included the institution of the secret ballot and in 1911 the passage of a bill that denied the House of Lords a veto over legislation. This was a gradual response motivated at least in part by the desire of the political parties to court popular support in a mass society. The Conservatives and the Liberals were both successful in winning votes from new electors, and they alternately formed a series of governments in the final decades of the nineteenth century. In response to social problems and social changes, government ministries from both parties introduced legislation that previously would have been regarded as unthinkable according to laissez-faire standards. Labor unions were formally recognized and regulatory measures enacted regarding work, housing, and public health. In addition, reforms eliminated the purchase of army commissions, removed religious tests from Oxford and Cambridge Universities, and gave the government, rather than religious denominations, control over elementary education through the Education Act of 1870.

One of the factors that contributed to the shifts in popular support between the Liberal and Conservative governments of the period was the "Irish question." In 1801, Ireland became part of the United Kingdom of Great Britain and Ireland. The Irish peasant was without recourse in his exploitation by English or absentee Anglicized Irish landlords. In addition, the Irish, although mainly Catholic, were made to tithe to the Church of Ireland, a sister church to the Church of England and a large landowning institution. Gladstone attempted in his first ministry to confront some of the problems. He succeeded in disestablishing the Church of Ireland, and he tried to institute home rule in 1886, but this attempt split the Liberal Party, as many members did not wish to endorse a political division of the British Isles. In 1914, home rule was granted, and the Ulstermen (Presbyterians) of Northern Ireland armed in protest against a predominantly Catholic independent Ireland. The specter of civil war loomed over the United Kingdom.

In France, the Third Republic, born of the bloodshed and hatred of war and insurrection, was beset from the beginning by major problems. Elected in February, the new National Assembly struggled to establish a government, but was interrupted almost immediately in its deliberations by the bloody insurrection in Paris in May. In 1873, the monarchist majority forced the resignation of Thiers, a staunch republican, who headed the new regime. He was replaced by Marshal MacMahon, and in 1875 constitutive laws, but not a constitution, were passed, and a republic was established by a margin of one vote. The new laws provided for a president, a bicameral parliament, and a cabinet headed by a premier. This Third Republic was to endure for sixty-five years, but its existence was volatile and often precarious. The years between 1875 and 1914 saw fifty cabinet changes. Amazingly, government policy achieved continuity due to the stability of ministerial posts and the existence of a permanent civil service. The republic did not have the support of monarchists, Catholic clergy, or professional army officers, but its moderation in policy did win over many members of the peasant and middle classes.

The last two decades of the century saw France shaken by two major crises. The first arose between 1886 and 1889 when General Boulanger gathered about him a diverse following of the disenchanted, ranging from monarchists and aristocrats to radical republicans and workers. Briefly, it seemed that the strong man on horseback might seize power, but he lost heart and fled the country. Pope Leo XIII in 1892 called for a rallying of French Catholics in support of the republic (*ralliement*), but hope for such an event was shattered with the explosion of the second great crisis, the Dreyfus affair. In 1894 a Jewish army officer, Alfred Dreyfus, was accused of selling military secrets to German intelligence. He was convicted of treason and deported to Devil's Island, although evidence soon came to light that pointed to the guilt of another officer. The army refused to reopen the case despite mounting protest from the public. A deep split within French society resulted as traditionalists, royalists, anti-Semites, and army supporters fought against the reopening of the case and hoped to disgrace the republican regime. Captain Dreyfus was stoutly and tenaciously defended by liberals, radicals, and socialists, who believed in him and who were determined in their efforts to see justice done and to bring down their adversaries. It was not until 1899, after several hellish years of imprisonment, that Dreyfus was pardoned, and in 1906 he was fully exonerated. In the eyes of his supporters, this resolution brought about an understanding that the rights of French citizens were safer under a republic than under an alternative type of conservative government. Thus, *l'affaire*, as the whole miserable episode came to be known, ultimately reinforced the republic and ruined the monarchical party. The army was put under the control of a constitutional authority, and many Catholic orders were dismantled. *L'affaire* served to reduce the prestige of the church, as its alliance with the monarchists in the perpetration of a miscarriage of justice and a campaign of hatred backfired. The republic had triumphed.

Political scandal was not the only challenge facing the republic. It was plagued by a rising tide of socialist agitation in the wake of industrialization.

4.1. Courtroom scene from the espionage trial of Captain Alfred Dreyfus (Library of Congress, Prints and Photographs Division [LC-USZ62-116133])

French workers wishing to establish a socialist republic were consistently thwarted and frustrated in their efforts. Low wages and abysmal working conditions resulted in strike action that was brutally suppressed. Still confronting problems of a longstanding nature presented by monarchists, church, and army, the government had to face the workers' discontent domestically. In addition, the increasing bellicosity of the German nation began to dominate the landscape of Europe as the specter of war loomed on the horizon.

Germany and Italy

The new German Empire was a federation of monarchies, all German states, in which Prussia was dominant. Bismarck, shrewd politician that he was, played on democratic and socialist sentiment in his battle for popular support and, in so doing, had members of the Reichstag (lower chamber) elected by universal manhood suffrage. In principle, he was little concerned about this arrangement as he believed that governing the country was the domain of the kaiser, Wilhelm I, and the chancellor, who in this case was none other than himself. The upper house, the Bundesrat, was in reality more powerful than the Reichstag.

Almost immediately following the proclamation of the new empire in 1871, the government became embroiled in a conflict with the Catholic Church. This struggle, known as the *kulturkampf*, hinged on an increase in papal power and the political activity of German Catholics. In the 1870s the dogma of papal infallibility was promulgated, and this signaled to Bismarck an imminent crisis in the historical struggle between church and state. The creation of a Catholic Center Party in 1871 proved a particular threat since it was based in the south of the empire. It represented southern interests as well as Catholicism and as such was most distasteful to Bismarck. On both grounds, it was hostile to the central government dominated by Protestant Prussia. During the early 1870s, the government set about stripping the church of its traditional powers. It expelled the Jesuits and took control of education and discipline. Civil marriage was made obligatory, and government financial aid to the church was suspended, while all religious orders were dissolved except the nursing orders. At the end of the decade, Bismarck decided that the government was not in danger from the church and that the support of the Center Party would be useful to his government in the new tariff policies that he wished to adopt. By the mid-1880s the *kulturkampf* had died out, but the supremacy of the state over the church in the new German Empire had been clearly established.

WAR, REVOLUTION, AND THE NATION-STATE

During the *kulturkampf*, the government encountered a new problem in the considerable growth of German socialism and the establishment in 1875 of the German Workingmen's Party. Within its ranks moderate socialists joined with Marxists to form the Social Democratic Party (SPD). The early socialists were beset by divisions within their ranks between the followers of Marx and those of the evolutionary socialists (Lassalle), but despite these differences, the party gained membership rapidly. Bismarck was deeply concerned with these events since he mistrusted even moderate socialism and viewed the recent Paris Commune as a truly horrific event. Viewed as anarchical and republican in nature, socialism in an empire of monarchies justified fear of revolution. In 1878, after two attempts to assassinate the emperor, both unrelated to the socialists, Bismarck succeeded in having antisocialist legislation passed in the Reichstag. The socialists were forbidden to gather in groups and to distribute printed material, but Bismarck realized that these measures alone did not have the strength to stem the rising tide of socialist support and activity. He cunningly preempted the demands of the socialists with a program of reform that included sickness insurance, insurance against periods of unemployment, and a pension plan for the elderly. With these reforms, Germany was in the forefront of social legislation, far ahead of England, France, and the United States. The move garnered much popular support due to the obviously paternalistic, "caring" attitude of the government, but the measure did not halt the growth of socialism in the form of the SPD. Realizing that once again his measures had failed to stem the tide, Bismarck, in 1890, after twelve years of campaigning against socialism, supported the repeal of the antisocialist laws. In that same year, a greater number of socialists were elected to the Reichstag than had been in 1878. Bismarck greatly feared a social revolution within the empire and he continued to do so up until the end of his political career. This event occurred abruptly in 1890 with the "dropping of the pilot," when Wilhelm II ordered him to resign. Wilhelm II, having succeeded to the throne in 1888, steered Germany on what was termed a "new course." He exhibited some startling personality traits manifested in his idea of his own personal power and prestige. As a result, he could not deal effectively with the shadow of Bismarck as elder statesman looming over him. As emperor, Wilhelm II dominated the next four chancellors and proved that he was certainly no democrat. His actions were rooted firmly in his belief in the power of the House of Hohenzollern, and the main forces in the empire were the traditional ones; power rested with the army, the Junkers, and the princes, as well as with the new German industrialists.

KEEPING IT DOWN!

SOCIALIST JACK IN THE BOX.

4.2.   Otto von Bismarck attempting to contain socialism (CORBIS/MAGMA)

Despite all this, democratic forces continued to grow in strength and number in the form of the SPD and the Progressive Party. They worked toward a reform of the illiberal constitution of 1850 and for control of the chancellery by the dominant party in the German parliament, the Reichstag. By 1912, the SPD polled one-third of the votes and became the largest single party in the Reichstag.

In Italy, the unification that took place in the 1870s had brought together a disparate conglomeration of bedfellows under the rule of Victor Emmanuel II. Despite the new geographical unity, many problems remained unsolved. Systems of administration had to be unified, as did systems of law, trade coinage, weights and measures, agriculture, and education. Technology, machine industry, and resources such as coal and iron were lacking in the newly unified country. Transportation and communication facilities were outmoded or nonexistent. In addition, there was as yet no feeling of commonality among the citizenry.

Illiteracy and poverty were common throughout the country, but most particularly in the South where about 85 percent of the population was illiterate. The North's rate was somewhat better at 55 percent. Such a condition presented obstacles to effective self-government. Increasing population was giving impetus to emigration, and added to these conditions was a major dispute raging between the government and the Roman Catholic Church. When the troops of Victor Emmanuel II marched into Rome in September 1870 and annexed it, thereby depriving the pope of his temporal power, what came to be called the "Roman question" was raised, disrupting the relations between church and state for more than half a century. The Italian parliament passed the Law of Guarantees, which granted the pope royal dignities, free communication with Catholics everywhere, the right to receive foreign embassies, possession of the Vatican palace, and other properties, as well as a subsidy from the state treasury equivalent to his former income from his lands. The person of the pope was declared sacred and inviolable, and the Vatican was granted the right of extraterritoriality, meaning that it could not be entered by Italian officials without papal consent. These conditions granted greater liberty to the Roman Church than it enjoyed in Spain, France, or Austria. Yet Pius IX was not satisfied. He insisted that he should be able to retain some part of Rome, and when the government would not agree, he refused to accept the settlement. In so doing, he refused to recognize the new Italian state and forbade Italians to participate in its affairs. The pope became a voluntary "prisoner" within the Vatican and forbade all Catholics to vote or hold office under the government.

The government consisted of the king as executive head, and he exercised authority through his ministers. They were responsible to a parliament of two houses, the Senate and the Chamber of Deputies. The Senate was composed of the royal family and of members appointed by the king for life, whereas the Chamber of Deputies consisted of some 500 elected members. Suffrage was restricted to adult males who could read and write and further limited by additional educational and property qualifications, with the result that only 2.5 percent of the population could vote. In 1882, restrictions were eased so that virtually every Italian who could read and write was granted suffrage, but it was only in 1912 that universal manhood suffrage was adopted, increasing the number of voters from three million to eight million.

In the meantime, politics in the new state fell into the hands of the anti-clerical parties, as many Italian Catholics refused to vote or to run for office. Moderately liberal governments ruled the new state until 1876; it can be said that for the most part Italian politics were characterized during this period by bribery and graft (*trasformismo*), and government was taken up with a movement called *irredentism*, an ongoing agitation to secure from Austria areas north and northeast of Venetia with largely Italian populations. In addition, there occurred in 1896 an ill-conceived imperialist venture into Ethiopia when the Italians moved inland after taking over Somaliland and Eritrea on the Red Sea. They confronted the Ethiopians at Adowa and were slaughtered. This thorough routing ensured that the Italians did not try this again for forty years.

Meanwhile, the stalemate between church and government continued until 1904, when the pope, aware of the growth of the social question and of radical tendencies, allowed Catholics to vote. It was not until much later (1929) that the Lateran Accord was signed, and an agreement was reached between the government of Mussolini and the church establishing an independent Vatican state.

Although there was limited economic expansion in the last quarter of the nineteenth century, banking scandals were so common as to prevent confidence in the economy. Socialist activism led to strikes, and the country remained poor, suffering from labor unrest and unresolved state-church problems. These unresolved problems, central to Italy's history in the nineteenth century, were due at least in part to the reactionary attitude of Pius IX, who did not recover from the shock of having been driven from Rome by the republicans in 1848. In 1878, Pius IX was succeeded by Leo XIII, whose main legacy was the formulation of Catholic social doctrine. It is in *Rerum Novarum* (*Of Modern Things*), which attacked poverty and condemned capitalism as its source, that the bases of Catholic socialism are to be found. In its turn, socialism was viewed as a double-edged sword, antireligious and materialistic, but nonetheless Christian in principle. The pope supported the formation of Catholic socialist parties and labor unions composed of Catholic workingmen, and in this way the church dealt with the rising tide of socialism. The rise and growth of syndicalism, which saw trade unionism as central to production and to government, was another important aspect of the Italian political landscape at this time. This movement took hold in Italy because the trade unions were weak and, having little to lose, were willing to subscribe to a sensationalist doctrine to attract membership. Such was the general condition of Italy on the eve of the Great War.

Austria-Hungary, Russia, and the Ottoman Empire

After the Ausgleich of 1867, the Austrian empire had a constitution but continued to be ruled as a traditional monarchy under the emperor, Franz-Josef (r. 1848–1916). In foreign affairs and military matters, there existed very little parliamentary restraint upon the emperor. As in Germany, the government faced a rising tide of socialism that was held in check in much the same manner: reforms featuring a social-insurance plan and paternalistic legislation were combined with repressive laws. The advance of socialism, however, was not the main problem facing the government. It was the disparate and varied minority groups that made the empire a mosaic of nationalities and languages. In reality the ruling groups, Austrians and Magyars, constituted a minority. The large Slavic population envied the position of the Hungarians after the Ausgleich, and the various Slavic groups also envied each other. The animosities among these dissatisfied groups resulted in ongoing turmoil and destabilization within the empire as various minorities demanded autonomy or independence or rights equal to those granted some other group(s). Furthermore, Austria lacked a viable middle class. Outside the city of Vienna, only two classes were discernible, the aristocracy and the peasantry. Within the city, the middle class provided a small impetus for liberal reform, but its members were determined to keep the many minorities of the empire bereft of the rights of constitutional government that they themselves enjoyed. These centrifugal forces, constantly at work within the empire, threatened to destroy it and cast minorities into the neighboring states.

But by 1900 the conflicts among various nationalities had served to immobilize the Reichsrat and the emperor was ruling by decree with the support of the civil service. In 1907 universal manhood suffrage was introduced in Austria, but the Reichsrat remained in a state of paralysis. Constitutionalism was a dead letter. It was able to exist in Hungary, but the price exacted was the subjugation of minorities to the dominance of the Magyars, who proved to be the real winners in the Ausgleich. They met the problems posed by the minorities not by concession, but by suppression. They instituted a systematic program of Magyarization through control of education and imposition of their language. Croatia was excepted from these policies and allowed to preserve its separate existence, its parliament, and its language.

Politically, an ever-expanding working class, represented by members of the SPD, received after 1870 the right to form trade unions and to strike. Further measures were passed in the 1880s by the existing government to protect the workers, but the SPD faced the usual dilemmas of socialists. One involved the question of whether to overthrow the existing government by revolutionary means or to wait until it would be possible to assume full power peacefully. In addition, the nationality question loomed large. In theory, the political beliefs of the SPD supposedly transcended this issue, but in reality remained intrusive, causing disturbances that were explosive and far-reaching in their impact.

Both parts of the empire were plagued with serious financial difficulties during the last quarter century. In Austria, the government struggled with a severe depression, and despite social legislation, the workers suffered enormously. Labor organizations proliferated as a result, and the more the government attempted to curb socialist political parties and trade unions, the more determined the people became to keep them. Expenditures for the army, bureaucracy, and public services were constantly increasing. Existing tax revenues were inadequate and the means of collection complex and confused. Indirect taxes on consumer goods, documents, and newspapers were the principal sources of state funding. The state increased its borrowing with the result that servicing the national debt became more and more expensive.

In Hungary, the Magyars imposed high tariffs, which resulted in increased food prices for all the peoples within the realm. The peasants could at least subsist, and some large landowners actually realized large profits, but the Magyar petty nobles experienced economic difficulties. The revolutionary upheaval in 1848 had resulted in the abolition of serfdom in 1853. Since the land holdings of the petty nobles were not large enough for their estates to function profitably without forced labor, many were forced to sell their estates. The great nobles took over with alacrity, and by 1900 owned about one-third of the land in Hungary. Many of the Magyar petty nobles entered the civil service where they remained, defending the settlement of 1867 and jealously defending the privileged status of their nation. As a result, in 1900 more than 90 percent of Hungary's bureaucrats and judges were Magyar.

Vienna had long been the center of cultural activity in the Habsburg domain, rich in the diverse talents of its many nationalities. This wealth of talent, pouring into Vienna from all areas of the realm, made Vienna a rival to Paris as an intellectual and artistic center. Musicians, artists, writers, and architects all gravitated to this lively center, which was also the home of scholars of the humanities and social and natural sciences. It had been home to composers Franz Joseph Haydn, Wolfgang Amadeus Mozart, Ludwig von Beethoven, and Franz Schubert in the eighteenth century. Later, toward the end of the nineteenth century, Viennese artists Gustav Klimt, Egon Schiele, and Oskar Kokoschka became world renowned, as were composers Richard Strauss, Richard Wagner, Anton Bruckner, and Gustav Mahler. These names are only representative of the talent native to Vienna, which was also the home of the famous founder of psychoanalysis, Sigmund Freud. The vibrant and creative intellectual life of the city gave it a reputation for warmth, light, and gaiety that few European cities could hope to match. At the same time, centered in Vienna, there existed a raging anti-Semitism that was perhaps the worst in all of Europe. In addition, despite the brilliance of Vienna's cultural life, both sectors of the empire continued to face formidable problems in the areas of finance and ethnic unrest. By 1914 it seemed unlikely that Austria could meet the challenges facing Europe. The government was incapable of putting a modern army into battle, and the weakness of the economy and government were starkly revealed.

The problems of ethnic unrest affected the Ottoman Empire as well. Long known as the "sick man of Europe," its demise had been considered imminent since at least the end of the eighteenth century. The patient, however, refused to die and kept hanging on year after year while circumstances internal and external to the empire, worked together to lengthen its lifespan. National groups could not overcome their differences long enough to unite in overthrowing the regime, and the rivalry between the Great Powers kept them sufficiently divided to prohibit any concerted action from that quarter. The inner disruption was a quite different matter. In general, the Ottoman government was not so intolerant as it is frequently painted to have been and did not interfere with the religions of conquered peoples, other than to have them pay a poll tax. Christians survived almost as always under Ottoman Muslim rule, and only in Albania was there a general acceptance of the Islamic faith of the conquerors among the masses, although many of the Christians were quite wealthy, more so than their Ottoman rulers.

The force destroying the Ottoman Empire was nationalism, with every national group insisting upon complete independence; there was absolutely no way that the Turks could please everyone. Rebellion was always uppermost in the minds of the subject peoples, as was demonstrated whenever military defeat demonstrated the weakness of the government. Problems with Serbia began in the early nineteenth century (1804). In 1821 the Greek revolt shook the empire to its foundations, and the sultan granted autonomy to the Serbs. In 1829 Greek independence was recognized. After the Crimean War, Moldavia and Wallachia elected a joint administration under Alexander Cuza, and the new entity, Rumania, was recognized in 1862 by the Ottoman government.

CHAPTER 4

The Treaty of Paris (1856) at the end of Crimean War had ensured that the independence and territorial integrity of the Ottoman Empire would be safeguarded and that any efforts to infringe upon Ottoman territory would be considered "a matter of general interest." This really was an attempt to bring the Ottoman Empire into the European family of states by means of a series of reforms. These reforms did not see the light of day, however, and conditions became worse within the empire. In 1875 there was a revolt of Slavs in Herzogovina. The revolt spread to Bulgaria and was quelled by the Turks in a most brutal and bloody manner, with dozens of villages destroyed and thousands of defenseless men, women, and children massacred in cold blood. This bloodbath carried in its wake a widespread demand for military action. Despite Gladstone's demand that they should be expelled from Europe, Russia ended up acting alone against the Turks. The tsar used the occasion to further expansionist aims by pushing closer to Constantinople and attempting to unite the Balkan Slavic nationalities (Serbs, Croats, Slovenes, Bulgars, Macedonians, and Montenegrins) as one group under the leadership of mother Russia.

The tsar's troops were within a day of Constantinople, the object of the campaign, when the tsar and the Ottoman sultan concluded the Treaty of San Stefano in March 1878. From this would emerge a large, self-governing Bulgaria under Russian control. The Ottoman Empire would retain only a small strip of territory in Europe. The other European powers strongly objected to this arrangement and revision. In June, a congress met in Berlin under the direction of Bismarck. The principle of nationality was recognized to some degree in the revision. On condition that there would be no religious or other discrimination in the granting of civil and political rights, Montenegro, Serbia, and Rumania were given recognition as completely independent states. The huge Bulgaria as designed by the Russians was divided into three separate areas: the autonomous principality of Bulgaria under the suzerainty of the sultan, but having a Christian governor; the province of Eastern Rumelia, which was to remain under the direct political and military authority of the sultan; and Macedonia, which was returned to the Ottoman government.

Although intent upon curbing Russia's expansion, the powers were quick to expand their own control of Ottoman possessions. England was given the right to occupy Cyprus, while Austria-Hungary received the right to administer the provinces of Bosnia and Herzegovina, although they remained nominally part of the Ottoman Empire. This latter peculiar arrangement was undertaken to prevent the formation of a strong Slavic state bordering on

Hungary. The Ottoman Empire was badly mutilated by the terms of this treaty and left with little land in Europe.

Internally, the reactionary regime of Sultan Abdul Hamid sparked protest from a group of young, Western-educated reformers and army officers who organized themselves into the Young Turk movement. In 1908 this group forced Abdul Hamid to restore the constitution and the parliament. The Young Turks unseated the sultan when he attempted a counterrevolution. It appeared to neighboring countries that the Ottoman Empire was increasing in power and would soon become a force to be reckoned with in the Balkans. As a result, these countries decided it was time to get on with their own agendas before the Young Turks became so strong as to thwart their objectives. In October 1908, a series of events undermined and exposed the weakness of the empire. Bulgaria declared complete independence from the Ottoman Empire, Emperor Franz-Josef annexed Bosnia-Herzogovina, and the Cretan Assembly declared union with Greece. Domestically, the early months of the new regime showed great promise, and the ideals of liberty and fraternity were paramount. However, economic reforms did not meet expectations, and the response to the demands of diverse national groups was rigid centralization. A great surge of nationalism within the ethnic groups gave rise to revolutionary agitation, and before long these animosities led to war.

In the Russian Empire the accession of Alexander II to the throne in 1855 marked the beginning of a period of reform. The defeat suffered by Russia in the Crimean conflict pointed to her antiquated state in an advancing world. This war had exposed the government as weak and corrupt, and the country as technologically far behind other European nations. Alexander attacked the institution of serfdom, which he knew could not continue, and he expressed the desire to abolish it from above, before it abolished itself from below. The problem was extreme in its complexity because he wished to achieve his objective without harming the interests of the nobles. In February 1861, after years of discussion, the tsar finally signed a decree that abolished serfdom (see appendix, Document XX). He went on to establish a home-rule system in thirty-three provinces of European Russia to be carried out by *zemstvos* ("local assemblies") composed of elected representatives of the nobles, peasants, and townsmen. This local level of government would be in charge of hospitals, roads, schools, bridges, and charitable institutions. In addition, Alexander reformed the secret service by limiting its power, relaxed the censorship of the press, reformed the judicial system, and extended education. In 1870s only 8 to 9 percent of the population could read and write. He did increase the number of primary schools, but by the end of his reign, the number of children in school had not increased significantly, with only 13.5 percent of school-age boys and 3.3 percent of school-age girls attending. Reforms in higher education yielded more significant results with the lifting of entrance restrictions and an increase in the number of available fellowships.

Alexander's reforms netted him much opposition, not only from those whose vested interests were under attack, but also from progressives and radicals who deemed the reforms inadequate. The tsar's most extreme enemies were individuals and groups who believed that all of the institutions of government and society must be destroyed so that a fresh start could be made. Among these, Michael Bakunin is remembered as the father of European anarchism, whose followers aimed at complete annihilation of institutions and all forms of authority. His theories inspired many young Russians to take down tsarism by assassinating Alexander (see appendix, Document XXI).

Attempts on the life of the tsar succeeded in 1881 when Alexander II was killed by a bomb. The new tsar, Alexander III, was determined to maintain the old system and worked to that end with remarkable success. Believing that the mission of government was to wipe out liberalism, a plague that had infiltrated Russia from the Western nations, he congratulated himself that the illiteracy of the people had prevented this doctrine from succeeding. This tsarist regime was reactionary to a degree that paralleled the reign of his grandfather, Nicholas I. He was dedicated to wiping out revolutionaries and bringing the various nationalities together through a process of Russification, which, despite outward signs of success, actually resulted in an enormous hatred of government by the tsar's non-Russian subjects. It was the Jewish people who suffered the most under Alexander III. At the end of the eighteenth century, it had been decreed that they could live only within the pale made up of fifteen provinces in the southwestern part of the empire. There they lived apart from their Christian neighbors.

In the mid–nineteenth century they were granted access to schools, universities, and technical institutions, and during the time of Alexander II, some had been allowed to move outside the pale. Many entered the liberal professions, especially medicine, law, and journalism. Alexander III restricted their rights and persecuted them for his belief that they were lazy and subversive. Violence against the Jewish people increased, and no attempt was made to halt it. In addition, the Jews were forced back within the pale.

In the meantime, the peasants were becoming increasingly dissatisfied as the realities of emancipation hit home. In the two years following the emancipation, there were 1,100 agrarian uprisings. The redemption payments and taxes were too high for most to pay, and the former serfs found themselves worse off than before. In addition, the size of landholdings decreased as the proportion of supposedly free men increased. Agricultural implements were primitive, and the soil was poor in many regions. The nobles leased land to the peasants at exorbitant rates, and the peasants were forced to pay. Starvation was a constant threat and a great hunger for land developed and was manifested in continued riots and attacks on landlords.

Alexander III died suddenly in 1894 and was succeeded by his son, Nicholas II. Despite the best intentions and to the great disappointment of the initially supportive masses, this new tsar, blinded by his belief in divine right, proved to be totally out of touch with the situation in the empire and showed a complete lack of understanding of the problems confronting him. When Nicholas dismissed the idea of a constitution as a "foolish dream," and the people realized that there would be no reform, thoughts of revolution began to surface. Sporadic uprisings grew in number and organized groups, whose aim was to depose the government, began to appear. The strongest of the moderate organizations was the Constitutional Democratic Party, or the Kadets, who advocated a constitutional monarchy on the English model. This group was composed of merchants, manufacturers, liberal gentry, and professionals within the bourgeoisie. The extreme group was the Social Revolutionary Party, which focused on the condition of the peasants and had as its basic objective the seizure of the lands of the nobility.

But a new force, the industrial proletariat, would eventually bring down the Romanov dynasty. Industry had been steadily on the increase since the Emancipation of 1861. Labor had been cheap, and a wealth of natural resources had attracted a good deal of foreign investment in Russia. Factories and railways were built, and industrial development was burgeoning in the last years of the century. By 1900, approximately 10 percent of the population was engaged in industry, and most harbored a burning hatred of government. The conditions under which they worked were horrendous, and there was little government intervention. The workers were ready for revolution, and the Marxists gained a great deal of support from this group. In 1898 the Marxists combined to form the Social Democratic Labor Party, which split into a moderate and a radical faction; the latter was led by Lenin, who insisted that a new social order should be established by force at once. His followers, the left wing, were called the Bolsheviks, meaning "majority," because there were a few more of them. Members of the smaller faction were known as the Mensheviks ("minority"), a label that stuck even after they gained a majority in the next congress held in London in 1903. Russia's obvious weakness and ultimate defeat in a war with Japan in 1905 was a staggering blow to the government. It seemed impossible at the time that such a great European power as Russia had been defeated by an Asian power so newly arrived on the world scene. This defeat led to political instability at home and served as an encouragement for the revolutionaries to accelerate their activities. They did so, and the outcome was to be a revolution that took place in the early weeks of 1905, even as the Russian government still struggled with Japan. Political discontent and growing food shortages resulted in a workers' demonstration on January 9, 1905, when a massive procession made its way to the Winter Palace in St. Petersburg to present a petition of grievances to the tsar. Troops opened fire, and hundreds of peaceful demonstrators were killed. Known as "Bloody Sunday," this event marked the beginning of a revolution in Russia. Workers called strikes and formed unions, ethnic minorities revolted, local governments called for parliamentary government, and the peasants turned violently against their landlords, often razing their houses. A general strike occurred in October 1905, and the government gave in. The tsar attempted to divide his opponents with warnings against extremists and with his October Manifesto. In this manifesto, he agreed to create a Duma ("legislative assembly") elected directly by a broad franchise, and he granted civil liberties to his people. This proved satisfactory to the moderates and was sufficient to buy their support for the government's repression of the workers, who rose in Moscow in December 1905. Real constitutional monarchy did not last. The tsar's chief adviser until 1906, Peter Stolypin, dispensed with village ownership of land and opened the door to individual ownership by enterprising peasants. The tsar, however, was not at heart a reformer, and after Stolypin was assassinated in 1911, he reverted to a military and bureaucratic form of rule. He had limited the power of the Duma in 1907, and it was not until World War I that the revolutionary forces within Russia were able to end the tsarist regime.

THE ROAD TO CONFLICT

The nineteenth century had been an era of relative peace once Napoleon was defeated in 1815. It wasn't until 1914 that widespread war once again engulfed Europe and eventually involved much of the world. Many factors contributed to this conflagration. Some were more immediate and could be said to have directly precipitated the conflict, while others stemmed from antagonism and friction rooted further back in history. These deeper causes of the war included the alliance system, the armaments race, nationalism, imperialism, and economic rivalry.

The New Imperialism

The domestic transformations that changed the shape of European society were accompanied in the late nineteenth century by an aggressive expansionist policy. The new imperialism resulted in European global hegemony, as areas not previously linked or accessible to European commerce were explored, as a global market developed, and as political empires were extended or established. These major developments were the consequence of complex interrelated forces in which economic factors played an important part. States used tariffs and other restrictions in an environment of increasing competition for markets and resources that were in demand for industrial developments. However, not every extension of imperialist control incorporated territory that was of economic value. Political and strategic considerations were also evident as nations sought to gain possessions overseas. To some extent these were regarded matter-of-factly as the measure of a great nation or as being necessary for the protection of existing conquests in the face of European rivalry.

Social adaptations of Darwin's theory, simplified to "survival of the fittest," was used to categorize the world's peoples as members of either superior or inferior races, with Europeans (whites) in the former category and, therefore, dominant over others. Europeans tried to make this attitude more acceptable by describing their role as that of a "civilizing" force among "primitive" peoples. This so-called responsibility was often referred to as the "white man's burden," a term taken from a poem of the same title by Rudyard Kipling.

The imperialistic attitudes of the European nations were the result of technological and military superiority, which had come about through industrialization. Improvements in transportation and communication took Europeans to all regions and, as medical advances reduced their susceptibility to tropical diseases such as malaria, conquests were made with greater ease. Rifles and machine guns accentuated the technological gap and turned many unequal battles into tragic massacres.

Political issues also became an occasion for encouraging foreign expansion as national leaders attempted to divert attention from domestic problems to colonial enterprises. In addition, governments were frequently advised by officials overseas to take assertive action or pressured by private

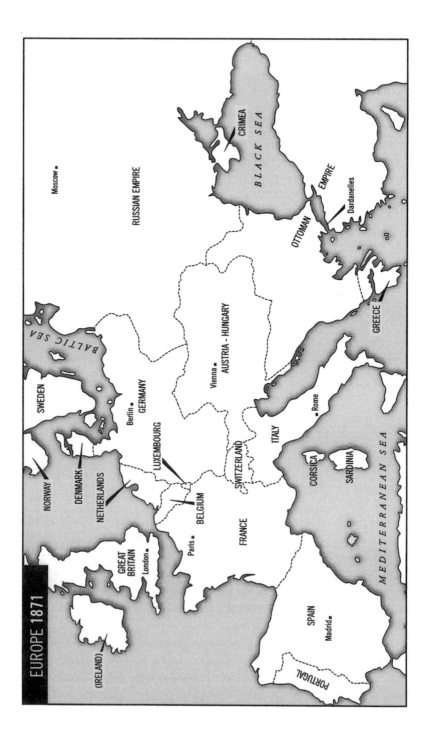

EUROPE 1871

BLACK SEA

CRIMEA

OTTOMAN EMPIRE

Dardanelles

RUSSIAN EMPIRE

Moscow ■

BALTIC SEA

SWEDEN

NORWAY

DENMARK

NETHERLANDS

Berlin ■
GERMANY

LUXEMBOURG

BELGIUM

SWITZERLAND

Vienna ■
AUSTRIA - HUNGARY

Rome ■

ITALY

GREECE

CORSICA

SARDINIA

MEDITERRANEAN SEA

GREAT BRITAIN

London ■

(IRELAND)

Paris ■

FRANCE

SPAIN

Madrid ■

PORTUGAL

firms seeking a competitive advantage. Humanitarian and religious motives were also frequently part of the "civilizing" responsibility of European nations. The spread of Christianity served to further inroads made into the indigenous cultures of conquered regions. The European press contributed to popular support by propagandizing colonial grandeur and emphasizing the tribulations and triumphs of explorers and missionaries in distant regions.

These motives and factors, often building on much earlier efforts at expansion, produced by 1900 a powerful European presence overseas. For example, China had traditionally been resistant to foreign incursion, but during the mid–nineteenth century, it had been the victim of an extremely aggressive thrust by European merchants. The valiant attempt of the Chinese to confine European trading activities to the port of Canton was unsuccessful, and the illegal import and sale of opium posed enormous problems to Chinese government and society. When the Chinese attempted to shut down the British traders to control the traffic in opium, the two countries ended up at war. The outcome of these Opium Wars was Chinese surrender and, in accordance with the Treaty of Nanking (1842), the cession of the island of Hong Kong to Great Britain and the opening of additional ports to foreign trade. Subsequently, due to unequal treaties and extraterritoriality provisions, other imperialistic nations gained access to China, and their establishment of foreign spheres of influence greatly compromised Chinese sovereignty. In India, the British had been present since the time of the founding of the East India Company (1600), which had ruled large areas of the country until the mid–nineteenth century. In 1857 and 1858, a series of uprisings, called collectively the Indian Mutiny, resulted in the imposition of rule through a governor-general responsible to the British cabinet.

The focus of French imperialist ambitions was northern Africa where Algeria, in debt to France, had first been invaded in 1830 and brought under French control by 1870. To the East, in 1881, Tunis became a French protectorate at the expense of a weakened Ottoman Empire. At the same time, Egypt was in debt to foreign bankers after a modernization program that had included the building of the Suez Canal by a French company. Egypt came increasingly under foreign influence and was eventually occupied and subjected to British political control after 1883.

The most intense arena of the new imperialism's "scramble for Africa" during the final decades of the nineteenth century was the sub-Saharan region. The British had taken possession of the Dutch settlements on the Cape of Good Hope in 1815 and later added Egypt. The French held possessions on the Mediterranean. Prior to 1880, 90 percent of the African continent remained free of European control; however, within twenty years almost the entire continent had been claimed by foreign powers. The British moved southward from Egypt and northward from the Cape. The former action brought them into a confrontation with the French at Fashoda in the Sudan in 1898. Diplomacy prevailed in resolving the dispute, with the French ultimately withdrawing their claim to the region in the interest of an Anglo-French alliance against the Germans. Encounters with Arab resistance were resolved by the imbalance of military technology, as in the Battle of Omdurman in 1898. In southern Africa, native resistance was similarly crushed, and the British prevailed in a three-year war against the Boers (Dutch settlers), who wished to avoid direct British rule. Only the presence of Germans in the east-coast colony of German East Africa prevented a British Cape-to-Cairo territorial link. The northwest coast was held largely by the French, with some British territories, while Germany established colonies in the Cameroons and Togo and further south in what was to be called German Southwest Africa. Portugal, which also held Mozambique on the east coast, retained Angola in the West. The only areas in Africa beyond European jurisdiction were Liberia, a black republic on the west coast established in 1822, and Abyssinia, which remained independent after repulsing an Italian effort at conquest. Italy controlled a section of the Horn of Africa, as well as Libya.

In Asia, imperialist expansion was less dramatic, but European hegemony, excluding China and Japan, was nearly as complete. The British pushed outward from India, establishing themselves in neighboring areas of central and southeast Asia. Their incursions into Persia and Afghanistan threatened to result in war with Russia, which had engaged in long-term overland expansion and succeeded in completing a railway through Outer Mongolia and Manchuria to the Pacific by 1860. France asserted control over Indochina, and confrontation with Britain following its expansion into Burma and Malaysia was avoided, in part, by independent Siam (Thailand) acting as a buffer between the two imperial powers. The Netherlands from its base in Java gradually gained control of most of the Indonesian archipelago.

Two non-European powers also made their presence felt in Asia. The United States had put forward in 1823 the Monroe Doctrine to counter any possible resurgence of European imperialism in the Western Hemisphere and later in 1899 had initiated an open-door policy in China. While appearing to protect the Chinese from possible annexation, this policy nonetheless allowed foreign powers to obtain special concessions and to impose spheres of influence on a nominally sovereign country. The United States also took possession of the Philippines following a war with

4.3. Central panel of the palace doors at Ikere depicts the reception of the first British official to visit the area by the Yoruba king. (Werner Forman/Art Resource, New York)

Spain in 1898 and then placed Cuba under its protection in 1901. The other non-European nation was Japan, which had been forcibly opened by American gunboats in 1853 and managed to modernize with incredible speed in the face of the encroachments from the West. In so doing, Japan was able not only to maintain its independence, but to prepare for successful conquests at the expense of China.

CHAPTER 4

The consequences of late nineteenth-century imperialism are so complex as to defy accurate assessment in a summary manner. It can be said with assurance that this imperialism marked the beginning of the long process of integrating industrialized and nonindustrialized societies into a single global economy. But there existed a great imbalance among the emerging relationships, and the whole process was accompanied by increasing economic disparity between the rich and the poor. While some physical benefits, such as technologies and medical and scientific advantages, were transferred from the industrial nations, this generally occurred at the expense of traditional economies. Through "plunder economics," the natural resources and human labor of the colonies were used to the advantage of the metropolitan centers. The colonial peripheries experienced economic change and only limited economic growth, while long-term economic development remained focused at the industrial core. The indigenous peoples lost their traditional rights to their lands, which were frequently expropriated for use by European settlers or landowners. Raw commodities such as rubber, cacao, palm oil, peanuts, coffee, sugar, tea, jute, and cotton were much sought after by Europeans. Trade was regulated through tariffs to protect the home market and ensure the sale of Europeans' manufactured goods in the colonies. Large segments of local populations became wage employees in foreign enterprises. Many who were not accustomed to the European concept of continuous employment or labor found themselves in situations of forced labor, although slavery as such had been declared illegal.

Political subjugation of colonial people was not a difficult task for Europeans, although compliance tended to be superficial. Industrial weaponry ensured that physical resistance would be suppressed. The predominant indigenous political experience of rule by small elites made rule by foreigners more readily acceptable. Forms of colonial administration were varied and included "indirect rule," whereby a protectorate was established and ruled by a native ruler closely supervised by a European official. This tended to occur more frequently in the British Empire, with Egypt and other African territories providing examples at different times. "Direct" rule, which featured a more centralized colonial administration, was favored by France and attempted in the North African possessions, Algeria in particular.

Traditional culture was disrupted in all instances. Even with the most benign intent, the assumption of superiority by the foreigners undermined the beliefs and customs of the native populations. In the case of relatively peaceful and more persuasive missionary efforts, significant proportions of the population were Christianized, as in the case of the Ibos of West Africa. In its most brutal form, foreign domination resulted in genocide, as in the Belgian Congo and German Southwest Africa. Responses to European domination varied. Traditionalists often engaged in overt, frequently futile acts of resistance or withdrew and attempted to foster native ways and language. Native leaders usually saw that it was necessary to adopt foreign elements to survive or ultimately to challenge the external forces. Some among them chose to cooperate with the foreigners, while others chose to limit acceptance of European concepts and practices to those that could be used to counter foreign oppression. The ideas of liberalism and nationalism proved particularly useful in the struggle for self-determination.

The benefits of imperialism certainly accrued to the wealthy and propertied classes of Europe, but evidence of a general prosperity based on these ventures is limited. More goods were manufactured using materials from distant lands, and as incomes increased, more consumers could purchase these products. The standard of living in Europe was rising, but the precise extent to which this was the result of imperialistic ventures is uncertain. Interest in these exploits and popular support for them were most intense during the scramble for Africa. Yet throughout this time, critical voices were heard. The earliest systematic criticisms were put forward by the British economist J. A. Hobson. In *Imperialism: A Study*, published in 1902, he argued that imperialism primarily served the private interests of a financial elite. In 1916, the Russian revolutionary Vladimir Lenin published *Imperialism: The Last Stage of Capitalism* in which he maintained that capitalism required continual economic expansion, and when domestic competition limited potential, foreign investment became necessary. According to Lenin, capitalism unavoidably required international exploitation. The voices of such critics were muted in the years preceding 1914 as nationalistic fervor mounted.

Alliances and Arms Race

The system of European alliances, which intensified in the decades preceding World War I, had originally been the work of Bismarck. He had created a formidable enemy in 1871 when Germany had taken Alsace-Lorraine from France after the Franco-Prussian conflict. Much of his effort thereafter was directed toward isolating France with the objective of warding off any attempted coalition between that country and others to the detriment of Germany. He was the driving force behind the formation of the Three Emperors' League (*Dreikaiserbund*) in 1872, composed of Austria-Hungary, Germany, and Russia, the aim of which was preserving peace and maintaining the status quo. After three years, due to strained relations between Russia and

Austria-Hungary arising from issues in the Balkans, the league dissolved, and Bismarck was forced to choose between the two rivals. In 1879 he concluded a secret treaty with Austria-Hungary. This new Dual Alliance provided for mutual assistance in case of an attack by Russia on either of the signatories with each party promising to assist the other with the "whole war-strength of their empires" and only to conclude peace together and upon mutual agreement. If either country was attacked by a power other than Russia, the ally was to assume a stance of "benevolent" neutrality.

In 1881, Bismarck revived the Three Emperors' League. Once again it disintegrated, and in 1887 he concluded a secret treaty with Russia known as the Reinsurance Treaty. In this treaty, Bismarck protected Germany from an alliance between France and Russia in the event that France should attack Germany, promising, in return, to back Russian interests in the Balkan countries. At the same time, he was careful to keep Britain on side by repeatedly offering an alliance, proclaiming that "no differences exist between Germany and England." The existence of the Reinsurance Treaty was widely known, but its terms were not revealed until the collapse of the Central Powers in World War I.

Meanwhile, in 1882, Bismarck further strengthened Germany's position by forming an alliance with Austria-Hungary and Italy. In this triple alliance, Germany and Austria-Hungary held power, as neither one had any high regard for Italy. However, they both felt it best to nail down as many allies as possible, and certainly the Italian government had somewhat the same feelings for its new allies, not being especially fond of either of the other two powers. Most of *italia irredenta* belonged to the Habsburg, and the Italian government was aware that if isolated, it would be quite powerless in its ambition to recover those territories. With that in mind, as well as the French seizure of Tunis, the Italian government became part of the alliance. Tunis had been an area marked out by Italy as her own and this dissension worked to Bismarck's advantage in bringing the Italians into the alliance. The Italians gained a clause stating that this treaty, signed in Vienna in May 1882 could not in any way be construed as being against Great Britain. In 1883 Rumania came on side contributing to a strong central-European bloc.

Had Bismarck remained chancellor, the Reinsurance Treaty would have in all probability been renewed, but with General Caprivi in that position after 1888, the treaty was allowed to lapse. France and Russia had been undergoing a rapprochement, and when the treaty was not renewed, Russia changed course. At least partially due to the Russian need for French investment capital, the two countries in 1891 signed an *entente*, which was vague in nature with no definite stipulations. This was followed in December 1893 by a formal military convention, which promised military support if either France or Russia was attacked by Germany or by Italy or Austria-Hungary in support of Germany. Wilhelm II suggested that a continental league for the preservation of peace be formed from this agreement, but nothing came of his suggestion.

After this alliance between France and Russia was formed, Britain was for the most part isolated diplomatically, and a decision was necessary with regard to which alliance the government should join. British imperialist ambitions clashed with those of France and Russia in several regions; on the other hand, German industrial development loomed as a major threat to Britain. When France and Russia initially did not respond to Britain's overtures, Britain signed an agreement with Japan in January 1902, forming a defensive alliance. This was unique in that it marked the first time that a great European power had allied itself with an Asiatic power on terms of equality.

In April 1904, the British and French overcame their differences and created the Anglo-French Entente Cordiale, recognizing Britain's position of dominance in Egypt and the position of France in Morocco. Britain, increasingly wary of Germany, began to feel that there was not much to fear from Russia due to the latter's defeat in the Russo-Japanese War of 1904–1905. Gradually, the two countries, with the encouragement of France, drew closer together. In 1907, the Anglo-Russian Convention was signed; with it the two countries settled their colonial rivalries in Persia, Afghanistan, and Tibet. Britain, France, and Russia, through an informal arrangement known as the Triple Entente, now appeared to be acting in concert.

After 1907 and the formation of the Triple Entente, Europe found itself divided into two hostile camps. Insecurity had been heightened by these alliances, although their goal had been exactly the opposite. The French regarded the Triple Alliance as standing between them and the recovery of Alsace-Lorraine, and the Germans saw it as an obstacle to their growth and destiny, or their "place in the sun." As a result, the European states became engaged in an armaments race in which they vied for prowess and security through the increased strength of their armed forces. After 1870, but before Europe was split decisively into two opposing blocs, armaments companies in Britain, France, and Germany realized enormous profits from the sale of weapons. Per capita spending for arms more than doubled in France between 1870 and 1914, while Germany's spending increased more than sixfold. The European states, with the exception of Great Britain, remodeled their armed forces along

Prussian lines, with France and Germany introducing conscription and doubling the size of their standing armies, thus keeping almost half a million men under arms in peacetime. Conscription was accompanied by the revamping of the general staff along the lines of the German model, and the professional officer class increased in prestige and influence. The military command was linked to the landed nobility in every country, but the relationship was strongest in Germany where it was notably conservative in outlook and stood always in the way of those with liberal aspirations.

During this era, the European public was schooled from childhood to accept the possibility of war and to support it if it occurred. This was reinforced by the fact that military training was mandatory. Furthermore, almost 5 percent of the national income of Germany and of France was spent on weapons on the eve of the war, to the detriment, of course, of funding for domestic needs. Improvements in technology changed the nature of warfare, and the military was convinced that the outcome of war would be determined by artillery; long-range howitzers, more powerful explosives, and torpedoes from submarines all contributed to the new style of warfare. In addition, the magazine rifle and the machine gun changed the function of the infantry, giving as they did a huge advantage to the defensive position and putting attacking armies in grave danger of sustaining enormous casualties. Tension was so high that no nation dared withdraw from the race for fear of being annihilated by the others in the event of open conflict.

The naval contest between Britain and Germany constituted a special phase of competition. Wilhelm II was not satisfied with having the strongest army in Europe, but wanted the best navy as well. His successive naval programs were worrisome to the British, who wished to retain dominion of the seas, a status that allowed the British to pride themselves on being a power in Asia, Africa, Australia, and North America, as well as in Europe. Furthermore, Britain was an island power, and it was dependent on imported food and shipping trade. This situation compelled the British to spend large sums to keep up with Germany and maintain their naval supremacy. In 1906 the British launched the first of the dreadnoughts, a series of battleships with increased range, speed, and firepower; the Germans retaliated the next year with their own dreadnoughts, and the naval race was on. Furthermore, the Germans planned to finance the completion of the railway running from Berlin to Baghdad, and the other powers saw this as a threat to their positions in the Middle East.

The saber rattling of the German kaiser and his insistence that Germany must reach supremacy in Europe began to worry the other leaders, and at the

4.4. Kaiser Wilhelm II and John Bull engage in a table game with miniature naval vessels and playing cards. (Library of Congress, Prints and Photographs Division [SWANN–no. 636])

instigation of the tsar, twenty-six of them met in The Hague in January 1899 to discuss armament reduction. The First Hague Conference had little practical impact, but it did lead to a vague agreement indicating that a reduction of armaments was highly desirable. In addition, a permanent court of international justice was established along with laws for the conduct of war, collection of war debts, stipulation of rights and obligations of neutrals. The results of the Second Hague Conference (1907) were also limited.

In a frenzy of competition, the European nations continued to increase their military forces. In 1912, Austria-Hungary recruited more soldiers, and Russia increased the size of the army and the length of enlistment. In 1913, France increased the length of enlistment from two to three years. In retaliation, the government of Germany, greatly disturbed by the actions of France and Russia, raised its standing army to close to 800,000 men. The greater European states now faced each other in full readiness for war, while the smaller states, believing war to be imminent, began to arm accordingly.[1]

Nationalism and Rivalry

Although nationalism in Germany and Italy tended to have a unifying effect, it had exactly the opposite results in other areas. Minority groups were motivated to create national states either on their own or in conjunction with others of their group who lived in other regions. Agitation and propaganda were common, with the result that states containing minority national groups were seriously undermined. The destabilizing effects of nationalism were especially evident in the Balkans, where the legacy of horrific wars further contributed to the political complexity of the region. The nineteenth century had witnessed the disruption of the Ottoman Empire by the forces of nationalism, and in the years immediately preceding World War I, the Austro-Hungarian Empire was hard hit by the same pressures. Serbia was blatant in her desire to annex the five million Serbs living within the empire and had the full support of the Russians, who had helped undermine the Ottomans and were now eagerly awaiting the disruption of Austria-Hungary. Germany, on the other hand, wished to keep Austria strong and did not wish to see the Turks expelled from Europe because of the importance of the Dardanelles, which gave access to the Black Sea. The forces of nationalism continued to grow as groups continued to strive for recognition, and the hatreds that accompanied these forces did not lessen with time.

During the period preceding the Great War, almost every alignment of European powers was strongly influenced by imperialistic ambitions and policies. The distribution of imperial possessions was uneven with the British Empire overseas accounting for one-fifth of the world's land surface and numbering 400 million people. France was next with six million square miles of territory and fifty-two million people, followed by Germany, Belgium, and Italy, each with one million square miles of land and about fourteen million people. Germany wished to dominate the Near East and by 1914 was the most powerful influence in the Ottoman Empire. France, Britain, and Austria-Hungary were most envious of this position. In addition, Austria wished to extend its influence into the Balkans. The alignment of France and Britain and of Britain and Russia fell into the same category of far-reaching imperialistic tendencies.

Local wars of the period, outside of Europe, were almost without exception due to imperialistic ambition. The British were at war in the Sudan, Burma, Afghanistan, and South Africa, while the French were fighting in Africa, Madagascar, and Cochin China (South Viet Nam). The Italians were in Abyssinia and Tripolitania, and the Japanese were at odds with China. The great powers were also constantly bickering among themselves over markets, territory, and spheres of influence, with a ruthless competition for raw materials that had them standing often on the verge of war in the years preceding 1914. Economic leadership shifted in the early twentieth century as the Germans outdistanced the French and began to gain on the British as an industrial and commercial power. Germany's advance resulted in fear and dissatisfaction in England, and this rivalry, added to the race to acquire territory, produced a situation of great instability.

THE GREAT WAR: 1914-1918

A series of immediate crises in North Africa and the Balkans hastened the coming of war. Morocco was of great economic and strategic importance because of its position on the south shore of the Mediterranean and on the west coast of Africa. In 1904, when British and French governments reached agreement regarding their possessions and spheres of influence in North Africa, both the Italian and Spanish governments were asked for their agreement, but the German government was not. The German government was greatly disturbed by this, with the result that the kaiser went to Tangier in March 1905 and made a speech, stating, among other things, that the sovereignty of Morocco had to be ensured and that he would do his best to see that politicoeconomic equality would be maintained. At the request of the kaiser, an international conference was held at Algeciras in June 1906, theoretically recognizing the sovereignty and independence of the sultan of Morocco; in reality, France and Spain received the right to police the coastal towns and establish a state bank. In this way the hold of France over Morocco was actually strengthened as a result of the conference, and the German government lost ground over the incident. Its attempt to shatter the entente had failed.

Next came a crisis that put relations between Russia and Austria-Hungary to the test. Austria-Hungary annexed Bosnia-Herzogovina in October 1908 without consulting with the other signatories to the 1878 Treaty of Berlin. This treaty had put the provinces under the administration of Austria-Hungary, although they remained a part of the Ottoman Empire. This annexation was in reaction to the Young Turk movement, which threatened to revitalize the Ottoman Empire. The Serbs were also against the annexation and regarded it as a severe blow to the Greater Serbian movement and to their hope of gaining access to the sea and of doubling their population by gaining the territory and its

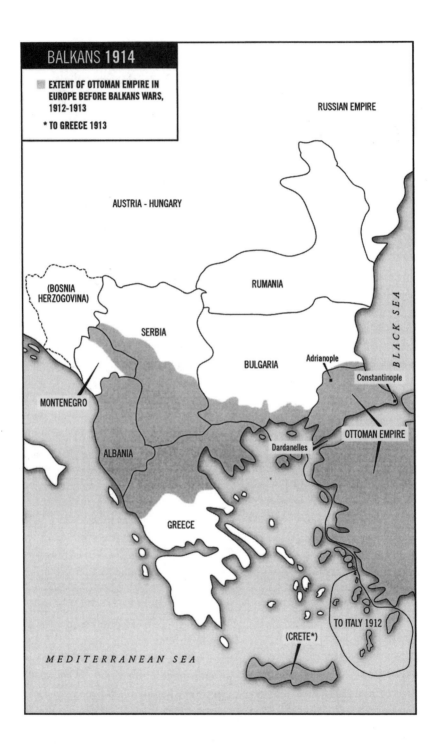

BALKANS 1914

EXTENT OF OTTOMAN EMPIRE IN
EUROPE BEFORE BALKANS WARS,
1912-1913

* TO GREECE 1913

RUSSIAN EMPIRE

AUSTRIA - HUNGARY

(BOSNIA
HERZOGOVINA)

RUMANIA

SERBIA

BLACK SEA

MONTENEGRO

BULGARIA

Adrianople

Constantinople

ALBANIA

OTTOMAN EMPIRE

Dardanelles

GREECE

TO ITALY 1912

(CRETE*)

MEDITERRANEAN SEA

inhabitants for themselves. When the news was announced, there were violent demonstrations in Belgrade with window-smashing at the Austrian embassy and the burning of the Austro-Hungarian flag.

The Serbs did not stand alone in their protest. If they had, the danger would not have been so great, but as matters stood, they were supported by the Russian government, which protested that the annexation violated the Treaty of Berlin and that the issue should be discussed at a European congress. Britain and France were also against the annexation, but the Austrian government would agree to such a congress only on the condition that the annexation be considered an accomplished fact. At Buchlau in 1908, the Russian and Austrian foreign ministers agreed that they would call a conference of all the powers. There the Russians would favor the Austrians' annexation of Bosnia, and in return the Austrian government would support the opening of the Dardanelles to Russian warships. The annexation followed promptly, whereas the Russians got nowhere in the Dardanelles due to British opposition. The result was further animosity between the powers. Eventually, cooler heads prevailed, and the crisis passed as the Russian government realized that the country had still not recovered sufficiently from the disastrous war with Japan (1904–1905) to again become embroiled in a major conflict. Britain and France did not wish to take part in a Balkan war in which they would bear the brunt of Serbian and Russian hostility, and the German kaiser eventually recovered from his initial outrage at Austria's unilateral aggression.

A second Moroccan crisis occurred in 1911 and is known as the "panther's leap." The Algeciras settlement of 1906 had pleased no one. The country continued in turmoil with the sultan's financial situation one of chaos and law and order being a spotty affair, with the police force achieving little success in their efforts. In the summer of 1911, the French army went into the capital city of Fez for the purpose of protecting the lives of foreigners, a move that the German government saw as an effort toward complete control of the country by the French. In response, they sent the gunboat *Panther* to the port of Agadir, ostensibly to protect Germans in the region. The French were supported by the British in their determination not to yield. It seemed that war was inevitable, but as it turned out, the Germans gave way. Later, an agreement was reached between the French and the Germans whereby the Germans consented to the occupation of Morocco by France and Spain. In return, Germany would receive a section of the French Congo. The British publicly condemned the German "menace."

Meanwhile, in late 1911, Italy attacked the Ottoman Empire in its North African territory of Tripoli. Resistance was strong, and victory was not proclaimed until October 1912. At the same time a group of Balkan states decided it was time to liberate members of their nationalities who were still living under Ottoman rule. They put aside their own bitter animosities and formed an alliance against the Turks. The Balkan League, composed of Bulgaria, Serbia, Montenegro, and Greece, mobilized against the Turks, despite the promise of that government to begin reforms immediately. The Ottoman Empire was defeated in the ensuing war, and the subsequent Treaty of London left the weakened empire with only Constantinople and a small amount of territory around it of its European possessions.

In June 1913 the Balkan League collapsed amidst disputes over territory gained from the Ottoman Empire, and a second Balkan war erupted. This time Bulgaria, seeking additional land, attacked Serbia and Greece. Montenegro and Rumania entered the fray on the side of Serbia and Greece, and then the Ottoman Empire, with the goal of regaining losses of the previous year, also set upon Bulgaria. This time Bulgaria was readily defeated, an independent Albania was recognized, and the Ottoman Empire regained some land (Adrianople). Neither of these nor other minor adjustments satisfied the competing nationalist goals of the states of the region.

Assassination and the Beginning of War

Relations between the major powers were perhaps less strained after the Balkan wars than they were in the aftermath of the Moroccan crisis. Austria-Hungary, despite its interest in the area, had avoided direct involvement. The other European powers had applied restraint and had been instrumental in working out the peace settlements. However, it is a definite possibility that Europe was already by 1913 standing on the brink of war. By this time many Europeans appear to have viewed a major conflict as inevitable. The division of the major powers into two blocs, however uncertain the respective commitments may have seemed, were regarded by many as providing the basis for an inevitable major conflict.

The emissary of American president Woodrow Wilson, Colonel House, wrote that the situation in Europe was one of militarism "run stark mad,'" and a mere spark would set the whole thing off. That "spark" proved to be the assassination of Archduke Franz Ferdinand, heir to throne of Austria-Hungary, on June 28, 1914, in Sarajevo, the capital of Bosnia. His murder was the work of the Black Hand, a pan-Serbian society whose dream was the establishment of a Greater Serbia and whose motto was "union or death." Franz Ferdinand's desire to keep Bosnia-Herzogovina within the Habsburg empire was a major

4.5.   Franz Ferdinand, Archduke of Austria, and his wife Sophie, Duchess of Hohen-
berg, about to get into the car, June 28, 1914 (Bettmann/CORBIS/MAGMA)

obstacle to their ambitions. He favored the transformation of the Dual Monarchy into a Triple Monarchy, which would contain an additional Slavic state of
about seven million people. This was viewed as a favorable arrangement by a
large number of Serbs; however, members of the Black Hand did not wish to
see happy Slavs in Bosnia. The pan-Serbians feared that the Archduke's plans
would end all hopes for a Greater Serbian state in Europe.

The assassination itself succeeded only in its second attempt. The first
attempt failed as the Archduke deflected the bomb thrown at the open car
in which he and his wife, Sophie, were riding. A ceremony of welcome ensued at city hall, and then the route that the procession would take was
changed in an effort to throw any other assassins off the trail. This might
have worked had anyone remembered to inform the driver of the change
of plans. As the car carrying Franz Ferdinand and Sophie turned into
Franz Josef Street, the royal couple came face to face with Gavrilo Prin-
cip, one of the Black Hand's appointed assassins. He raised his revolver
and, from a distance of not more than five feet, fired twice, putting one
bullet in Franz Ferdinand's neck and another in Sophie's abdomen.

Word of the murders spread rapidly, and the Austrian government accused
the Serbian government of complicity in the assassination. In actuality, the

Serbian cabinet had been aware of the plot, but had not approved of it. The Austrians feared that retaliation would bring the Russians into the conflict on the side of Serbia and so, with this in mind, the Austrian government decided to consult Germany and seek her support before taking action.

It is well known that Bismarck had refused flatly to become involved in the problems of the Balkans and that he had once declared that the whole Balkan question was "not worth the bones of a single Pomeranian grenadier." Kaiser Wilhelm, however, held a different opinion and did not wish to see his Austrian ally weakened, firmly believing that Serbian nationalism had to be halted or the disintegration of the Austrian Empire would be the ultimate price. In addition, he felt that the Russians would back down, as they were not prepared for war. Thus, the German government issued a blank cheque to the Austrians in the matter of handling the situation, assuring them of wholehearted support. The Austrian Crown Council drew up an ultimatum to the Serbs that they were certain to refuse, or so the Austrians thought. All anti-Austrian materials were to be suppressed in Serbia, and the Austrians were to oversee the process. This ultimatum was not sent to the German government for approval; rather, it was sent directly to the Serbs with a forty-eight hour time limit for approval. Refusal and war were deemed to be imminent (see appendix, Documents XXII and XXIII).

Amazingly, the Serbian government accepted all of the terms with the exception of two, but they offered to negotiate even those points. The German kaiser was optimistic and believed that war had been averted. However, the Austrians declared the Serbian response to be unsatisfactory and declared war on June 28. Russia was determined to stand behind Serbia, not only in support of fellow Slavs, but also in the hope of winning Constantinople. When the Austrian government declared war, its Russian counterpart ordered immediate mobilization in the South, that mobilization being tantamount to a declaration of war.

Representatives of the German and British governments tried desperately to prevent a general war. The German Chancellor, Bethmann-Hollweg, stated in a telegram to the Austrian government that the Germans were ready to live up to their obligations, but would refuse to be drawn "frivolously" and with no regard for their advice into a general war. Meanwhile, the British government was attempting to prevent a general mobilization of the Russian forces because such action would cause the German government to declare war. After vacillating between partial and general mobilization, the tsar gave in to his ministers and on July 30 signed the order for a general mobilization. The Russian government would not rescind the order even after receiving a conciliatory telegram from the German kaiser.

In accordance with the German war plan, named after Count Alfred Von Schlieffen, who formulated it in 1905, and because they were terrified of a two-front war, the Germans thought that their only hope of ensuring success would be to head westward. If they could settle the score with France in the first six weeks, they could then move to the East according to the plan and deal with the Russian army, which, they thought, would be much slower in deployment due to the size of the country and its less developed railways. As a consequence, the German government sent out two ultimatums on July 31. One went to the Russian government, the other to France. The Russians were informed that if they did not suspend mobilization within twelve hours, they would be facing German mobilization. The other asked that the French government give a promise of neutrality in the event of a war between Russia and Germany and that they do so within eighteen hours. The Germans also asked whether the French would agree to give the Germans the fortresses of Toul and Verdun as a sign of good faith. At the same time, Britain was preparing to intervene. On July 31, Lord Grey, British foreign minister, sought assurances from both France and Germany that these countries would respect Belgian neutrality. The Germans did not respond, although the French immediately answered in the affirmative. The Austro-Hungarian government ordered general mobilization eighteen hours after the Russians, but it seems that no one paid any attention. Instead, everyone was watching Germany as the Germans paid the price for the suspicion and mistrust that had been accumulating for years.

On August 1, the French government, having rejected the German ultimatum, ordered general mobilization. Fifteen minutes later, the Germans did the same. The Russian government did not even respond to the German ultimatum, and Russian troops were moving westward even before the time limit had expired. It has been said that the war had at that point become a war of the generals, with von Moltke, the German chief of staff, superseding Bethmann-Hollweg, the German chancellor. In Austria, Count Conrad was the chief of general staff. In Russia, their counterpart was Grand Duke Nicholas, and in France it was Marshal Joffre.

The British entered the conflict at midnight on August 4, after the Germans had invaded Belgium during the early morning hours. The Germans responded to an ultimatum from the British government requesting that they cease their attack on Belgium by explaining that a quick defeat of France was necessary to their plan. This was the justification for the invasion of Belgium; it offered a speedy route to the ultimate target. The Germans were asking the British to understand the Schlieffen Plan and to act accordingly. With the

British declaration of war, Europe was plunged into a bloody conflict that eventually included many countries other than the original combatants. The Central Powers (Germany and Austria-Hungary) were only able to draw the Ottoman Empire (1914) and Bulgaria (1915) to their cause. Italy, not bound by any military commitments as a signatory to the Triple Alliance, initially remained neutral. However, in 1915 Italy was persuaded by Britain's assurances of territorial gains to join the Allies. The Triple Entente within the next three years had also added Portugal, Rumania, Japan, and the United States as its allies. What was to be a brief, localized war became a world conflagration. On August 4, 1914, Lord Grey, the British foreign minister, is reported to have said, "the lights are going out all over Europe." There is no way he could have guessed the extent of the debacle to come.

The aggressive mindset of many Europeans on the eve of World War I meant that news of the outbreak of war was often met with enthusiasm. However, there were statesmen who foresaw the suffering that would result from such an event and were horrified at the ineptitude that had unleashed it. Lloyd George stated that this war "was something into which [the nations] glided, or rather staggered and stumbled." In 1914, each nation had its own strengths and weaknesses with which to contend. At the outset, the British, due to their naval superiority, enjoyed an advantage at sea. The Germans had the land advantage with their enormous striking force and huge reserves. In addition, theirs was a tradition in which military science held a place of major importance in education. As for Austria, the military suffered from the great diversity of nationalities within the realm as reflected in the composition of the forces. Omnipresent was the danger of internal hostilities and mutiny. Although the population from which it drew was about twenty-five million people smaller, the French military, amazingly enough, ranked second to that of Germany. This meant that its reserves were necessarily small. The British army was small, but well-equipped and well-trained. Russia had the largest military in terms of numbers, being twice as large as that of Germany, but it lacked both equipment and skilled soldiers.

It was recognized that in the event of war, the heavily fortified frontier between Germany and France would be a major obstacle to the German military advance. Von Schlieffen had advocated circumventing this problem by means of a rapid march through Belgium and onward to Paris, where peace would be dictated to the French before Britain could act. After this victory in the West, the German forces would turn eastward and deal with the Russians, who would have been held in check in the meantime by Austrian forces. So, in accordance with the plan, and despite the threat of Russian mobilization, on August 3 the bulk of the German forces headed west, recognizing that speed was everything and determined to knock out the French with one quick blow. To draw the French troops to the South, the German cavalry crossed the French border between Luxembourg and Switzerland on the night and early morning of August 1 and 2, but the main attack was to come through Luxembourg and Belgium. The Belgian government had refused to accede to the German demand to allow the passage of their troops through the country, but by August 20 the Germans had smashed through the Belgian fortifications at Liège and entered Brussels. The job was soon finished as the siege howitzers demolished the fortresses at Namur, marking the end of Belgian resistance.

However, the stand taken by the Belgians had served to delay the German advance and had given the Allies valuable time to get their armies into position. The French positioned five armies, and the British transported their troops across the channel. At Charleroi on August 22, the French and the Germans clashed, and the next day the Germans and the British met at Mons. The French and the British were unable to halt the advancing Germans, and General Joffre, the allied commander, ordered a general retreat. The Allies fell back to within twenty-five miles of Paris, and the government moved to Bordeaux. Joffre strengthened his forces and ordered his soldiers to stand firm against the Germans if Paris were to be saved. Two million men were engaged in the ensuing Battle of the Marne (September 6–12), and the French drove the Germans back until they reached the Aisne. This battle is considered by some to be the most decisive of the war because it halted the German drive on Paris and, in so doing, destroyed any hope of a quick victory over France. The German general Erich von Falkenhayn later said that the war was lost at the Marne.

Industrialized Warfare

After the Marne, the war turned into one of attrition as trench warfare replaced the war of movement. Although the original lines of trenches had been built between the Aisne and the Swiss border, it was necessary to extend these later to protect against the machine gun and the quick-firing field gun. In 1915, second- and third-line trenches appeared as a safeguard for retreat in the event that troops could not hold the first line. The troops lived underground in horrendous conditions, emerging only long enough to attack the enemy across no man's land, the area of barbed wire that separated the opposing sides. The horror of this type of warfare wreaked destruction both physically and mentally on the millions of young men sent to the western front (see appendix, Document XXIV).

Meanwhile, the German war plan also failed in the East as the Russians moved much faster than the Germans had anticipated. The Russians won victories by moving two separate armies deep into East Prussia. The Germans were determined to retrieve this area, and General Hindenburg, who had grown up in the region and was reputed to have known every pond, lane, and cow path there, was brought out of retirement and appointed leader. The armies of Hindenburg and his chief of staff, General Ludendorff, met the Russians under Generals Samsonov and Rennenkampf at Tannenberg and Masurian Lakes, where the Russian troops were decisively defeated.

The Russians fared better against the armies of the Austro-Hungarians. Russian troops overran Galicia and drove into Hungary. The Austrian troops were pushed back in the Balkans by the Serbs, but in November 1914, when the Ottoman Empire entered the war, the Dardanelles were closed to the Russians and critical supply lines were severed. In March 1915, the British first lord of the Admiralty, Winston Churchill, tried a daring plan to force the straits open, but this attempt failed. In April, a landing was made by allied troops on the Gallipoli peninsula, but the Turks put up such an effective resistance that the troops could not get any further than the beaches, and the campaign became a tragic and bloody failure, costly in human lives and in war materials.

In general terms, 1915 was a year of reverses for the Allies. Although Italy entered the war in May, having been won over by promises of obtaining *italia irredenta,* it did not lend as much strength as had been hoped to the Allied cause. Bulgaria entered the war on the side of the Central Powers in September 1915. The Russian front was forced steadily back by the German troops with the German howitzers leveling the Russian forts and blasting the Russians out of their trenches. At the end of 1915 the Central Powers were in a position of strength. They had thwarted the Allied hope of opening a passage into the Black Sea by taking the Dardanelles, had reversed earlier losses, and forced the collapse of the Serbian army. In addition, they succeeded in taking most of Poland from the Russian armies. In the West, their armies checked or drove back the Allied forces on all fronts, and the Central Powers were able to hold their position successfully.

In February 1916, the Germans made an all out attack on Verdun that began with a massive artillery bombardment, and after several days a German victory seemed inevitable. But the French, whose motto was "they shall not pass," fought with a determination that slowed the German advance and resulted in heavy losses. By June, it was clear that, despite enormous casualties, there would be no decisive victory. In the East, the Central Powers were more successful, beating back the Russians and dealing a deathblow to Rumania immediately upon her entrance into the war on August 27, 1916. By the end of the month, the province of Wallachia, with its wealth of oil and rich farmland, was in the hands of the Central Powers.

Meanwhile, on July 1, in the West, the British and French forces began their battle against the Germans in the area of the Somme. This battle continued for four months, and more than one million men were lost, with German casualties numbering 500,000, British 400,000, and French 200,000. It was here that tanks, introduced by the British, were used in action for the first time, but not very successfully due to wet and muddy conditions. They were capable of crashing through barbed wire and tracking over trenches, but they were used so inefficiently and in such small numbers that they made very little difference in the battle. Although the Germans had known success in 1916, their resources and manpower were completely exhausted as a result of the heavy fighting. The generals were aware of this, but the government was not.

4.6. Troops leaving the trenches during the Battle of the Somme (National Archives of Canada/PA207187)

The British navy had control of the sea, and the Allies used this naval superiority to stop the Central Powers from importing the goods necessary to their survival and their war effort. The Allies believed that if they could blockade Germany and cut off food and raw materials, they would then be able to force a surrender. In March 1915, the British government announced its determination to prevent commodities of any kind from reaching or leaving Germany. This violated international law, which stated that neutrals could continue to trade with Germany. The Germans had not been idle, and they initiated submarine warfare early in the war. In September 1914, the German U-boat (U for *untersee,* meaning "underwater") made its impact known with the sinking of three armored British cruisers off the coast of Holland. Then, merchant ships became targets, and unrestricted submarine warfare began. In March 1915, twenty-seven ships were torpedoed, and in April, eighteen more went down. On May 7, 1915, the Cunard liner *Lusitania* went down off the coast of Ireland. The toll was 1,198 men, women, and children, of whom 124 were Americans. The American people and their government were outraged, and after the strong protests of President Wilson to the German government, that government promised that liners would not be destroyed without warning and without regard for the safety of noncombatants. Unrestricted submarine warfare was suspended. The Germans then began to use their surface fleet in a more aggressive manner. The Battle of Jutland, which pitted dreadnoughts against one another, was fought in May 1916 and was the only great naval battle of World War I. British losses were greater than the Germans', but the battle proved a strategic victory for Britain. The Germans did not risk another such battle for the duration of the war. However, at the end of January 1917, the Germans resumed unrestricted submarine warfare.

The activities of the Germans at sea, along with other factors, were instrumental in bringing about an event that entirely changed the course of war. On April 6, 1917, the United States declared war against Germany. The immediate provocations for this action were the attempts of the German government by means of the Zimmerman telegram to form an alliance with the government of Mexico for purposes of war against the United States. As spoils of war, Mexico was promised Texas, New Mexico, and Arizona (roughly). On March 12, the steamer *Algonquin* was torpedoed off the English coast, and four days later three more American ships went down. The American public demanded a declaration of war against the Germans and the war message of President Wilson stated:

4.7.   Lead vessel of a convoy near England receives semaphore signals from an airship. (National Archives of Canada/PA006291)

[The American people] enter this war only where we are clearly forced into it because there are no other means of defending our rights. . . . It is a fearful thing to lead this great, peaceful people into war, into the most terrible and disastrous of all wars, civilization itself seeming to be in the balance.

The first weeks were disastrous for the Allied nations. For some time one out of four ships leaving British ports was sunk. The Germans were able to build the U-boats more quickly than the Allies were able to find and destroy them. In May 1917, the Allies began to use the convoy system, in which merchant ships went out in large numbers, sailing under the protection of warships, and this cut losses enormously.

The Germans now realized that they were in trouble. Submarine warfare had not achieved the desired goal of a quick and decisive victory. It had failed to break the blockade, and the nation was hungry. The Austrians were also short of food, and the dissension within the forces meant that they were at the end of their ability to fight. Ludendorff decided that the best and only hope lay with the ground forces and with concentration on the French. Time was of the essence to beat the arrival of American troops. Throughout the early weeks of 1918, due to the withdrawal of Russia from the war (see Revolution in Russia), the Germans moved their troops westward, and by the third week of March preparations for the assault were complete. In the weeks that followed, the Germans drove through the French lines until they were again on the Marne. They had taken many prisoners and left many casualties in their wake and at one time they dropped shells on Paris from a distance of seventy-five miles, using the ominous "Big Bertha" cannon. This show of force was demoralizing to the French, just as the Germans had intended. It looked as if a German victory was only a matter of time.

All was not as it appeared, however, as reinforcements were pouring into Europe from America. The drive on the Marne had exhausted German manpower and material. Between March and September 1918, one and a half million Americans arrived in Europe. These troops were not experienced fighting forces; rather, they had only basic training and no experience of combat. The British and French military leaders did not hold them in high esteem, and the Allied commander in chief, Marshal Foch, did not wish to use the American troops for attack. He feared that they would simply disintegrate under heavy fire. To his surprise, their tenacity and determination in battle soon drove the Germans back from their position on the Marne. As in the beginning of the war, the Germans could not advance past the Marne, this time due to the incredible drive of the raw American troops.

On September 26, an assault of the combined Allied forces of American, French, Belgian, and British Imperial troops was launched. By September 30, the Allies had penetrated the Hindenburg line and were seven miles behind German lines. The day before, the Central Powers had lost the first of their allies when Bulgaria dropped out of the war. The German high command requested an immediate armistice because General Ludendorff believed it would be advantageous to make the request while the German line was still holding.

The Allied position was based on President Wilson's Fourteen Points. He made it plain that the war was with the government of Germany and not with the people ("War on the German government, peace to the German people"). The first three points called for "open covenants of peace, openly arrived at," "absolute freedom of navigation upon the sea," equality of trade with the removal of all economic barriers. The last of the points called for "a general association of nations . . . formed under specific covenants for the purpose of affording mutual guarantees of political independence and territorial integrity to great and small states alike." To Wilson, this was the most important point of all; it formed the basis of the League of Nations and was the cornerstone of the Wilsonian peace. Internationalism was to triumph over nationalism in the new order, and although Wilson certainly had his critics, in general his pronouncements resonated with a war-weary world and brought hope for a new beginning (see appendix, Document XXV).

The German people were the most enthusiastic about the promise of peace, and when it was threatened by their government's brief resumption of submarine warfare, they protested vehemently. When Wilson demanded a change of government as a prerequisite to the peace, the majority of Germans, but mainly those on the political left, demanded the abdication of the kaiser. It must be remembered that the German people already had a democratic tradition and willing and capable citizens well prepared to participate in government. On November 3, there was a mutiny of the German fleet at Kiel. In Bavaria, the ruler was deposed and a republic proclaimed. On November 8, revolutionaries gained control in Berlin. The kaiser, having sought asylum with the army and having been refused, abdicated on November 9 and fled to Holland.

Revolution in Russia

In Russia, an experiment with constitutional government after the revolution of 1905 was hesitant and brief. The tsarist regime soon returned to a reliance on a combination of state bureaucracy and military in attempting to maintain control. An important element of the former was the Okhrana sections of the Police Department, which engaged in a variety of investigative operations, including antirevolutionary surveillance at home and abroad. The armed forces were used to suppress disturbances. The tsar and his government were increasingly regarded as oppressive and unable or unwilling to address the problems facing the country.

The opening stages of the war were met with a degree of patriotic fervor and at least a façade of greater national unity. Diverse groups and classes, even portions of the ruling class, assumed their interests would be served by a quick conflict. Some believed war would allow the government to shore up support for traditional structures and institutions, while others hoped it would convulse the tsarist regime and destroy the remnants. The demands placed on the country by the war were soon to openly strain and exacerbate the social, economic, political, and military weaknesses of the state.

In 1914, Russia had the largest army of all the European powers, and by 1917 the government had conscripted more than fifteen million men, who were for the most part poorly trained, ill-equipped, illiterate peasants. Even in 1915 conscripts were being sent to the front without rifles under direction to obtain arms from fallen "comrades." In the first two years, more than seven million were captured, wounded, or killed. For Russia, the first major encounter and disaster of the war took place at Tannenburg and Masurian

Lakes in September 1914. Nearly 100,000 Russians were captured. From then on, the Central Powers, primarily Germany, advanced into Russian territory. As the military situation deteriorated, Tsar Nicholas decided to take personal command of the military effort, and in September 1915, he left St. Petersburg (renamed Petrograd to remove its German connotation) to take responsibility at Mogilev, the army's headquarters. Here, removed from the capital, but still distant from the front, the tsar became increasingly isolated. Nicholas had not previously demonstrated political competence, and his military direction did not serve to improve the country's war effort. The Allies attempted to assist by sending equipment and dedicating some resources to Russia; however, shortages of war materials and deficiencies in skills compounded the problems of discipline and morale, making desertions increasingly common as the war went on.

The initial patriotic outbursts were not sustained in the face of popular discontent and division, which quickly resurfaced as the political leadership failed in its attempts to build popular support. The tsar appeared to realize the potential of popular participation in this national crisis when *zemstvos* and municipal committees were allowed to participate in *Zemgor,* a central body established with the intention of assisting with the administrative coordination of the war effort. But this body, like industrial committees formed to improve output, was regarded with great suspicion. From the tsar's perspective, it could provide an opportunity to mobilize and express opposition that would otherwise be thwarted. Members of the Duma, with the exception of some from left-wing parties, expressed support for the war by approving loans as the conflict began. By the summer of 1915, a grouping of liberal and center parties formed the Progressive Bloc within the Duma and presented a reform aiming for a "government of public confidence" that was to have introduced elements of parliamentary accountability for the tsar and the Council of Ministers. The tsar's response was to dismiss any ministers who appeared to favor such measures and to prorogue the Duma in September 1915. The tsar's departure to assume military command left the Empress Alexandra as head of government in Petrograd. Several factors served to undermine the capacity of the regime to attend to the war and the ever-present domestic problems. The frequent absence of the tsar from the capital, a government entrusted to an empress whose German ancestry posed serious questions of loyalty, and the exclusion of members of representative bodies from effective decision making contributed to the government's inefficiency.

These political troubles were compounded by the presence of the tsarina's strange advisor Grigori Efimovich Rasputin (1872–1916). His influence rested on his capacity as a *starets* ("holy man" or "healer"), able, the tsarina was convinced, to alleviate the hemophilia from which the heir to the throne, Alexei (1904–1919), suffered. Rasputin's charismatic and mystical impact brought attention to religious beliefs and personal behavior that caused scandal and left the royal court subject to criticism. But in the frequent absence of the tsar, Alexandra accepted political advice from Rasputin, at the same time having no time for the Duma and labeling its members "hopeless chatterboxes." Appointments to and dismissals from the Council of Ministers resulted in confusion, which made competent administration impossible and further discredited the regime. The growing concern regarding the disreputable figure of Rasputin resulted in an extreme right-wing conspiracy, which included Prince Yusopov, a relative of the tsar. This group of conspirators succeeded in assassinating Rasputin in December 1916. This disposal of the unsavory adviser did not reduce the practical problems of governance in Petrograd or command at Mogilev.

The government's response to military needs was not a constant succession of failures. The munitions crisis of 1914 was addressed by an administrative reorganization and a redirecting of resources, which dramatically improved military production and delivery to the front. However, these gains were made at the expense of civilian productivity and investment. Military requirements absorbed any increases in production, and by 1917 there were severe shortages of basic household goods. Transport deficiencies were an additional contributing factor to economic problems as loss of territory and infrastructure in the western regions of the country required rerouting of military and civilian supplies. The existing system deteriorated, and new rails, rolling-stock, and locomotives were not produced to meet demand. Refugees and the movement of people in search of wartime jobs in the cities further stressed capacity.

It was in the supply of food that the regime encountered its most severe challenge. Although food production does not appear to have immediately diminished with the onset of war, the government's inconsistent policies contributed to confusion and uncertain responses in the agricultural sector. Grain exports ended as the war began, and the 1915 harvest exceeded pre-war levels, resulting in adequate supply for domestic needs. But peasants reacted to the procuring and pricing policies by trying to avoid regulations and moving toward an approach of subsistence production. As 1917 approached, the government attempted to address rising shortages through rationing; however, this policy was neither universally applied nor effectively enforced.

In urban centers, long queues formed for rationed foodstuffs that were frequently in supply when shops opened or alternatively available on the open or black market at exorbitant prices. At the same time, the government had not implemented a consistent war-time policy on wages with the result that levels of real income had declined even in the most favored sectors. In addition, the government's reliance on domestic borrowing and issuing of currency to finance the war resulted in an inflationary spiral and distrust of the currency. Disillusionment with the government and discontent with the economy spread throughout society. Soldiers, workers, and peasants were joined by middle-class and liberal aristocrats in denouncing the tsarist regime.

February Revolution and Provisional Government

The immediate developments that led to revolution grew out of the increasingly frequent demonstrations, strikes, and food riots during January and February 1917. In Petrograd there were calls for a general strike, and on February 23 (International Women's Day), 10,000 women marched, and some factories closed.[2] Two days later there was a general strike, and Nicholas II ordered the suppression of disorder in the capital. As the size of the demonstration grew in the following days, thousands of soldiers and some officers refused the tsar's orders to fire on the crowds and instead joined in the protests. On February 26, the tsar ordered the Duma dissolved, but the majority of its members moved to an alternate location and continued to meet. On February 27, the Petrograd Soviet of Workers' and Soldiers' Deputies was established led by more moderate socialists, including Mensheviks.[3] The tsar decided to return to Petrograd, but by the time he was en route, his forces were no longer in control in either Petrograd or Moscow.

On March 1 a Duma committee formed a Provisional Government and the Petrograd Soviet issued Order No. 1, which called upon troops to replace traditional military discipline with election of committees in all army units for the purpose of considering and implementing decisions. Authority had slipped from the tsar's hands, and on March 2 he abdicated in favor of his younger brother, Grand Duke Mikhail, who declined the following day in the hostile atmosphere of the capital. Once in Petrograd, the tsar and his immediate family were placed under house arrest and subsequently transferred to the Siberian town of Tobolsk in the summer. The Romanov dynasty had come to an end.

On March 4 the Provisional Government declared Russia to be a republic, but it was unclear which institutions were to exercise effective political power in post-tsarist Russia. The Provisional Government and the Petrograd Soviet constituted potential dual centers of authority. The Provisional Government actually consisted of a series of political combinations and coalitions between March and October 1917 governing in anticipation of the election of the Constituent Assembly, which would determine a new institutional framework. The nominal head of the new government was Prince Georgii Lvov (1861–1925), prominent as chair of the All-Russian Union of Zemstva formed in 1915 with Pavel Milyukov (1859–1943), who assumed he would dominate as leader of the largest "bourgeois" party, the Constitutional Democrats, or Kadets. However, it was Alexander Kerensky (1881–1970) who emerged to provide continuity through the government's lifespan, initially as minister of justice, then war, and from July as prime minister. Kerensky's political affiliation was with the Party of Socialist Revolutionaries. Radical in its populist origins, which included political terrorism and an agrarian socialist orientation, the party was characterized by factional disputes. Kerensky, among others, accepted the need for a transitional phase of "bourgeois democracy" as a prelude to a final socialist revolution. This position resulted in Social Revolutionary–Menshevik cooperation in both the Provisional Government and soviets.

The new government inherited all of the problems of the tsarist regime, the first of which was the conduct of the war if Russia was to continue in the conflict. Although a separate peace was a consideration for some members of the Provisional Government, Russia remained in the war. However, this government soon demonstrated that it was no more effective than the tsarist regime had been in responding to offensives of the Central Powers. Monarchist officers were purged, and Order No. 1 of the Petrograd Soviet was partially incorporated by the Provisional Government into its commands to the army. This fuelled the disintegration of authority in the front lines. Large-scale desertion accelerated as discipline and morale continued to decline. Many of the ten million mostly peasant soldiers simply wished to return home to their families in anticipation of land distribution and reforms to follow.

The process of reform had begun immediately with the proclamations democratizing political and social life. Equality of adult citizens before the law, democratic elections, freedom of religion and the press, and judicial and penal reforms were all undertaken. In addition, plans to make education accessible and to introduce a basic social-welfare system were introduced. The

Provisional Government moved quickly to address food-supply problems by establishing a state monopoly over grain surpluses. However, pricing policies were not consistent, and transport and distribution problems continued to result in shortages. The land-reform issue was not fully addressed, and in many areas peasants continued with unsanctioned expropriations. Labor unrest also persisted as the government came to view inflationary wage settlements and the actions of workers' committees in factories as responsible for diminishing productivity.

In addition to confronting specific military and economic problems, the Provisional Government was faced with the challenge of asserting centralized power. Tsarist civil authority was overthrown across the empire as news spread, primarily by telegraph, of the events in Petrograd. Locally organized bodies calling themselves committees of public organization, or committees of public safety, assumed power. Their composition varied, but they all turned their attention to the immediate questions of food and public order. The Provisional Government set about forming elected local governments either to replace or incorporate the spontaneously formed committees, but the latter did not always disband, with the result that tension and questions of legitimacy persisted. The growth of separatism and demands for self-determination among national minorities further complicated matters.

After the soviet movement resurfaced in February 1917, soviets were formed in cities and towns across Russia and numbered almost 1,000 by October 1917. In June, a congress of soviets convened, which claimed to represent twenty million workers and soldiers, and a meeting of representatives of peasant soviets was held soon afterward. These gatherings reinforced the authority of soviet organizations. Although there was tension between soviets and the Provisional Government, there had been for the most part no direct challenge to the power of the Provisional Government. Everyone was waiting for the elections on September 17 for the Constituent Assembly to determine the future governance of Russia. The soviets were, however, the scene of political struggles between the Social Revolutionary–Menshevik coalition on the one hand and the Bolsheviks on the other.

The Bolsheviks and Lenin played a negligible role in the February Revolution and the establishment of the Provisional Government. Assisted by the German government, Lenin did not return from exile in Switzerland until April. His subsequent issuance of the famous *April Theses* gave the party a clear direction and distinguished it from the Mensheviks and Socialist Revolutionaries. There was to be, Lenin maintained, no further waiting for economic development through a period of "bourgeois democracy." He called for the crushing of the Provisional Government, an immediate end to participation in the war, workers' control in the workplaces, nationalization of private property, agricultural land reforms, and the right of national self-determination. In addition, in the *April Theses* Lenin demanded that word "Communist" replace "Bolshevik" in general usage.

This was a definite program expressed in slogans such as "peace, land, bread" and "all power to the Soviets," which Bolshevik agitators used tirelessly in the following months to bring the soldiers, the sailors, the workers, and the peasants on side. The Provisional Government lurched through a series of political crises in the spring and summer of 1917. The April Crisis led to the formation of the first coalition, with Kerensky emerging in a stronger position following protests and demonstrations that opposed a continuation of a "decisive victory" war strategy. The new policy, "revolutionary defensism," was intended to give priority to the protection of revolutionary gains, while maintaining military capacity. This would endure until there was "peace without annexations and indemnities." This marked a shift to the left, but was not acceptable to the Bolsheviks, who continued to criticize the Provisional Government.

In mid-June, Kerensky, then war minister, initiated a new offensive that failed within weeks. In the politically uncertain atmosphere, some Bolsheviks attempted an attack on the Provisional Government on July 2, but most troops failed to heed their appeals, and the uprising failed. The Bolshevik Party Headquarters and the offices of its newspaper (*Pravda*) were closed. A number of Bolshevik leaders were arrested, and Lenin fled to Finland. These so-called July Days seemingly removed the Bolsheviks from the political arena. However, some Bolsheviks escaped, while others were released, and the party was able to take advantage of the Kornilov affair, which began to unfold the following month.

General Lavr Kornilov (1870–1918) had been made commander in chief in July with the understanding that he would be given the authority to restore discipline in the army. In August, vague and confusing communications culminated in Kornilov's refusal to accede to Kerensky's demand for his resignation. This apparently mutinous position was portrayed as an attempted military coup by supporters of the revolution. Bolsheviks joined Mensheviks and Social Revolutionaries in preparing to resist the forces of counterrevolution. There was, however, no popular support in response to Kornilov's appeal to the Russians at the end of August, and his forces were readily disarmed as they neared Petrograd. The severity of the threat is uncertain, but Kerensky was further discredited by this incident, and it also resulted in the postponement of elections of representatives to the Constituent Assembly until November 17. The Bolsheviks were able to present themselves as having been instrumental in preserving the revolution.

October Revolution and Civil War

By September the Bolsheviks had gained majorities in many urban soviets, including those of Petrograd and Moscow, and in October Lenin returned to Petrograd convinced that the next crisis would provide the circumstances for a Bolshevik seizure of power (see appendix, Document XXVI). The decision was made to coordinate the move against the Provisional Government with the Second All-Russian Congress of Soviets scheduled to meet in the latter part of October. Preparations were made through the Petrograd Soviet's Military Revolutionary Committee under the leadership of Leon Trotsky (1879–1940), who had been elected president of the Petrograd Soviet in September 1917. Although a conspicuous revolutionary, Trotsky had been a critic of Lenin and the Bolsheviks. After the February Revolution, he became convinced that Lenin best understood the developing situation, and he joined the Bolsheviks.

Kerensky was anticipating a coup attempt, but when on the night of October 25–26 Bolshevik insurgents occupied communications and transportation centers and stormed the Winter Palace, the forces he had been counting on did not respond. Kerensky and some ministers fled, others were apprehended, and the Provisional Government collapsed. Power was formally transferred to the Second Congress of Workers' and Soldiers' Deputies on October 26. However, actual power was retained by the Council of People's Commissars under Lenin's leadership. Lenin issued three decrees within twenty-four hours, and all were adopted by the congress. First, the new government offered to conclude immediate peace with all nations on the grounds that there were no indemnities and no annexations. Second, private property was to be abolished and land use was to be transferred to the peasants. Third, control of production was to be given to soviets or committees composed of workers. News of the *coup d'état* and further developments, referred to as the October Revolution by the Bolsheviks, together with Lenin's decrees, was spread to key areas and persons by sending troops and dispatching telegraph directives to local soviets and Bolshevik committees. Moscow and other urban centers were secure within days. The Bolsheviks hoped that the Constituent Assembly elections scheduled for November 1917 would provide a means of legitimizing the party's political

4.8. Bolshevik soldiers on the streets of Moscow during the October revolution (Library of Congress, Prints and Photographs Division [LC-USZ62-120888])

actions. The results were disappointing, with the Bolsheviks gaining only 25 percent of the votes while the Social Revolutionaries obtained the single largest portion at 38 percent. Lenin's reaction was to dissolve the assembly forcibly at the end of its first day, on January 5, 1918. His promise of peace was achieved at a very high cost to the country. An initial truce was arranged in October 1917, but fighting resumed briefly in February 1918, with the result that the Central Powers made significant advances in the war. The capital was moved to Moscow, and new negotiations commenced. Lenin had to accept the harsh demands of the German government, and on March 18 the

Treaty of Brest-Litovsk was signed. The Russians lost substantial territory in the process (Poland, Ukraine, Finland, and the Baltic provinces), to the point that European Russia was essentially dismembered.

The overthrow of the Provisional Government and the spreading of the revolutionary message did not ensure consolidation of power by the Bolshevik Party. In the summer of 1918 the party changed its name to the Communist Party, according to Lenin's preference, as a way of distinguishing its followers from other less-radical leftists. Opposition to the Communist coup d'état was varied, and the new regime was presented with a variety of political and military foes. The disparate domestic forces that formed the military opposition came to be known as the Whites. In the first two years of the civil war (1917–1919), operating in varying strengths and under independent regional leaderships, the Whites experienced some success, as they were in a position to proceed against the Reds from the South, Northwest, and mid-Siberia. Some aid was sent to the Whites by the Allied powers whose primary interest was the reopening of an eastern front, although the Communist call for international revolution had long aroused concern. In August 1918, British, American, and Canadian troops landed at Archangel with the stated intention of protecting supplies that had been forwarded. They did not play an active battlefield role in the civil war.

The most curious intervention by foreign forces was that of the Czech Legion. This was a corps of over 40,000 men who had been captured or recruited by the Russians and given permission to form a separate unit by the Provisional Government. Complications arose when the Communists gained power and in May 1918, the Czechs began to fight their way along the Trans-Siberian Railway toward the Pacific, leaving a number of self-appointed non-Bolshevik governments in their wake. In the West, a Polish republic was proclaimed as the war ended, and the new government indicated its intention of recovering all of the territories lost during the partitions of the eighteenth century. These goals soon broadened as the first leader, Josef Pilsudski (1867–1935), sent Polish forces well into the Ukraine. The Bolsheviks responded forcefully; however, with aid from western European powers, mainly France, the Poles counterattacked and succeeded in driving the Red Army back. Additional territory initially relinquished at Brest-Litovsk and that was not regained included Finland, Estonia, Latvia, and Lithuania. All were recognized as independent states at the Paris Peace Conference. Nationalistic groups in the Ukraine also attempted to establish a separate state, but Red Army forces remained present and ultimately prevailed.

The issue of self-determination and nationalist conflicts played a role in the civil war in other parts of the former empire, but these remained militarily secondary. The Communists appeared more sympathetic toward the aspirations of non-Russian than did the Whites. For example, they returned land that had previously been seized to the Chechens. However, such actions did not herald the implementation of a lasting, consistent policy. Nationalities fought among themselves, particularly in the Transcaucasus region. In some regions the civil war actually consisted of a number of simultaneous conflicts.

Despite the appearance of overwhelming forces in the early stages, the White leadership never agreed upon common goals or strategy and failed to cooperate with each other. Meanwhile, the Red Army was put under the direction of Leon Trotsky, whose organizational and morale-building skills helped shape it into an effective fighting force. Its military units operated from the Russian heartland with the advantages of a large population, interior lines of transportation, and a consistent battlefield strategy. The Whites also did very little to gain popular support among the peasant masses. Campaigns of "White Terror" were launched to eradicate resistance and bring about compliance through fear. Anti-Semitism was used as a vehicle to direct opposition against Communists since some of the leaders were Jews. In the final phases of the civil war, White forces in the Ukraine, the Baltic region, and Siberia were all defeated. By 1921 there were only remnants of conflict remaining as the opposition had been all but eliminated. The Red Army then turned its attention to local nationalist conflicts within its borders and furthered the process of imposing central authority. The very last elements of White resistance faded into exile in 1922, when Japanese troops left Russian territory and returned home.

The revolutionary determination of the Communists was expressed not only in their military campaigns, but in a revolutionary terror directed against all opponents of the new regime. These political victims ranged from their immediate leftist rivals, who in many cases had been partners of the Communists, to royalists and to the royal family itself, which was assassinated on July 17, 1918, after having been moved to Ekaterinberg. In August, after an attempt on Lenin's life, the "Red Terror" intensified. According to records, the new secret police, the *Cheka*, killed at least 15,000, but some estimates suggest a figure closer to 300,000. Persecution went far beyond those who could simply be labeled "class enemies," which inspired greater compliance through widespread fear. The Communists were also effective in using propaganda to gain popular support and mobilize people. They could appeal to patriotism in response to the foreign intervention and a dreaded return to the misery and repression of the past. Although uncertainties continued for the new regime, there did not appear to be any significant, immediate challenges to its authority by the end of 1921.

In the "official" Soviet view, the revolution was a verification of the laws of history as discovered by Karl Marx and further explicated by Vladimir Lenin. The leaders of the Communist Party were regarded as having been in the vanguard, expressing the will of the masses and guiding them toward the inevitable establishment of a socialist state. To non-Marxist historians, the developments did not lend themselves to analysis based on deterministic principles. They argued for greater complexity in the interpretation of the actions of individual figures, including their relationship to the largely illiterate population. The roles of these individuals were further complicated due to the problems of modernization and the strains of an industrialized war. In addition, many analysts have examined the role of mass and local organizations prior to their subordination to centralized Communist authority. The recent disintegration of the Soviet Union has provided access to additional material, which will ensure that interpretive controversies continue.

THE END OF THE GREAT WAR

While Russia was embroiled in its civil war, the Great War was ending. Representatives of the allied nations met in Paris to formulate the terms of an armistice, and on November 8, 1918, Marshal Foch read the terms to members of the German Armistice Commission in a railway car in the forest at Compiègne. The Germans, given seventy-two hours in which to sign, did so at 5 A.M. on November 11; in accordance with the terms of the armistice, firing was to cease six hours later. At 11 A.M. silence fell along the western front, and the horror of the war that had threatened world civilization came at last to an end.

Then, the final accounting began. The world was shocked as the realization dawned that almost ten million men were dead. The number of wounded was about twenty-one million. The cost of the war was estimated at $330 billion, but no price tag could possibly be attached to the human suffering that had been endured. The peace process that followed revealed the depth of the animosity toward Germany for the misery she had wrought. Wilson's "just" peace proved ephemeral as the representatives struggled to reach consensus.

The Peace of Paris

Peacemaking at Paris 1919 resulted in the signing of five treaties: St. Germain with Austria, Trianon with Hungary, Neuilly with Bulgaria, Sèvres with the Ottoman Empire, and Versailles with Germany. The Big Four—United States, Great Britain, France, and Italy—were the countries most central to the negotiations, although representatives from twenty-seven nations had assembled in Paris. Russia was not represented. Secret treaties, previously agreed upon, proved to be grievous stumbling blocks to the peace process, and Wilson's belief that days of "secret covenants" and "conquest and aggrandizement" were past was proven incorrect. Nonetheless, by May 1919 the Treaty of Versailles with Germany had been drafted, and the Germans were called to Versailles to receive it. Its harsh terms stunned the Germans, but the allied nations refused to make more than slight modifications (see appendix, Document XXVII).

Article 231 caused the most grief. Known as the War Guilt Clause, it assigned sole responsibility to Germany for all loss and damage resulting from the war. The Germans found it difficult to accept such colossal blame. They felt that it besmirched their honor as a people, and it was to continue to rankle long after the peace talks were over and the representatives had dispersed. The tentacles of this treaty proved far reaching, and it opened the way for agitation and for the feeling among the German people that their nation should strive to escape it.

The Treaty of Versailles also contained terms requiring that the German nation make restitution for property destroyed by their armies in areas they had occupied. Locomotives, trucks, railways cars, farm machines, and livestock were turned over in vast numbers. The best part of the merchant marine was surrendered. The fleet was destroyed by the Germans themselves at Scapa Flow. Payments in the form of coal, dyestuffs, and chemicals were required of the Germans, and control of their ocean cables was turned over to the victors.

The area and population of the German Empire was reduced by approximately one-tenth. The provinces of Alsace and Lorraine went back to France. Some small areas went to Belgium, and the Saar Valley, known for its valuable coal deposits, was placed under the League of Nations for a period of fifteen years, after which the inhabitants would vote on their fate. In the East, Germany had to give up all the areas of Poland gained by the partitions, and a corridor that separated East Prussia from the rest of Germany was formed to provide Poland with access to the Baltic Sea. Danzig became a free city, part of Upper Silesia went to Poland, the city of Memel went to Lithuania, and part of Schleswig went to Denmark following a plebiscite.

Germany was required to renounce her rights and titles to all overseas possessions. These were not transferred directly to the victorious powers, but were awarded to them as mandates by the League of Nations. The territories were to be administered until such time as the indigenous populations were deemed ready for self-government. Japan acquired Shandung province in China, much to the chagrin of the Chinese, who had participated on the western front with the Allies in the hope of regaining these areas after the war. Japan also got the German holdings in the Pacific that were north of the equator. Islands south of the equator went to Britain or her self-governing dominions. German East Africa went to the British as well, while German Southwest Africa went to the Union of South Africa under a League of Nations mandate. The French received the German Cameroons.

The reparations commission, which had been formed at the end of the war, set about assessing the damage and evaluating the ability of the German people to pay for losses suffered by the Allied nations. "Germany understands that she will make compensation for all damage done to the civilian population." In 1921, the commission set the sum at $33 billion. There was no precedent for such a large sum. The punitive mindset of many of the victors led to demands that Germany be made to pay it down to the last penny. In 1924 and 1929 the sum was reduced to more reasonable amounts, but by 1931, Germany was refusing to meet these obligations.

The Germans surrendered their fleet, what was left of it after Scapa Flow, to the British, and the Allied troops held the left bank of the Rhine. They also held bridgeheads on the right bank at Mainz, Coblenz, and Cologne. The German army was reduced in size to 100,000 men, and the navy became nothing more than a few small, obsolete ships. Germany could have no submarines or military aircraft, and all fortifications were dismantled in areas occupied by Allied troops. Provision was made for these troops to withdraw gradually over a period of fifteen years. The Allies, however, could remain or reoccupy the areas in the event that it was deemed necessary to maintain the peace.

Germany kept its general territorial shape after the settlements issuing from the war were complete. The greatest changes took place in the lands of the Habsburgs, and the far-reaching effects of the decisions made at Paris have continued to affect the course of events in the region. National self-determination was certainly a primary principle in drawing the new frontiers. However, well-defined areas containing distinct nationalities were rare within the boundaries of Austria-Hungary. Rather, there were broad regions of mixed nationalities, and islands containing a single nationality scattered throughout the empire. These islands were often surrounded by peoples of a completely different origin. It was not possible to create states that would satisfy all nationalities.

In addition, factors other than ethnicity came into play in determining national boundaries. Consideration had to be given to the economic viability of the new states, as well as to their ability to defend themselves. These factors were in turn related to the strategic concerns of major powers. Paramount among these were the possible reemergence of German power in the future and the uncertain motives of the Communist government in Moscow. The intention was to establish a semblance of order among the states of Europe. It was inevitable that some of the ethnic populations would be situated on the wrong side of national boundaries since the borders of fourteen states were either created or modified in the new territorial arrangements. Four major successor states rose from the ruins of the Austro-Hungarian Empire: Austria, Hungary, Czechoslovakia, and Yugoslavia (Kingdom of the Serbs, Croats, and Slovenes until 1929). Italy gained a segment of territory from the former Habsburg domain as well. Russia was transformed into the Union of Soviet Socialist Republics and lost Finland, Estonia, Latvia, Lithuania, and Poland. The smaller states of Greece, Albania, and particularly Rumania expanded, while Bulgaria, which had joined the Central Powers, lost some territory.

Since ethnic minorities were present in all countries, there was no possible way that their competing cultural, strategic, political, and economic goals could be reconciled to the satisfaction of all. Despite the fact that the new Czechoslovakia had been founded according to the wishes of the Czechs and Slovaks, there were within its boundaries three million ethnic Germans. Another one million lived in Poland. Linguistic islands existed in Rumania and Yugoslavia as well, and one in three Hungarians was now living outside Hungary in a neighboring state. Nor was national independence realized in the former Ottoman territories. Arabs and Jews in the Middle East were placed under either British or French jurisdiction through the mandate system established as part of the League of Nations. Turkey fell into revolution and then into war with Greece before its position on the Anatolian peninsula was affirmed in 1923. The final settlement involved uprooting and exchanging Greek and Turkish populations from their traditional homelands. The territorial arrangements made in the wake of World War I are not the sole cause of recent or continuing problems in the Balkans and Middle East. They are,

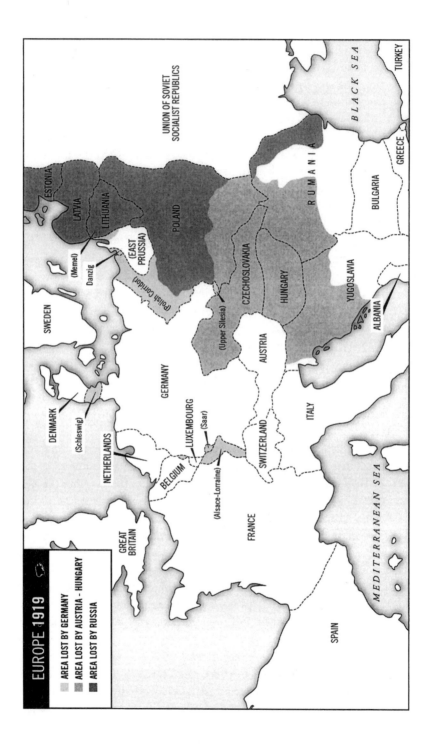

EUROPE 1919

AREA LOST BY GERMANY
AREA LOST BY AUSTRIA - HUNGARY
AREA LOST BY RUSSIA

GREAT
BRITAIN

NETHERLANDS

DENMARK
(Schleswig)

SWEDEN

BELGIUM

LUXEMBOURG
(Saar)

(Alsace-Lorraine)

FRANCE

SPAIN

GERMANY

SWITZERLAND

ITALY

(Memel)

Danzig

(EAST
PRUSSIA)

(Polish Corridor)

(Upper Silesia)

AUSTRIA

ESTONIA

LATVIA

LITHUANIA

POLAND

CZECHOSLOVAKIA

HUNGARY

UNION OF SOVIET
SOCIALIST REPUBLICS

R U M A N I A

YUGOSLAVIA

ALBANIA

BULGARIA

GREECE

TURKEY

B L A C K   S E A

M E D I T E R R A N E A N   S E A

however, part of the legacy that witnessed the collapse of four empires and the uneven application of new principles to old problems.

The Fourteen Points did not evolve as President Wilson had foreseen, and in the end the American Congress refused to ratify any of the treaties hammered out in Paris in 1919. The Republican-dominated Senate reflected the isolationist mood that was overtaking the American people, and it refused to support the work of its Democratic president. Some examples of how the settlement that emerged differed from the original intent of the Fourteen Points are of interest. First, the ideal of "open covenants, openly arrived at" came to mean instead talks held in secret to the point where lesser delegates were kept in total ignorance until the settlement was completed. Another point promising adequate guarantees for disarmament ended disarming only the vanquished. The "impartial" adjustment of colonial claims meant in actuality that the victors divided the spoils. Point 6 called for the evacuation of Russian territory and opportunity for the Russian people to be granted political development; in reality, allied governments interfered in Russia in their determination to overthrow the Soviet regime.

Domestic Effects of the War

The nature of warfare in this first major power conflict of the industrial age produced unanticipated battlefield consequences, and the impact on civilian populations was unprecedented. The term *homefront,* referring to the involvement of civilians in the war effort, is indicative of this development. Previous wars had certainly devastated countryside and town; however, none, with the exception of the French *levée en masse* in April 1793, had brought about this degree of national mobilization and coordination of resources to serve the military front.

World War I imposed fundamental changes on European society, not the least of which involved the enormous contribution of women to the nations at war. There is no way that mobilization could have succeeded without them. The immediate effect of the war on lower-class women who were already working was unemployment, since their work was normally in the production of luxury goods. The need for such commodities was superseded by the need for war supplies. But as the war continued, the need for labor increased, and women were soon an integral part of war industry. In Germany, women began to sew such items as cartridge belts, uniforms, and hospital linens. French women went to work in the service of the war industry by knitting for soldiers and by assuming new duties within the country. They did postal work and blacksmithing, as well as airplane repair and ploughing. Of those employed in the armaments industry in Great Britain, 60 percent were women. Although their wages were much lower than those of men, usually by about half, they worked as plumbers, steamfitters, undertakers, and police officers. In Russia, where the professions and middle-class occupations remained for the most part closed to women, participation in industry was quite acceptable, and battalions of women were put to work to maintain order in large cities. By 1917, about one-third of the workforce was composed of women.

Women's auxiliaries of the armed forces were most advanced in Great Britain, and the members served mostly as secretaries and kitchen help. However, it was in the area of nursing that women made their greatest contribution. Many of the nurses came from the upper classes of the nations at war and included members of the royal houses of Germany, Belgium, and Great Britain. One of the most famous was Edith Cavell, who was court-martialed and shot for having aided Allied soldiers in escaping. The nurses worked on the frontlines, nursing and driving ambulances, and they sometimes died in the line of duty.

War brought a certain equality to women, at least in recognition of the types of tasks that they were able to perform. Women were performing in so many areas of the war economy that the traditional debate about their capabilities was brought to an end. British trade unions feared that women would keep their jobs once the war was over and, therefore, asked for some government guarantee that women would relinquish their jobs to men once hostilities had ceased. Politically, war accomplished for women in several countries of Europe what years of agitation had not. Women were enfranchised by the new government in Russia in 1917; the next year British women thirty years of age and over were allowed to vote, and in 1928 all restrictions were dropped; in 1919, German women were enfranchised. In addition, between 1918 and 1919, women in Austria, Sweden, Luxembourg, and the Netherlands obtained the right to vote. In Belgium, war widows who had not remarried, women who had been prisoners of the Germans, and mothers whose sons had been killed in the war were enfranchised. The women of France and Italy were not given the right to participate until much later, at the close of World War II, in 1944 and 1945, respectively.

Although World War I did not end gender inequalities, women did make some lasting progress. They were able to dress in a more practical manner and to bob their hair, thus giving them freedom of movement and from the prison of elaborate hairdressing. They were able to wear makeup, a practice

4.9. A 1919 cartoon comments on Belgium's rejection of universal female suffrage despite women having borne the sufferings of war equally. (Library of Congress, Prints and Photographs Division [CD1–Kirby, no. 2])

that had hitherto been associated with prostitutes. During the war, with the shortage of men, women had become accustomed to going out without chaperones, and this continued. Nonetheless, the plight of women did not improve in the working world where they worked long hours under terrible conditions for wages lower then those of men. Although they had succeeded in gaining the franchise, economic inequality and discrimination continued.

Government economic intervention in various forms was used to direct resources and labor for use in the war effort. This trend toward economic planning witnessed a proliferation of government agencies far beyond the regulatory and protectionist measures implemented before 1914. In Great Britain the economic coordination of allocating resources, fixing prices, and rationing goods was achieved through a network of panels, councils, and committees. The idea of laissez-faire was sacrificed to wartime necessity. Germany, which already had greater economic intervention prior to 1914, experienced even more rigorous regulation, as the impact of the blockade produced increasingly severe shortages. German government controls resulted in such a mobilization of resources, development of substitute products, and supervision of industrial firms that the programs were called "war socialism." Allied governments were forced to go beyond merely raising taxes and proceeded to borrow extensively, particularly from the United States. The long-term consequence was to upset the balance of trade to the detriment of the standard of living in European nations in the years following World War I.

The most direct intervention in the lives of the citizens was the imposition of conscription, which served to add hundreds of thousands to the numbers of soldiers already present in the standing armies of 1914. Further, civilians experienced restrictions far beyond economic regulation. The free flow of ideas, which had expanded through the nineteenth century, was now severely limited. Governments faced the challenge of maintaining morale among their populations during the protracted struggle, and they used all the techniques and media available to them to take advantage of mass literacy. Propaganda and censorship shaped messages that demonized opponents and sustained the emotional enthusiasm required to endure privations and casualties. The pressures of the conflict engendered internal dissatisfaction, and by 1916 strike activity among workers was on the rise. In Great Britain military force was used to crush an uprising in Ireland where the desire for home rule, which had been authorized by Parliament in 1914, but deferred for the duration of the war, ignited a rebellion in 1916.

The authoritarian monarchies collapsed while the liberal democracies underwent leadership changes in the form of coalitions or national union governments committed to national mobilization for the war effort. In Great Britain David Lloyd George became prime minister of the coalition government by the end of 1915, and in France Georges Clemenceau once more became prime minister in 1917. Both proved effective in providing the firm leadership and authoritarian measures that appeared to be the price of organizing the war effort.

4.10. A weary world struggles through a storm toward peace and security. (Library of Congress, Prints and Photographs Division [CD1–Pease, no. 43])

In Germany, the new government, called the Weimar Republic, under Friedrich Ebert, espoused democratic ideals in its rejection of the old system of government under the kaiser. Unfortunately, this new government in Germany became linked in the minds of the German people with the humiliation of the Treaty of Versailles and its War Guilt Clause. The Weimar government was never able to live down this image, and in the years to come it was hamstrung due to its failure to secure the support of the people. The hallmark of its first five years was violence.

It is not surprising that in the aftermath of the catastrophic events of 1914 to 1918 the primary concerns of nations were economic recovery and readjustment. The details of this challenge overshadowed people's lives in the years immediately following the Great War. Relations among European states were tense with concerns about a humiliated and possibly resurgent Germany and the uncertainty of the newly constituted Soviet Union. The League of Nations, with Great Britain and France playing major roles, settled some disputes and provided a modicum of hope for a new era in international relations. In Europe generally, however, the decade after the settlement was to see the exacerbation of old animosities, of problems that had never seen resolution, as well as the appearance of new hostilities. The landscape had undergone irrevocable change and Europeans found themselves participating in the search for a new world order and attempting to find their place within it.

NOTES

1. Total mobilization through to the end of the war: Austria-Hungary, 7,800,000; France, 8,400,000; Germany, 11,000,000; and Britain, 8,900,000. See Chris Cook and John Stevensen, *The Longman's Handbook of European History: 1763–1985* (London: Longman's, 1987).

2. Russia had retained the Julian, or old-style, calendar, which by the twentieth century lagged thirteen days behind the Gregorian, or new-style calendar. The dates used here are in the old style until 1918, when the Soviet government decreed that February 1, 1918, old style was to become February 14, 1918, new style. All subsequent dates are in accordance with the Gregorian calendar.

3. These soviets had initially played a role in Russia during the 1905 revolution, when local strike committees broadened the scope of their activities and membership. They came to be representative of working-class interests in general and were referred to as Soviets (Councils) of Workers' Deputies.

APPENDIX

DOCUMENT I: BARON CHARLES DE SECONDAT DE MONTESQUIEU

Source: *The Spirit of Laws.* Translated by Thomas Nugent. Revised by J. V. Pritchard. New York: The Colonial Press, 1899.

In every government there are three sorts of power; the legislative; the executive, in respect to things dependent on the law of nations; and the executive, in regard to things that depend on the civil law.

By virtue of the first, the prince or magistrate enacts temporary or perpetual laws, and amends or abrogates those that have been already enacted. By the second, he makes peace or war, sends or receives embassies; establishes the public security, and provides against invasions. By the third, he punishes criminals, or determines the disputes that arise between individuals. The latter we shall call the judiciary power, and the other simply the executive power of the state.

The political liberty of the subject is a tranquility of mind, arising from the opinion each person has of his safety. In order to have this liberty, it is requisite the government be so constituted as one man need not be afraid of another.

When the legislative and executive powers are united in the same person, or in the same body of magistrates, there can be no liberty; because apprehensions may arise, lest the same monarch or senate should enact tyrannical laws, to execute them in a tyrannical manner.

Again, there is no liberty, if the power of judging be not separated from the legislative and executive powers. Were it joined with the legislative, the life and liberty of the subject would be exposed to arbitrary control; for the judge would then be the legislator. Were it joined to the executive power, the judge might behave with violence and oppression.

There would be an end of every thing, were the same man, or the same body, whether of the nobles or of the people to exercise those three powers, that of enacting laws, that of executing the public resolutions, and that of judging the crimes or differences of individuals.

Most kingdoms in Europe enjoy a moderate government, because the prince, who is invested with the two first powers, leaves the third to his subjects. In Turkey, where these three powers are united in the sultan's person, the subjects groan under the weight of a most frightful oppression.

In the republics of Italy, where these three powers are united, there is less liberty than in our monarchies. Hence their government is obliged to have recourse to as violent methods for its support, as even that of the Turks; witness the state inquisitors, and the lion's mouth into which every informer may at all hours throw his written accusations.

In what a situation must the poor subject be in, under those republics! The same body of magistrates are possessed, as executors of the laws, of the whole power they have given themselves in quality of legislators. They may plunder the state by their general determinations; and as they have likewise the judiciary power in their hands, every private citizen may be ruined by their particular decisions.

The whole power is here united in one body; and though there is no external pomp that indicates a despotic sway, yet the people feel the effects of it every moment.

Hence it is that many of the princes of Europe, whose aim has been leveled at arbitrary power, have constantly set out with uniting in their own persons, all the branches of magistracy, and all the great offices of state.

The executive power ought to be in the hands of a monarch; because this branch of government, having need of expedition, is better administered by one than by many: on the other hand, whatever depends on the legislative power, is oftentimes better regulated by many than by a single person. . . .

But if there was no monarch, and the executive power was committed to a certain number of persons selected from the legislative body, there would be an end then of liberty; by reason the two powers would be united, as the same person would actually sometimes have, and would moreover be always able to have, a share in both.

Were the legislative body to be a considerable time without meeting, this would likewise put an end to liberty. For one of these two things would naturally follow; either that there would be no longer any legislative resolutions, and then the state would fall into anarchy; or that these resolutions would be taken by the executive power, which would render it absolute.

It would be needless for the legislative body to continue always assembled. This would be troublesome to the representatives, and moreover would cut out too much work for the executive power, so as to take off its attention from executing, and oblige it to think only of defending its own prerogatives, and the right it has to execute.

Again, were the legislative body to be always assembled, it might happen to be kept up only by filling the places of the deceased members with new representatives; and in that case, if the legislative body was once corrupted, the evil would be past all remedy. When different legislative bodies succeed one another, the people who have a bad opinion of that which is actually sitting, may reasonably entertain some hopes of the next: But were it to be always the same body, the people, upon seeing it once corrupted, would no longer expect any good from its laws; and of course they would either become desperate, or fall into a state of indolence.

The legislative body should not assemble of itself. For a body is supposed to have no will but when it is assembled; and besides, were it not to assemble unanimously, it would be impossible to determine which was really the legislative body, the part assembled, or the other. And if it had a right to prorogue itself, it might happen never to be prorogued; which would be extremely dangerous, in case it should ever attempt to encroach on the executive power. Besides, there are seasons, some of which are more proper than others, for assembling the legislative body: It is fit therefore that the executive power should regulate the time of convening, as well as the duration of those assemblies, according to the circumstances and exigencies of state known to itself.

Were the executive power not to have a right of putting a stop to the encroachments of the legislative body, the latter would become despotic; for as it might arrogate to itself what authority is pleased, it would soon destroy all the other powers.

But it is not proper, on the other hand, that the legislative power should have a right to stop the executive. For as the execution has its natural limits, it is useless to confine it; besides, the executive power is generally employed in momentary operations. The power therefore of the Roman tribunes was faulty, as it put a stop not only to the legislation, but likewise to the execution itself; which was attended with infinite mischief.

But if the legislative power in a free state has no right to stop the executive, it has a right, and ought to have the means of examining in what manner its laws have been executed; an advantage which this government has over that of Crete and Sparta, where the Cosmi and the Ephori gave no account of their administration.

But whatever may be the issue of that examination, the legislative body ought not to have a power of judging the person, nor of course the conduct of him who is entrusted with the executive power. His person should be sacred, because as it is necessary for the good of the state to prevent the legislative body from rendering themselves arbitrary, the moment he is accused or tried, there is an end of liberty.

DOCUMENT II: CESARE BECCARIA

Source: *An Essay on Crimes and Punishments.* Translated from the Italian with a commentary attributed to Voltaire, translated from the French. 2nd ed. London: 1769.

The torture of a criminal during the course of his trial is a cruelty consecrated by custom in most nations. It is used with an intent either to make him confess his crime, or to explain some contradictions into which he had been led during his examination, or to discover his accomplices, or for some kind of metaphysical and incomprehensible purgation of infamy, or, finally, in order to discover other crimes of which he is not accused, but of which he may be guilty.

No man can be judged a criminal until he be found guilty; nor can society take from him the public protection until it has been proved that he has violated the conditions on which it was granted. What right, then, but that of power, can authorize the punishment of a citizen so long as there remains any doubt of his guilt? This dilemma is frequent. Either he is guilty, or not guilty. If guilty, he should only suffer the punishment ordained by the laws, and torture becomes useless, as his confession is unnecessary. If he be innocent his crime has not been proved. Besides, it is confounding all relations to expect that a man should be both the accuser and the accused; and that pain should be the test of truth, as if truth resided in the muscles and fibers of a wretch in torture. By this method the robust will escape, and the feeble be condemned.

DOCUMENT III: ADAM SMITH

Source: *An Inquiry into the Nature and the Causes of the Wealth of Nations.* Edited by C. J. Bullock. New York: P. F. Collins & Sons, 1909.

By restraining, either by high duties, or by absolute prohibitions, the importation of such goods from foreign countries as can be produced at home, the monopoly of the home-market is more or less secured to the domestic industry employed in producing them. Thus the prohibition of importing either live cattle or salt provisions from foreign countries secures to the graziers of Great Britain the monopoly of the home-market for butcher's meat. The high duties upon the importation of corn, which in times of moderate plenty amount to a prohibition, give a like advantage to the growers of that commodity. The prohibition of the importation of foreign woolens is equally favorable to the woolen manufacturers. The silk manufacture, though altogether employed upon foreign materials, has lately obtained the same advantage. The linen manufacture has not yet obtained it, but is making great strides towards it. Many other sorts of manufacturers have, in the same manner, obtained in Great Britain, either altogether, or very nearly a monopoly against their countrymen. . . .

That this monopoly of the home-market frequently gives great encouragement to that particular species of industry which enjoys it, and frequently turns towards that employment a greater share of both labor and stock of the society than would otherwise have gone to it, cannot be doubted. But whether it tends either to increase the general industry of the society, or to give it the most advantageous direction, is not, perhaps, altogether so evident.

The general industry of the society never can exceed what the capital of the society can employ. As the number of workmen that can be kept in employment by any particular person must bear a certain proportion to his capital, so the number of those that can be continually employed by all the members of a great society, must bear a certain portion to the whole capital of that society, and never can exceed that proportion. No regulation of commerce can increase the quantity of industry in any society beyond what its capital can maintain. It can only divert a part of it into a direction into which it might not otherwise have gone; and it is by no means certain that this artificial direction is likely to be more advantageous to the society than that into which it would have gone of its own accord.

Every individual is continually exerting himself to find out the most advantageous employment for whatever capital he can command. It is his own advantage, indeed, and not that of the society, which he has in view. But the study of his own advantage naturally, or rather necessarily leads him to prefer that employment which is most advantageous to the society.

First, every individual endeavors to employ his capital as near home as he can, and consequently as much as he can in the support of domestic industry; provided always that he can thereby obtain the ordinary, or not a great deal less than the ordinary profits of stock.

Thus upon equal or nearly equal profits, every wholesale merchant naturally prefers the home-trade to the foreign trade of consumption, and the foreign trade of consumption to the carrying trade. In the home-trade his capital is never so long out of his sight as it frequently is in the foreign trade of consumption. He can know better the character and situation of the persons whom he trusts, and if he should happen to be deceived, he knows better the laws of the country from which he must seek redress. . . . Home is in this manner the center, if I may say so, round which the capitals of the inhabitants of every country are continually circulating, and towards which they are always tending, though by particular causes they may sometimes be driven off and repelled from it towards more distant employments. But a capital employed in the home-trade, it has already been shown, necessarily puts into motion a greater quantity of domestic industry, and gives revenue and employment to a greater number of the inhabitants of the country, than an equal capital employed in the foreign trade of consumption: and one employed in the foreign trade of consumption has the same advantage over an equal capital employed in the carrying trade. Upon equal, or only nearly equal profits, therefore, every individual naturally inclines to employ his capital in the manner in which it is likely to afford the greatest support to domestic industry, and to give revenue and employment to the greatest number of people of his own country.

Secondly, every individual who employs his capital in the support of domestic industry, necessarily endeavors so to direct that industry, that its produce may be of the greatest possible value.

The produce of industry is what it adds to the subject or materials upon which it is employed. In proportion as the value of this produce is great or small, so will likewise be the profits of the employer. But it is only for the sake of profit that any man employs a capital in the support of that industry of which the produce is likely to be of the greatest value, or to exchange for the greatest quantity either of money or of other goods. . . .

As every individual, therefore, endeavors as much as he can both to employ his capital in the support of domestic industry, and so to direct that industry that its produce may be of the greatest value; every individual necessarily labors to render the annual revenue of the society as great as he can. He generally, indeed, neither intends to promote the public interest, nor knows how much he is promoting it. By preferring the support of domestic to that of foreign industry, he intends only his own security; and by directing that industry in such a manner as its produce may be of the greatest value, he intends only his own gain, and he is in this, as in many other cases, led by an invisible hand to promote an end which was no part of his intention. Nor is it always the worse for the society that it was no part of it. By pursuing his own interest he frequently promotes that of the society more effectually than when he really intends to promote it. I have never known much good done by those who affected to trade for the public good. It is an affectation, indeed, not very common among merchants, and very few words need be employed in dissuading them from it. . . .

To give the monopoly of the home-market to the produce of domestic industry, in any particular art or manufacture, is in some measure to direct private people in that manner they ought to employ their capitals, and must, in almost all cases, be either a useless or a hurtful regulation. If the produce of domestic can be brought there as cheap as that of foreign industry, the regulation is evidently useless. If it cannot, it must generally be hurtful. It is the maxim of every prudent master of a family, never to attempt to make at home what it will cost him more to make than to buy. The tailor does not attempt to make his own shoes, but buys them from a shoemaker. The shoemaker does not attempt to make his own clothes, but employs a tailor. The farmer attempts to make neither the one nor the other, but employs those different artificers. All of them find it for their interest to employ their whole industry in a way in which they have some advantage over their neighbors, and to purchase with a part of its produce, or what is the same thing, with the price of a part of it, whatever else they have occasion for.

DOCUMENT IV: MARY WOLLSTONECRAFT

Source: *A Vindication of the Rights of Women.* Introduction by Elizabeth Robin Rennel. London: Walter Scott, 1891.

Consider—I ADDRESS YOU as a legislator—whether, when men contend for their freedom, and to be allowed to judge for themselves respecting their own happiness, it be not inconsistent and unjust to subjugate women, even though you only believe that you are acting in the manner best calculated to promote their happiness? Who made man the exclusive judge, if woman partake with him the gift of reason?

own happiness, it be not inconsistent and unjust to subjugate women, even though you only believe that you are acting in the manner best calculated to promote their happiness? Who made man the exclusive judge, if woman partake with him the gift of reason?

In this style, argue tyrants of every denomination, from the weak king to the weak father of a family; they are all eager to crush reason; yet always assert that they usurp its throne only to be useful. Do you not act a similar part, when you force all women, by denying them civil and political rights, to remain immured in their families groping in the dark? For surely, sir, you will not assert that a duty can be binding which is not founded on reason? If, indeed, this be their destination, arguments may be drawn from reason; and thus augustly supported, the more understanding women acquire, the more they will be attached to their duty—comprehending it—for unless they comprehend it, unless their morals be fixed on the same immutable principle as those of man, no authority can make them discharge it in a virtuous manner. They may be convenient slaves, but slavery will have its constant effect, degrading the master and the abject dependent.

But, if women are to be excluded, without having a voice, from a participation of the natural rights of mankind, prove first, to ward off the charge of injustice and inconsistency, that they want reason–else this flaw in your NEW CONSTITUTION will ever show that man must, in some shape, act like a tyrant; and tyranny, in whatever part of society it rears its brazen front, will ever undermine morality.

I have repeatedly asserted, and produced what appeared to me irrefragable arguments drawn from matters of fact, to prove my assertion, that women cannot, by force, be confined to domestic concerns; for they will, however ignorant, intermeddle with more weighty affairs, neglecting private duties only to disturb, by cunning tricks, the orderly plans of reason which rise above their comprehension.

Besides, whilst they are only made to acquire personal accomplishments, men will seek for pleasure in variety, and faithless husbands will make faithless wives; such ignorant beings, indeed, will be very excusable when, not taught to respect public good, nor allowed any civil rights, they attempt to do themselves justice by retaliation.

The box of mischief thus opened in society, what is to preserve private virtue, the only security of public freedom and universal happiness?

Let there be, then, no coercion *established* in society, and the common law of gravity prevailing, the sexes will fall into their proper places. And, now that more equitable laws are forming your citizens, marriage may become more sacred; your young men may choose wives from motives of affection, and your maidens allow love to root out vanity. The father of a family will not then weaken his constitution and debase his sentiments by visiting the harlot, nor forget, in obeying the call of the appetite, the purpose for which it was implanted. And the mother will not neglect her children to practice the arts of coquetry, when sense and modesty secure her the friendship of her husband.

But, till men become attentive to the duty of a father, it is vain to expect women to spend that time in their nursery which they, "wise in their generation," choose to spend at their glass; for this exertion of cunning is only an instinct of nature to enable them to obtain indirectly a little of that power of which they are unjustly denied a share; for, if women are not permitted to enjoy legitimate rights, they will render both men and themselves vicious, to obtain illicit privileges.

DOCUMENT V: FREDERICH THE GREAT'S ADDRESS TO HIS GENERALS AND STAFF OFFICERS ON DECEMBER 3, 1757, BEFORE HIS VICTORY AT LEUTHEN

Source: James Harvey Robinson. *Readings in European History.* Vol. 2. Boston: Ginn and Company, 1906.

You are aware, gentlemen, that Prince of Lorraine has succeeded in taking Sweidnitz, defeating the duke of Bevern and making himself master of Breslau, while I was engaged in checking the advance of the French and imperial forces. A part of Schleswig, my capital, and all the military stores it contained, are lost, and I fell myself in dire straits indeed if it were not for my unbounded confidence in your courage, your constancy, and your love for the fatherland, which you have proved to me on so many occasions in the past. These services to me and to the fatherland have touched the deepest fibers of my heart. There is hardly one among you who has not distinguished himself by some conspicuous deed of valor, wherefore I flatter myself that in the approaching opportunity also you will not fail in any sacrifice that your country may demand of you.

And this opportunity is close at hand. I should feel that I had accomplished nothing if Austria were left in possession of Schleswig. Let me tell you then that I propose, in defiance of all the rules of the art of war, to attack the army of Prince Karl, three times as large as ours, wherever I find it. It is here no question of the numbers of the enemy nor of the importance of the positions they have occupied; all this I hope to overcome by the devotion of my troops and the careful carrying out of my plans. I must take this step or all will be lost; we must defeat the enemy, else we shall all lie buried under his batteries. So I believe—so I shall act.

Communicate my decision to all the officers of the army; prepare the common soldier for the exertions that are to come, and tell him that I feel justified in expecting unquestioning obedience from him. Remember that you are Prussians and you cannot show yourselves unworthy of that distinction. But if there be one or other among you who fears to share with me any and all danger, he shall at once be given discharge without reproach from me. . . .

I was convinced that no one of you would wish to leave me; I count then absolutely, on your faithful help and on certain victory. Should I not return to reward you for your devotion, the fatherland itself must do it. Return now to camp and repeat to your troops what you have heard from me. . . . The regiment of the cavalry that does not immediately on the receipt of orders throw itself upon the enemy I will have unmounted immediately after the battle and make it a garrison regiment. The battalion of the infantry that even begins to hesitate, no matter what the danger may be, shall lose its flags and its swords and have the gold lace stripped from its uniforms.

And now, gentlemen, farewell; erelong we shall either have defeated the enemy or we shall see each other no more.

DOCUMENT VI: MARIA THERESA'S LETTER TO HER SON REGARDING THE PARTITION OF POLAND

Source: James Harvey Robinson. *Readings in European History.* Vol. 2. Boston: Ginn and Company, 1906.

Firmian will receive a lengthy document with instructions in regard to our present situation, our engagement towards Russia, Prussia, and the Turks, but particularly in regard to this unfortunate partition of Poland, which is costing me ten years of my life. It will make plain the whole unhappy history of that affair. How many times have I refused to agree to it ! But disaster after disaster heaped upon us by the Turks; misery, famine, and pestilence at home; no hope of assistance either from France or England, and the prospect of being left isolated and threatened with a war both with Russia and Prussia, it was all these considerations that finally force me to accede to that unhappy proposal, which will remain a blot on my whole reign. God grant that I be not held responsible for it in the other world! I confess that I cannot keep from talking about this affair. I have taken it so to heart that it poisons and embitters all my days, which even without that are sad enough. I must stop writing about it at once, or I shall worry myself into the deepest melancholy.

DOCUMENT VII: GEORGE III'S LETTER TO LORD NORTH ON THE NECESSITY OF SUBDUING THE AMERICAN COLONIES (JUNE 11, 1779)

Source: James Harvey Robinson. *Readings in European History*. Vol. 2. Boston: Ginn and Company, 1906.

I should think it the greatest instance among the many I have met with of ingratitude and injustice, if it could be supposed that any man in my dominion more ardently desired the restoration of peace and solid happiness in every part of this empire than I do; there is no personal sacrifice I could not readily yield for so desirable an object; but at the same time no inclination to get out of the present difficulties, which certainly keep my mind very far from a state of ease, can incline me to enter upon what I look upon as the destruction of the empire. I have heard Lord North frequently drop that the advantages to be gained by this contest could never repay the expense; I own that, let any war ever be so successful, if persons will sit down and weigh the expenses, they will find, as in the last, that it has impoverished the state, enriched individuals, and perhaps raised the name only of the conquerors. But this is only weighing such events in the scale of a tradesman behind his counter: it is necessary for those in the station it has pleased Divine Providence to place me to weigh whether expenses, though very great, are not sometimes necessary to prevent what might be more ruinous to a country than the loss of money.

The present contest with America I cannot help seeing as the most serious in which any country has ever engaged. It contains such a train of consequences that they must be examined to feel its real weight. Whether the laying of a tax was deserving all the evils that have arisen from it, I suppose that no man could allege that, without being thought more fit for bedlam than a seat in the Senate; but step by step the demands of the Americans have risen. Independence is their object; that certainly is one which every man, not willing to sacrifice every object to a momentary and inglorious peace, must concur with me in thinking that this country can never submit to. Should America succeed in that, the West Indies must follow them, not independence, but must for its own interest be dependent upon North America. Ireland would soon follow the same plan and be a separate state; then this island would be reduced to itself, and soon would be a poor island indeed, for, reduced in her trade, merchants would retire with their wealth to climates more to their advantage, and shoals of manufacturers would leave this country for the new empire.

These self-evident consequences are not worse than what can arise should the Almighty permit every event to turn out to our disadvantage; consequently this country has but one sensible, one great line to follow, the being ever ready to make peace when to be obtained without submitting to terms that in their consequence must annihilate this empire, and with firmness to make every effort to deserve success.

DOCUMENT VIII: VISCOUNT NOAILLES'S SPEECH IN THE NATIONAL ASSEMBLY, AUGUST 4, 1789

Source: *Réimpression de l'Ancien Moniteur.* Vol. 1. Translated by Shirley Roessler.

The goal of the decree which has just been heard by the Assembly is to stop the agitation in the provinces, to assure public liberty, and to confirm the landowners in their true rights.

But how can one hope to do this without knowing the cause of the insurrection which is manifest in the realm? And how can it be remedied without applying the remedy to its cause?

The communities have made some demands. It is not a constitution that they desire. That request came only from the bailiwicks. What have they [the communities] demanded? That taxes be suppressed, that subdelegates be abolished, that seigniorial rights be lightened or changed. These communities have seen their representatives occupied for more than three months with what we call and what is in effect the common good, but the common good appears to be the thing that the people desire most and which they ardently wish to obtain.

In spite of all the differences which have existed among the representatives of the nation, the rural areas saw only the representatives working for them and the powerful persons in opposition.

What resulted from this state of affairs? They [the people] believed it necessary to arm themselves against force and today they no longer know restraint. As well, the result of the situation is that the realm vacillates at this moment between the destruction of society and a government that will be admired and imitated throughout Europe.

How can this government be established? By public tranquility. How can one hope to achieve this tranquility? By calming the people, in showing them that no one resists them except when restraint is necessary. To bring about this tranquility which is so necessary, I propose

1. that it be said, before the projected proclamation of the committee, that the representatives of the nation have decided that the taxes will be paid by all the individuals of the realm, in proportion to their revenues.
2. that public burdens will be in the future borne equally by all
3. that all feudal tithes will be redeemable by the communities in money or exchanged on the price of a just estimate taken over an average of ten years
4. that seigneurial *corvées*, mainmorts and other servitudes will be destroyed without compensation

DOCUMENT IX: THE REVOLUTIONARY CALENDAR

After the fall of the Bastille, 1789 was known as the First Year of Liberty. When royalty was abolished in France on September 21, 1792, the Fourth Year of Liberty became the Year I of the Republic, the two terms sometimes being used concurrently. When the Revolutionary Calendar was adopted in October 1793, its effect was retrospective to the first anniversary of the abolition of royalty, so that September 22, 1793, became the first day of the month of Vendémaire of the Year II of the Republic. Thereafter the months of the Year II ran as follows:

- Vendémiaire 1–30 the month of vintage = September 22–October 21
- Brumaire 1–30 the month of fog = October 22–November 20
- Frimaire 1–30 the month of frost = November 21–December 20
- Nivôse 1–30 the month of snow = December 21–January 19
- Pluvôse 1–30 the month of rain = January 20–February 18
- Ventôse 1–30 the month of wind = February 19–March 20

- Germinal 1–30 the month of budding = March 21–April 19
- Floréal 1–30 the month of flowers = April 20–May 19
- Prairal 1–30 the month of meadows = May 20–June 18
- Messidor 1–30 the month of harvest = June 19–July 18
- Thermidor 1–30 the month of heat = July 19–August 17
- Fructidor 1–30 the month of fruit = August 18–September 16
- September 17–21 inclusive = sans culottides

DOCUMENT X: MADAME DE REMUSAT COMMENTING ON ATTITUDES TOWARD NAPOLEON BONAPARTE

Source: James Harvey Robinson. *Readings in European History.* Vol. 2. Boston: Ginn and Company, 1906.

I can understand how it is that men worn out by the turmoil of the Revolution, and afraid of that liberty which had long been associated with death, looked for repose under the dominion of an able ruler on whom fortune was seemingly resolved to smile. I can conceive that they regarded his elevation as a decree of destiny and fondly believed that in the irrevocable they should find peace. I may confidently assert that those persons believed quite sincerely that Bonaparte, whether as consul or emperor, would exert his authority to oppose the intrigues of faction and would save us from the perils of anarchy.

None dared utter the word "republic," so deeply had the Terror stained that name; and the government of the Directory had perished in the contempt with which its chiefs were regarded. The return of the Bourbons could only be brought about by the aid of a revolution; and the slightest disturbance terrified the French people, in whom enthusiasm of every kind seemed dead. Besides, the men in whom they had trusted had one after the other deceived them; and as, this time, they were yielding to force, they were at least certain that they were not deceiving themselves.

The belief, or rather the error, that only despotism could at that epoch maintain order in France was wide spread. It became the mainstay of Bonaparte; and it is due to him to say that he also believed it. The factions played into his hand by imprudent attempts which he turned to his own advantage. He had some grounds for his belief that he was necessary; France believe it, too; and he even persuaded foreign sovereigns that he constituted a barrier against republican influences, which, but for him, might spread widely. At the moment when Bonaparte placed the imperial crown upon his head there was not a king in Europe who did not believe that he did not wear his crown more securely because of that event. Had the new emperor granted a liberal constitution, the peace of nations and of kings might really have been forever secured.

DOCUMENT XI: TESTIMONY GIVEN BEFORE THE ASHLEY MINES COMMISSION, WHICH INVESTIGATED LABOR CONDITIONS

Source: *Parliamentary Papers.* Vols. XV–XVII. 1842.

No. 116.—Sarah Gooder, aged 8 years

I'm a trapper in the Gawper pit. It does not tire me but I do have to trap without a light and I'm scared. I go at four and sometimes at half past three in the morning, and come home at five and a half past. I never go to sleep. Sometimes I sing when I've light, but not in the dark; I dare not sing then. I don't like being in the pit. I am very sleepy when I go sometimes in the morning. I go to Sunday-schools and Reading made Easy. *She knows her letters and can read little words.* They teach me to pray. *She repeated the Lord's Prayer, not very perfectly, and ran on with the addition:* "God bless my father and mother, and sister and brother, uncles and aunts and cousins, and everybody else, and God bless me and make me a good servant. Amen." I have heard tell of Jesus many a time. I don't know why he came on earth, I'm sure, and I don't know why he died, but he had stones for his head to rest on. I would like to be at school far better than in the pit.

No. 137.—Thomas Wilson Esq., of the Banks, Silk Stone, Owner of Three Colliers

The employment of females of any age in and about the mines is most objectionable, and I should rejoice to see it put an end to; but in the present feeling of the colliers, no individual should succeed in stopping it in a neighborhood where it prevailed, because the men would immediately go to those pits where their daughters would be employed. The only way to effectively put an end to this and other evils in the present colliery system is to elevate the minds of the men; and the only means to attain this is to combine sound moral and religious training and industrial habits with a system of intellectual culture much more perfect than can at present be obtained by them.

I object on general principles to government interference in the conduct of any trade, and I am satisfied that in the mines it would be productive of the greatest injury and injustice. The art of mining is not so perfectly understood as to admit of the way in which a colliery shall be conducted being dictated any person, however experienced, with such certainty as would warrant an interference with the management of private business. I should also decidedly object to placing collieries under the present provisions of the Factory Act with respect to the education of children employed therein. First, because if it is contended that coal-owners, as employers of children, are bound to attend to their education, this obligation extends equally to all other employers, and therefore it is unjust to single out one class only; secondly, because if the legislation asserts a right to interfere to secure education, it is bound to make that interference general; and thirdly, because the mining population is in this neighborhood so intermixed with other classes, and it is in such small bodies in any one place, that it would be impossible to provide separate schools for them.

No. 134.—Isabel Wilson, 38 years old, Coal Putter

When women have children thick (fast) they are compelled to take them down early, I have been married 19 years and have 10 bairns; seven are in ife. When on Sir John's work I was a carrier of coals, which caused me to miscarry five times from the strains, and was gai ill for each. Putting is no so oppressive; last child was born on Saturday morning, and I was at work on the Friday night.

Once met with an accident; a coal brake my cheek-bone, which kept me idle some weeks.

I have wrought below 30 years, and so has the guid man; he is getting touched in the breath now.

None of the children read, as the work is no regular. I did read once, but no able to attend to it now; when I go below lassie 10 years of age keeps house and makes the broth or stir-about.

Nine sleep in two bedsteads; there did not appear to be any beds, and the whole of the other furniture consisted of two chairs, three stools, a table, a kail-ot and a few broken basins and cups. Upon asking if the furniture was all they had, the guid wife said, furniture was of no use, as it was so troublesome to flit with.

No. 26.—Patience Kershaw, aged 17, May 15

My father has been dead about a year; my mother is living and has ten children, five lads and five lassies; the oldest is about thirty, the youngest is four; three lasses go to mill; all the lads are colliers, two getters and three hurriers; one lives at home and does nothing; mother does nought but look after home.

All my sisters have been hurriers, but three went to the mill. Alice went because her legs swelled from hurrying in the cold water when she was hot. I never went to day-school; I go to Sunday-school, but I cannot read or write; I go to pit at five o'clock in the morning and come out at five in the evening; I get breakfast of porridge and milk first; I take my dinner with me, a cake, and I eat it as I go; I do not stop or rest any time for the purpose; I get nothing else until I get home, and then have potatoes and meat, not every day meat. I hurry in the clothes I have now got on, trousers and ragged jacket; the bald place upon my head is made by thrusting the corves; my legs have never swelled, but sisters' did when they went to mill; I hurry the corves a mile and more under ground and back; they weigh 300 cwt. I hurry 11 a-day; I wear a belt and chain at the workings to get the corves out; the getters that I work for are naked except their caps; they pull off their clothes; I see them at work when I go up; sometimes they beat me, if I am not quick enough, with their hands; they strike me upon my back; the boys take liberties with me sometimes they pull me about; I am the only girl in the pit; there are about 20 boys and 15 men; all the men are naked; I would rather work in the mill than the in coal-pit. (Note in the appendix: This girl is an ignorant, filthy, ragged, and deplorable-looking object, and such an one as the uncivilized natives of the prairies would be shocked to look upon.)

No. 7.—Benjamin Miller, Underlooker at the Mr. Wooley's, Near Staley Bridge, April 14, 1841

How do you account for women being used so frequently as drawers in the coal-pits? One reason is, that a girl of 20 will work for 2s. a-day or less, and man of that age would want 3s. 6d: It makes little difference to the coalmaster, he pays the same whoever does the work; some would say he got his coal cheaper, but I am not of that opinion, the only difference is that the collier can spend 1s. to 1s. 6d. More at the alehouse, and very often the woman helps him to spend it.

Do women ever become coal-getters? Not one woman in a hundred ever becomes a coal-getter, and that is one of the reasons men prefer them.

DOCUMENT XII: PROCLAMATION OF INDEPENDENCE ISSUED BY THE GREEK NATIONAL ASSEMBLY

Source: James Harvey Robinson. *Readings in European History.* Vol. 2. Boston: Ginn and Company, 1906.

We, descendants of the wise and noble peoples of Hellas, we who are contemporaries of the enlightened and civilized nations of Europe, we who behold; the advantages which they enjoy under the protection of the impenetrable aegis of the law, find it no longer possible to suffer without cowardice and self-contempt the cruel yoke of Ottoman power which has weighed upon us for more than four centuries, a power which does not listen to reason and knows no other law than its own will, which orders and disposes everything despotically and according to its caprice. After this prolonged slavery we have determined to take arms to avenge ourselves and our country against frightful tyranny, iniquitous in its very essence, an unexampled despotism to which no other rule can be compared.

The war which we are carrying on against the Turk is not that of a faction or the result of sedition. It is not aimed at the advantage of a single part of the Greek people; it is a national war, a holy war, a war the object of which is to reconquer the rights of individual liberty, of property and honor, rights which the civilized people of Europe, our neighbors, enjoy to-day; rights of which the cruel and unheard of tyranny of the Ottomans would deprive us— us alone—and the very memory of which they would stifle in our hearts.

Are we, then, less reasonable than other peoples, that we remain deprived of these rights? Are we of a nature so degraded and abject that we should be viewed as unworthy to enjoy them, condemned to remain crushed under a perpetual slavery and subjected, like beasts of burden or mere automatons, to the absurd caprice of a cruel tyrant who, like an infamous brigand, has come from distant regions to invade our borders? Nature has deeply graven these rights in the hearts of all men; laws in harmony with nature have so completely consecrated them that neither three nor four centuries—nor thousands nor millions of centuries—can destroy them. Force and violence have been able to restrict and paralyze them for a reason, but force may once more resuscitate them in all the vigour which they formerly enjoyed during many centuries; nor have we ever ceased in Hellas to defend these rights by arms whenever opportunity offered.

Building upon the foundation of our natural rights, and desiring to assimilate ourselves to the rest of the Christians of Europe, our brethren, we have begun a war against the Turks, or rather, uniting all our isolated strength, we have formed ourselves into a single armed body, firmly resolved to attain our end, to govern ourselves by wise laws, or to be together annihilated, believing it to be unworthy of us, as the descendants of the glorious peoples of Hellas, to live henceforth in a state of slavery fitted rather for unreasoning animals than for rational beings.

Ten months have elapsed since we began this national war; the all-powerful God has succored us; although we were not adequately prepared for so great an enterprise, our arms have everywhere been victorious, despite the powerful obstacles which we have encountered and still encounter everywhere. We have had to contend with a situation bristling with difficulties, and we are still engaged in our efforts to overcome them. It should not, therefore, appear astonishing that we were not able from the very first to proclaim our independence and take rank among the civilized peoples of the earth, marching forward side by side with them. It was impossible to occupy ourselves with our political existence before we had established our independence. We trust these reasons may justify, in the eyes of the nations, our delay, as well as console us for the anarchy in which we have found ourselves. . . .

Epidaurus, January 15/27, 1822: the First Year of Independence

DOCUMENT XIII: KARL MARX AND FRIEDRICH ENGELS

Source: *Manifesto of the Communist Party.* Edited and annotated by Frederick Engels. Chicago: Charles Kerr & Company, 1888.

A spectre is passing through Europe–the spectre of Communism. All the powers of old Europe have joined in a holy crusade against this spectre: Pope and Tsar, Metternich and Guizot, French radicals and German police-spies.

Bourgeoisie and Proletarians

The history of all hitherto existing society is the history of class struggles. . . .

The modern bourgeois society, that has sprouted from the ruins of feudal society, has not done away with class antagonisms. It has but established new classes, new conditions of oppression, new forms of struggle in place of the old ones.

Our epoch, the epoch of the bourgeoisie period, possesses, however, this distinctive feature; it has simplified the class antagonisms. Society as a whole is more and more splitting into two great hostile camps, into two large classes directly facing each other: Bourgeoisie and Proletariat. . . .

Modern industry has established the world market, for which the discovery of America paved the way. The market has given an immense development to commerce, navigation, to communication by land. This development has, in its turn, reacted on the extension of industry; and in proportion as industry, commerce, navigation, railways extended, in the same proportion the bourgeoisie developed, increased its capital, and pushed into the background every class handed down from the Middle Ages.

We see, therefore, how the modern bourgeoisie is itself the product of a long chain of developments, of a series of revolutions in the modes of production and of exchange.

Each step in the development of the bourgeoisie was accompanied by corresponding political advance of that class. An oppressed class under the sway of the feudal nobility, an armed and self-governing association in the mediaeval communes (i.e., free cities), here independent urban republic (as in Italy and Germany), there taxable "third state" of the monarch (as in France), afterwards, in the period of manufacture proper, serving either the semi-feudal or absolute monarchy as a counterpoise against the nobility, and, in fact, cornerstone of the great monarchies in general, the bourgeoisie has at last, since the establishment of Modern Industry and of the world market, conquered for itself, in the representative State, exclusive political sway. Finally, with the establishment of large industry and the world market the bourgeoisie conquered exclusive political domination for itself in modern states with representative governments. The executive of the modern State is but a committee for managing the common affairs of the whole bourgeoisie.

The bourgeoisie, historically, has played a most revolutionary role in history.

The bourgeoisie, wherever it has got the upper hand, has put an end to all feudal, patriarchal, idyllic relations. It has pitilessly torn assunder the motley feudal ties that bound man to his "natural superiors," and has left remaining no other nexus between man and man than naked self-interest, than callous "cash payment." It has drowned the most heavenly ecstasies of religious fervor, of chivalrous enthusiasm, of philistine sentimentalism, in the icy water of egotistical calculation. It has resolved personal worth into exchange value, and in place of the numberless indefeasible chartered freedoms, has set up that single, unconscionable freedom—Free Trade. In one word, for exploitation, veiled by religious and political illusions it has substituted naked, shameless, direct, brutal exploitation. . . .

The bourgeoisie, during its rule of scarce one hundred years, has created more massive and more colossal productive forces than have all preceding generations together. Subjection of Nature's forces to man, machinery, application of chemistry to industry and agriculture, steam navigation, railways, electric telegraphs, clearing of whole continents for cultivation, canalization of rivers, whole populations conjured up to order out of the ground—what earlier century had even a presentiment that such productive forces slumbered in the lap of social labor? . . .

The weapons with which the bourgeoisie felled feudalism to the ground are now turned against the bourgeoisie itself.

But not only has the bourgeoisie forged the weapons that bring death to itself; it has also called into existence the men who are to wield those weapons—the modern working class—the proletarians.

In proportion as the bourgeoisie (i.e., capital) is developed, in the same proportion is the proletariat, the modern working class, developed, a class of laborers, who live only so long as they find work, and who find work only as long as their labor increases capital. These laborers, who must sell themselves piecemeal, are a commodity, like any other article of commerce and are consequently exposed to all the vicissitudes of competition, to all the fluctuations of the market.

Proletarians and Communists

In what relation do the Communists stand to the proletariat in as a whole?

The Communists do not form a separate party opposed to other working class parties.

They have no interests separate and apart from those of the proletariat as a whole.

They do not set up any sectarian principles of their own, by which to shape and mould the proletarian movement.

The Communists are distinguished from the other working class parties by this only: 1. In the national struggles of the proletarians of the different countries, they point out the common interests of the entire proletariat independent of all nationality. 2. In the various stages of development which the struggle of the working class against the bourgeoisie has to pass through, they always and everywhere represent the interests of the movement as a whole.

The Communists, therefore, are on the one hand, practically, the most advanced and resolute section of the working class parties of every country, that section which pushes forward all others; on the other hand, theoretically, they have over the great mass of the proletariat the advantage of clearly understanding the line of the march, the conditions and the ultimate general results of the proletarian movement.

The most immediate aim of the Communists is the same as that of all the other proletarian parties: formation of the proletariat into a class, overthrow of the bourgeois supremacy, conquest of political power by the proletariat. . . .

In this sense the theory of the Communists may be summed up in a single sentence: Abolition of private property.

We Communists have been reproached with the desire of abolishing the right of personally acquired property as the fruit of a man's own labor, which property is alleged to be the ground work of all personal freedom, activity, and independence.

Hard-won, self-acquired, self-earned property! Do you mean the property of the petty artisan or that of the small peasant a form of property that preceded the bourgeois form? There is no need to abolish that: the development of industry has to a great extent already destroyed it, and is still destroying it daily.

Or do you mean modern bourgeois private property?

But does wage-labor create any property for the laborer? Not a bit. It creates capital, that is, that kind of property, which exploits wage-labor, and which cannot increase except upon condition of getting a new supply of wage-labor, for fresh exploitation. Property, in its present form, is based on the antagonism of capital and wage-labor. Let us examine both sides of this antagonism.

To be a capitalist, is to have not only a purely personal, but also a social status in production. Capital is a collective product, and only by the united action of many members, nay, in the last resort, only by the united action of all members of society, can it be set in motion.

Capital is therefore not a personal, it is a social power.

When, therefore, capital is converted into common property, into the property of all members of society, personal property is not thereby transformed into social property. It is only the social character of property that is changed. It loses its class-character. . . .

The charges against Communism made from a religious, a philosophical and generally, from an ideological standpoint are not deserving of serious consideration.

Does it require deep intuition to comprehend that man's ideas, views, and conceptions, in one word, man's consciousness, changes with every change in the conditions of his material existence in his social relations and in his social life? What else does the history of ideas prove, than that intellectual production changes in character in proportion as material production is changed? The ruling ideas of each age have ever been the ideas of the ruling class. . . .

In short, the Communists everywhere support revolutionary movement against the existing social and political order of things.

In all these movements they bring to the front, as the leading question in each, the property question, no matter what its degree of development at the time.

Finally, they labor everywhere for the union and agreement of the democratic parties of all countries.

The communists disdain to conceal their views and aims. They declare openly that their ends can be attained only by the forcible overthrow of all existing social conditions. Let the ruling classes tremble at the prospect of a Communistic Revolution. The proletarians have nothing to lose but their chains. They have a world to win.

Working men of all countries, unite!

DOCUMENT XIV: THE PEOPLE'S CHARTER, 1842

Source: R. G. Gammage. *History of the Chartist Movement 1837–1854.* London: Truslove & Hanson, 1894.

Be it therefore enacted:

That from and after the passing of this Act, every male inhabitant of these realms be entitled to vote for the election of a Member of Parliament; subject, however, to the following conditions:

1. That he be a native of these realms, or a foreigner who has lived in this country upwards of two years, and has been naturalized.
2. That he be twenty-one years of age.
3. That he be not proved insane when the lists of voters are revised.
4. That he be not undergoing the sentence of the law at the time when called upon to exercise the electoral right.

5. That his electoral rights not be suspended for bribery at elections, or for personation, of for forgery of election certificates, according to the penalties of this Act.

Arrangement for Nominations

XI. That no other qualification be required than the choice of electors, according to the provisions of this Act, providing that no persons, (excepting Cabinet Ministers), be eligible to serve in the Commons' House of Parliament, who in the receipt of any emolument derivable from any place or places held under government, or of retired allowances arising therefrom.

Arrangements for Elections

XIII. That when any voter's certificate is examined by the registration clerk, and found to be correct, he shall be allowed to pass on to the next barrier, where a balloting ball shall be given him by the person appointed for that purpose; he shall then pass on to the balloting box, and with all due dispatch, shall put the balloting ball into the aperture opposite the name of the candidate he wishes to vote for, after which he shall without delay, leave the room by the door assigned for the purpose.

Duration of Parliament

I. Be it enacted, that the Members of the House of Commons chosen as aforesaid, shall meet on the first Monday in June each year, and continue their sittings from time to time as they may deem it convenient, till the first Monday in June following, when the next new Parliament *shall* be chosen; they shall be eligible to be re-elected.

Payment of Members

Be it enacted
I. That every member of the House of Commons be entitled, at the close of the session, to a writ of expenses on the Treasury. For his legislative duties in the public service; and shall be paid per annum.

DOCUMENT XV: DECREES ISSUED BY THE PROVISIONAL GOVERNMENT ON FEBRUARY 25, 1848, RELATING TO FRENCH WORKERS

Source: James Harvey Robinson. *Readings in European History.* Vol. 2. Boston: Ginn and Company, 1906.

The provisional government of the French republic decrees that the Tuileries shall serve hereafter as a home for the veterans of labor.

The provisional government of the French republic pledges itself to guarantee the means of subsistence of the workingman by labor.

It pledges itself to guarantee labor to all citizens.

It recognizes that workingmen ought to enter into associations among themselves in order to enjoy the advantage of their labor.

The provisional government returns to the workingmen, to whom it rightfully belongs, the million which was about to fall due upon the civil list.

The provisional government of the French republic decrees that all articles pledged at the pawn shops since the first of February, consisting of linen, garments of clothes, etc., upon which the loan does not exceed ten francs, shall be given back to those who pledged them. The minister of finance is ordered to meet the payments incidental to the execution of the present edict.

The provisional government of the French republic decrees the immediate establishment of national workshops. The minister of public works is charged with the execution of the present decree.

DOCUMENT XVI: A CONGRESS OF LABOR LEADERS ISSUE A SOCIALIST PROGRAM AT GOTHA IN 1875

Source: James Harvey Robinson. *Readings in European History.* Vol. 2. Boston: Ginn and Company, 1906.

Proceeding from these principles, the socialist labor party of Germany endeavors by every lawful means to bring about a free state and a socialistic society, to effect the destruction of the iron law of wages by doing away with the system of wage labor, to abolish exploitation of every kind, and to extinguish all social and political inequality.

The socialist labor party of Germany, although for the time being confining its activities within national bounds, is full conscious of the international character of the labor movement, and is resolved to meet all the obligations which this lays upon the laborer, in order to bring the brotherhood of all mankind to its full realization.

The socialist labor party of Germany, in order to prepare the way for the solution of the social question, demands the establishment of socialistic productive associations with the support of the state and under democratic control of the working people. These productive associations, for both industry and agriculture. Are to be created to such an extent that the socialistic organization of all labor may result therefrom.

The socialist labor party of Germany demands the following reforms in the present social organization: (1) the greatest possible extension of political rights and freedom in the sense of the above-mentioned demands [these included universal suffrage for all above twenty years of age, secret ballot, freedom of press, free and compulsory education]; (2) a single progressive income tax, both state and local, instead of all the existing taxes, especially the indirect ones, which weigh heavily upon the people; (3) unlimited right of association; (4) a normal working day corresponding with the needs of society, and the prohibition of work on Sunday; (5) prohibition of child labor and all forms of labor by women which are dangerous to health and morality; (6) laws for the protection of the life and health of workmen, sanitary control of workmen's houses, inspection of mines. Factories, workshops, and domestic industries by officials chosen by the workmen themselves, and an effective system of enforcement of the same; (7) regulation of prison labor.

DOCUMENT XVII: IN 1851 HERBERT SPENCER EXPRESSES THE VIEW THAT UNIMPEDED STRUGGLE IS A REQUISITE FOR PROGRESS

Source: *Social Statics.* New York: D. Appleton and Co., 1910.

Pervading all Nature we may see at work a stern discipline which is a little cruel that it may be very kind. That state of universal warfare maintained throughout the lower creation, to the great perplexity of many worthy people, is at bottom the most merciful provision which circumstances admit of. It is much better that the ruminant animal, when deprived of age by the vigour which made its existence a pleasure, should be killed by some beast of prey, than that it should linger out a life made painful by infirmities, and eventually die of starvation. By the destruction of all such, not only is existence ended before it becomes burdensome, but room is made for a younger generation capable of the fullest enjoyment; and moreover, out of the very act of substitution happiness is derived for a tribe of predatory creatures. Note, further, that their carnivorous enemies not only remove from herbivorous herds individuals past their prime, but also weed out the sickly, the malformed, and the least fleet or powerful. By the aid of which purifying process, as well as by the fighting so universal in the pairing season, all vitiation of the race through the multiplication of its inferior samples is prevented; and the maintenance of a constitution completely adapted to surrounding conditions, and therefore most productive of happiness, is ensured.

The development of the higher creation is a progress towards a form of being, capable of a happiness undiminished by these drawbacks. It is in the human race that the consummation is to be accomplished. Civilization is the last stage of its accomplishment. And the ideal man is the man in whom all the conditions to that accomplishment are fulfilled. Meanwhile, the well being of existing humanity and the unfolding of it into this ultimate perfection, are secured by that same beneficial though severe discipline, to which the animate creation at large is subject. It seems hard that an unskillfulness hit with which all his efforts he cannot overcome, should entail hunger upon the artisan. It seems hard that a laborer incapacitated by sickness from competing with his stronger fellows, should have to bear the resulting privations. It seems hard that widows and orphans should be left to struggle with life or death. Nevertheless, when regarded not separately but in connexxion with the interests of universal humanity, these harsh fatalities are seen to be full of beneficence—the same beneficence which brings to graves the children of diseased parents, and singles out the intemperate and debilitated as the victims of an epidemic.

There are many very amiable people who have not the nerve to look at this matter fairly in the face. Disabled as they are by their sympathies with present suffering, from duly regarding ultimate consequences, they pursue a course which is injudicious, and in the end even cruel. We do not consider it true kindness in a mother to gratify her child with sweetmeats that are likely to make it ill. We should think it a very foolish sort of benevolence which led a surgeon to let his patient's disease progress to a fatal issue, rather than inflict pain by an operation. Similarly, we must call those spurious philanthropists who, to prevent misery, would entail greater misery on future generations. That rigorous necessity which, when allowed to operate, becomes so sharp a spur to the lazy and so strong a bridle to the random, these pauper's friends would repeal, because of the wailings it here and there produces. Blind to the fact that under the natural order of things society is constantly excreting its unhealthy, imbecile, slow, vacillating, faithless members, these unthinking, though well-meaning, men advocate an interference which not only stops the purifying process, but even increases the vitiation—absolutely encourages the multiplication of the reckless and incompetent by offering them an unfailing provision, and discourages the multiplication of the competent and provident by heightening the difficulty of maintaining a family. And thus, in their eagerness to prevent the salutary sufferings that surround us, these sigh-wise and groan-foolish people bequeath to posterity a continually increasing curse.

DOCUMENT XVIII: VICTOR EMMANUEL'S ADDRESS AT THE OPENING SESSION OF THE ITALIAN PARLIAMENT ON FEBRUARY 18, 1861

Source: James Harvey Robinson. *Readings in European History*. Vol. 2. Boston: Ginn and Company, 1906.

Senators and Deputies:

Free and almost entirely united by the wonderful aid of Divine Providence, the harmonious cooperation of the people, and the splendid valour of the army, Italy confides in our uprightness and wisdom. Upon you it devolves to give her uniform institutions and a firm foundation. In extending greater administrative liberties to peoples that have had various usages and institutions, you will take care that political unity, the aspiration of so many centuries, may never be diminished.

The opinion of civilized nations is favorable to us. The just and liberal principles now prevailing in the councils of Europe are favorable to us. Italy herself will in turn become a guarantee of order and peace, and will once more be an efficient instrument of universal civilization.

The emperor of the French firmly upholding the principle of nonintervention,—a maxim eminently beneficial to us,—nevertheless deemed it proper to recall his envoy. If this fact was a cause of chagrin to us, it did not change our sentiments of gratitude toward him or diminish our confidence of his affection for the Italian cause. France and Italy, with their common origins, traditions, and customs, formed on the plains of Magenta and Solferino a bond that will prove indissoluble.

The government and people of England, that ancient country of freedom, warmly sanction our right to be the arbiters of our own destines; and they have lavishly bestowed upon us their good offices, the grateful remembrances of which will be imperishable.

A loyal and illustrious prince having ascended the throne of Prussia, I dispatched to him an ambassador in token of respect for him personally and of sympathy with the noble German nation, which I hope will become more and more secure in the conviction that Italy, being established in her natural unity, cannot offend the rights or interests of other nations. . . .

Valiant youths, led on by a captain who has filled with his name the most distant countries, have made it evident that neither servitude nor long misfortune has been able to weaken the fibre of the Italian peoples. These facts have inspired the nation with great confidence in its own destinies. I take pleasure in manifesting to the first parliament of Italy the joy that fills my heart as king and soldier.

DOCUMENT XIX: THE EMS TELEGRAM

Source: Otto Von Bismarck, Prince. *Bismarck: The Man and the Statesman.* Translated by A. J. Butler. Vol. 2. London: Smith, Elder & Co., 1898.

The Heinrich Abeken [Privy Councilor] text of the telegram delivered to Bismarck at Ems, July 13, 1870
His Majesty the King writes to me:

> Count Benedetti spoke to me on the Promenade in order to demand from me, finally in a most importunate manner, that I should authorize him to telegraph at once that I bound myself for all future time never again to give my consent if the Hohenzollerns should renew their candidature. I refused at last somewhat sternly, as it is neither right nor possible to undertake engagements of this kind á tout jamais. Naturally I told him that I had as yet received no news and as he was earlier informed about Paris and Madrid than myself, he could clearly see that my government once more had no hand in the matter.

Bismarck's Edited Version

After the news of the renunciation of the hereditary Prince of Hohenzollern had been officially communicated to the imperial government of France by the imperial government of Spain, the French Ambassador at Ems further

demanded of His Majesty the King that he would authorize him to telegraph to Paris that His Majesty the King bound himself for all future time
never again to give his consent if the Hohenzollerns should renew their
candidature.

His Majesty the King thereupon decided not to receive the French ambassador again and sent to tell him through the aide-de-camp on duty that
His Majesty had nothing further to communicate to the ambassador.

DOCUMENT XX: ALEXANDER II ON THE EMANCIPATION
OF THE RUSSIAN SERFS

Source: *Annual Register*. London: Longmans, 1861.

By the grace of God, we, Alexander II, Emperor and Autocrat of all the Russians, King of Poland, Grand Duke of Finland, etc. to all our faithful subjects,
make known:

Called by Divine Providence and by the sacred right of inheritance to the
throne of our ancestors, we took a vow in our innermost heart to respond to
the mission which is entrusted to us as to surround with our affection and
our Imperial solicitude all our faithful subjects of every rank and of every
condition, from the warrior, who nobly bears arms for the defence of the
country to the humble artisan devoted to the works of industry; from the official in the career of the high offices of the State to the laborer whose plough
furrows the soil. . . .

We thus came to the conviction that the work of a serious improvement of
the condition of the peasants was a sacred inheritance bequeathed to us by
our ancestors, a mission which, in the course of events, Divine Providence
called upon us to fulfil. . . .

In virtue of the new dispositions above mentioned, the peasants attached
to the soil will be invested within a term fixed by the law with all the rights
of free cultivators. . . .

At the same time, they are granted the right of purchasing their close,
and, with the consent of the proprietors, they may acquire in full property
the arable lands and other appurtenances which are allotted to them as a
permanent holding. By the acquisition in full property of the quantity of
land fixed, the peasants are free from their obligations towards the proprietors for land thus purchased, and they enter definitely into the condition of free peasants—landholders.

DOCUMENT XXI: LETTER FROM THE "EXECUTIVE COMMITTEE OF THE WILL OF THE PEOPLE" TO TSAR ALEXANDER III

Source: Vera Figner. *Memoirs of a Revolutionist*. New York: International Publishers, 1927. Reprinted with permission.

In the course of ten years we have seen how, notwithstanding the most severe persecutions, notwithstanding the fact that the government of the late Emperor sacrificed everything, freedom, the interests of all classes, the interests of industry, and even its own dignity, everything, unconditionally, in its attempt to suppress the revolutionary movement, that movement has nevertheless tenaciously grown and spread, attracting to itself the best elements of the nation, the most energetic and self-denying people of Russia, and for three years now has engaged in desperate partisan warfare with the government. You know well, your Majesty, that it is impossible to accuse the government of the late Emperor of lack of energy. They have hanged our followers, both guilty and innocent; they have filled our prisons and distant provinces with exiles. Whole dozens of our followers have been seized and hanged. They have died with the courage and calmness of martyrs, but the movement has not been suppressed, it has grown and gained strength. . . .

[T]here exists among us now no actual government, in the true meaning of the word. A government, according to its fundamental principle, should express only the aspirations of the people, should accomplish only the will of the people. While in Russia, pardon us for the expression, the government has degenerated into a veritable camarilla, and deserves to be called a band of usurpers far more than does the Executive Committee.

Whatever may have been the intentions of the Sovereign, the acts of the government have had nothing in common with the popular welfare and desires. The Imperial Government has subjugated the people to the state of bondage, it has delivered the masses into the power of the nobility; and now it is openly creating a pernicious class of speculators and profiteers. All its reforms lead to but one state of more complete exploitation. It has brought Russia to such a point that at the present time the popular masses find themselves in a state of utter beggary and ruin, not free even at their own domestic firesides from the most insulting surveillance, powerless even in their own communal village affairs. Only the spoiler, the exploiter, is favored by the protection of the law and the government. The most revolting depredations remain unpunished. But what a terrible fate awaits the man who sincerely thinks and plans for the public welfare! You know well, your Majesty, that it is not only the socialists who are exiled and persecuted. What kind of a government is this, then, which protects such an "order?" Is it not rather a band of rascals, an absolute usurpation?

This is the reason why the Russian government has no moral influence, no support in the people; this is why Russia gives birth to so many revolutionists; this is why even such a fact as regicide awakens joy and sympathetic approval in an enormous part of the population. Yes, your Majesty, do not deceive yourself with the declarations of fawners and flatterers. Regicide is very popular in Russia.

DOCUMENT XXII: THE AUSTRIAN ULTIMATUM TO SERBIA DELIVERED ON JULY 23, 1914

Source: Charles F. Horne and Walter F. Austin, eds. *The Great Events of the Great War*. Vol. 1. National Alumni, 1923.

The history of recent years, and in particular the painful events of the 28th of June last, have shown the existence of a subversive movement with the object of detaching a part of the territories of Austria-Hungary from the Monarchy. The movement, which had its birth under the eye of the Serbian government, has gone so far as to make itself manifest on both sides of the Serbian frontier in the shape of acts of terrorism and a series of outrages and murders. . . .

It results from the depositions and confessions of the criminal perpetrators of the outrage of the 28th of June that the Sarajevo assassinations were planned in Belgrade; that the arms and explosives with which the murderers were provided had been given to them by Serbian officers and functionaries belonging to the *Narodna Odbrana*; and finally, that the passage into Bosnia of the criminals and of their arms was organized and effected by the chiefs of the Serbian frontier service.

The above mentioned results of the magisterial investigation do not permit the Austro-Hungarian Government to pursue any longer the attitude of expectant forbearance which they have maintained for years in the face of machinations hatched in Belgrade, and thence propagated in the territories of the Monarchy. The results, on the contrary, impose on them the duty of putting an end to the intrigues which form a perpetual menace to the tranquillity of the monarchy.

To achieve this end, the Imperial and Royal Government see themselves as compelled to demand from the Royal Serbian Government a formal assurance that they condemn this dangerous propaganda against the Monarchy; in other words, the whole series of tendencies, the ultimate aim of which is to detach from the Monarchy territories belonging to it: and that they undertake to suppress by every means this criminal and terrorist propaganda.

In order to give a formal character to this undertaking, the Royal Serbian Government shall publish on the front page of their "Official Journal" 13–26 of July the following declaration:

The Royal Serbian Government condemn the propaganda directed against Austria-Hungary, that is to say, the general tendency of which the final aim is to detach from the Austro-Hungarian Monarchy territories belonging to it, and they sincerely deplore the fatal consequences of these criminal proceedings.

The Royal Serbian Government [acknowledges] that Serbian officers and functionaries participated in the above-mentioned propaganda and thus compromised the good neighborly relations to which the Royal Government were solemnly pledged by the declaration of the 31st of March, 1909.

The Royal Government, who disapprove and repudiate all idea of interfering or attempting to interfere with the destinies of the inhabitants of any part whatsoever of Austria-Hungary, consider it their duty formally to warn officers and functionaries, and the whole population of the Kingdom, that henceforward they will proceed with the utmost rigor against persons who may be guilty of any such machinations, which they use their efforts to anticipate and suppress.

This declaration shall simultaneously be communicated to the Royal army as an order of the day by His Majesty the King, and shall be published in the "Official Bulletin" of the army.

The Royal Serbian Government shall further undertake:

(1) To suppress any publication which incites to hatred and contempt of the Austro-Hungarian Monarchy. . . .

(2) To dissolve immediately the society styled *Narodna Odbrana*, to confiscate all its means of propaganda, and to proceed in the same manner against other societies and their branches in Serbia which engage in propaganda against Austria-Hungary. . . .

(3) To eliminate without delay from public instruction in Serbia, . . . everything that serves or might serve to foment propaganda against Austria-Hungary;

(4) To remove from the military service and from the administration in general all officers and functionaries guilty of propaganda against the Austro-Hungarian Monarchy, and whose deeds the Austro-Hungarian Government reserves to themselves the right of communicating to the Royal Government;

(5) To accept the collaboration in Serbia of representatives of the Austro-Hungarian Government for the suppression of the subversive movement directed against the territorial integrity of the Monarchy;

(6) To take judicial proceedings against accessories to the plot of the 28th of June who are on Serbian territory. . . .

(7) To proceed without delay to the arrest of Major Voislav Tankositch and of the individual named Milan Ciganovitch, a Serbian State employee. . . .

(8) To prevent by effective measures the cooperation of Serbian authorities in the illicit traffic in arms and explosives across the frontier, to dismiss and punish severely the officials of the frontier service of the Frontier Service . . . guilty of having assisted the perpetrators of the Sarajevo crime by facilitating their passage across the frontier;

(9) To furnish the Imperial and Royal Government with explanations regarding the unjustifiable utterances of high Serbian officials . . . who . . . have not hesitated since the crime of the 28th to express themselves in interviews in terms of hostility to the Austro-Hungarian Government; and, finally,

(10) To notify the Imperial and Royal Government without delay of the execution of the measures comprised under the preceding headings.

The Austro-Hungarian Government expect the reply of the Royal Government at the latest by 5 o'clock on Saturday evening the 25th of July.*

DOCUMENT XXIII: PRINCE REGENT ALEXANDER OF SERBIA'S TELEGRAM SENT TO TSAR NICHOLAS ON JULY 24, 1914

Source: Charles F. Horne and Walter F. Austin, eds. *The Great Events of the Great War*. Vol. 1. National Alumni, 1923.

The Austro-Hungarian Government yesterday evening handed to the Serbian Government a note concerning the "attentat" of Sarajevo. Conscious of

---

*Subsequently deferred to 6 o'clock.

its international duties, Serbia from the first days of the horrible crime declared that she condemned it, and that she was ready to open an inquiry on her territory if the complicity of certain of her subjects were proved in the investigation begun by the Austro-Hungarian authorities. However, the demands contained in the Austro-Hungarian note are unnecessarily humiliating for Serbia and incompatible with her dignity as an independent state. Thus we are called upon in peremptory tones for a declaration of the Government in the "Official Journal," and an order from the Sovereign to the army wherein we should repress the spirit of hostility against Austria by reproaching ourselves for criminal weakness in regard to our perfidious actions. Then we have to admit Austro-Hungarian functionaries into Serbia to participate with our own in the investigation and to superintend the execution of the other conditions indicated in the note. We have received a time-limit of forty-eight hours to accept everything, in default of which the legation of Austro-Hungary will leave Belgrade. We are ready to accept the Austro-Hungarian conditions which are compatible with the position of an independent State as well as those whose acceptance shall be advised us by your Majesty. All persons whose participation in the "attentat" shall be proved will be severely punished by us. Certain of these demands cannot be carried out without changes in our legislation, which require time. We have been given too short a limit. We can be attacked after the expiration of the time-limit by the Austro-Hungarian Army, which is concentrating on our frontier. It is impossible for us to defend ourselves, and we supplicate your Majesty to give us your aid as soon as possible. The highly prized good will of your Majesty, which has so often shown itself toward us, makes us hope firmly that this time again our appeal will be heard by his generous Slav heart.

In these difficult moments I voice the sentiments of the Serbian people, who supplicate your Majesty to interest himself in the lot of the Kingdom of Serbia.

Alexander

DOCUMENT XXIV: PRIVATE DONALD FRASER

Source: *The Journal of Private Fraser 1914–1918 Canadian Expeditionary Force.* Edited by Reginald H. Roy. Nepean, Ontario: CEF Books, 1998. Reprinted with permission.

Tuesday, October 12, 1915

At this stage it may be well to mention what the ordinary infantryman in the firing line has to go through and what his nerves have to stand. Old No Man's Land had an average width of 150 to 250 yds.; in many parts of the line it would come as close as 35 to 75 yds. As a rule, the narrower No Man's Land, the weaker the wire. The distance between is so little that fixing up wire is impossible. Ready made wiring obstacles have to be thrown over and, of course, they cannot be expected to be very effective. In fact, later on, Fritz had the audacity to fix on one of our wiring obstacles and pulled it on to his side. Anyway, besides being liable to be shelled at any moment, the man in the firing line is liable to have bombs, grenades, and trench mortars [bombs] thrown at him. Machine-guns may open up and rip the sand bags at pleasure. Clamped rifles go off now and then, trained at likely spots the infantryman has to pass. Any moment a swarm of Huns may rush him. He is liable to be blown up by a mine tunnelled underneath [the trench]. On dark nights the enemy could crawl into his trench without being seen. It is the same when it is foggy. He exists under these conditions, wet or dry, often in mud and slush over the knees and almost frozen with cold. Sometimes he sleeps on the firing step or in the bottom of the trench with practically no covering or protection. When he gets wet, his clothes have to dry on him—at times he is worked off his feet digging, draining, making dug-outs, carrying timber, corrugated iron, etc. And has to run the gauntlet of being sniped on many occasions. Knowing that at any moment he may be hurled into oblivion, his nerves are keyed to a certain pitch and his existence is one of suspense. No wonder the average man's stay in the trenches is a few months. . . .

Monday, April 3, 1916

When day broke, the sights that met our gaze were so horrible and ghastly that they beggar description. Heads, arms and legs were protruding from the mud at every yard and dear knows how many bodies the earth swallowed. Thirty corpses were at least showing in the crater and beneath its clayey waters other victims must be lying killed and drowned. A young, tall, slim English lieutenant lay stretched in death with a pleasant, peaceful look on his boyish face. Some mother's son gone to glory. He was wearing a gold signet ring, having an eagle with outstretched wings engraved thereon. It was removed by Munro, who thinking it of no value, handed it to Doull, who has it in his possession today. It was so narrow it could fit very few fingers. Another

English second lieutenant was lying at the edge of the crater, huddled, up with his legs uppermost. One of the most saddening cases was a stretcher bearer near half a dozen dead Tommies, a little to the right of the trench leading to crater 7. He was sitting with a bandage between his hands in the very act of bandaging his leg, when his life gave out, and his head fell back, his mouth open, and his eyes were gazing up to heaven, as if in piteous appeal. There he sat in a natural posture as if in life, the bandage in his hands, and the Red Cross bag by his side. Lovett was his name, and he belonged to the King's Liverpool. Another strange, appalling spectacle was a couple of Tommies sitting on the firing step; the head of one fallen forward on his chest, and between his fingers he still held a cigarette. There he was as if asleep, yes but in a sleep that knows no awakening. His comrade beside him was in a sitting position but inclining sideways. Both were unmarked and must have met their doom by concussion.

In the support line an Imperial with a Balaclava cap on was lying on a stretcher, dead. Eight bodies of British soldiers were collected in the crater for burial, when a shell came over and burst among them, plastering Weber and Doull with gangrened flesh. At daybreak one of the bombers was shocked to find himself standing between a dead German and English officer, whilst close by was a German private and English Tommy. What trench mats there were seemed to rest on bodies. One could not dig anywhere without coming a cross a human corpse. Huddled together amongst the dead our men passed their lonely vigil in the early hours of April 4th. "Amidst life is death" was indelibly printed on the minds of everyone present on that fateful morning. . . .

Friday, June 2, 1916

Artillery fire was fairly heavy during the early morning of [June] 6th. About 7:00 o'clock a bombardment of unprecedented ferocity began and the range was of uncanny accuracy. The shells were bursting in or near the trench and the gunfire would run from end to end. It played along the line as if worked by a hose. Gunfire so precise and methodical in its execution strikes terror, even into the bravest hearts. Stuck in a trench, with shells creeping gradually nearer and nearer to you from the right, and through a piece of good fortune you escape, only to go through the same ordeal as the fire sweeps back from the left, is unnerving to the last degree. All the time you hear the noise from the guns and brace yourself for the burst, which you expect every moment on top of you. Such was the situation we had to face until 2:00 P.M. when the assault came. This systematic shellfire which aims at complete destruction of a helpless foe, has swelled our hospitals and asylums to the brim. No fighting is so tense as at these moments and never has the reason hung on so fine a thread. To get up over the parapet and rush to certain death at the hands of machine-gunners or riflemen would be a welcome mental relief to remaining stoically in a trench with an avalanche of shells smashing and burying everything before it. Standing up to shellfire of such method and accuracy is the hardest part by far of a soldier's trials. . . .

Thursday, September 14, 1916

Lying low in the shell hole contemplating events with now and then a side glance at my sandy moustached comrade, lying dead beside me, his mess tin shining and scintillating on his back, a strange and curious sight appeared. Away to my left rear, a huge grey object reared itself into view, and slowly, very slowly, it crawled along like a gigantic toad, feeling its way across the shell-stricken field. It was a tank, the "Creme de menthe," the latest invention of destruction and the first of its kind to be employed in the Great War. I watched it coming towards our direction. How painfully slow it travelled. Down and up the shell holes it clambered, a weird, ungainly monster, moving relentlessly forward. Suddenly men from the ground looked up, rose as if from the dead, and running from the flanks to behind it, followed in the rear as if to be in on the kill. The last I saw of it, it was wending its way to the Sugar Refinery. It crossed Fritz's trenches, a few yards from me, with hardly a jolt. . . .

Monday, April 9, 1917

When in line with Neuville St. Vaast bordering Guillemot trench the enemy sent over a few shells bursting a hundred yards behind us. At first we took them for whiz-bangs on account of their rapid flight and did not pay much attention, but as the range was being lessened, the writer and a few others dropped into a shallow trench a little to our rear. Pausing there for a minute or two I was on the point of climbing out of the trench when a shell hit with a dull pop burst on the parapet almost in my face. My breathing stopped at once. With mouth open I could neither breathe in nor out. Breathing was paralysed. It was a peculiar sensation. In a flash I knew it was a gas shell and it completely fouled the air. In a fraction of a second, in fact my quickness astonished me, I had my respirator on and was breathing freely, but not before

I caught site of Porter on my left, who looked as if he was a goner and had not the strength to do anything. He was on the elderly side and I thought should not have been in this action. However, we were signaled at the moment to move on and I expected to hear later that Porter had breathed his last. . . .

DOCUMENT XXV: WOODROW WILSON

Source: "Speech on the Fourteen Points." *Congressional Record* 65th Cong. 2nd sess. 1918.

We entered this war because violations of right had occurred which touched us to the quick and made the life of our own people impossible unless they were corrected and the world secured once for all against their recurrence. What we demand in this war, therefore, is nothing peculiar to ourselves. It is that the world be made fit and safe to live in; and particularly that it be made safe for every peace-loving nation which, like our own, wishes to live its own life, determine its own institutions, be assured of justice and fair dealing by the other peoples of the world as against force and selfish aggression. All the peoples of the world are in effect partners in this interest, and for our own part we see very clearly that unless justice be done to others it will not be done to us. The programme of the world's peace, therefore, is our programme; and that programme, the only possible programme, as we see it, is this:

   I. Open covenants of peace, openly arrived at, after which there shall be no private international understanding of any kind but diplomacy shall proceed always frankly and in the public view.

   II. Absolute freedom of navigation upon the seas, outside territorial waters, alike in peace and in war, except as the seas may be closed in whole or in part by international action for the enforcement of international covenants.

   III. The removal, so far as possible, of all economic barriers and the establishment of an equality of trade conditions among all the nations consenting to the peace and associating themselves for its maintenance.

   IV. Adequate guarantees given and taken that national armaments will be reduced to the lowest point consistent with domestic safety.

V. A free, open-minded, and absolutely impartial adjustment of all colonial claims, based upon a strict observance of the principle that in determining all such questions of sovereignty the interests of the populations concerned must have equal weight with the equitable claims of the government whose title is to be determined.

VI. The evacuation of all Russian territory and such a settlement of all questions affecting Russia as will secure the best and freest cooperation of the other nations of the world in obtaining for her an unhampered and unembarrassed opportunity for the independent determination of her own political development and national policy and assure her a sincere welcome into the society of free nations under institutions of her own choosing; and, more than a welcome, assistance also of every kind that she may need and may herself desire. The treatment accorded Russia by her sister nations in the months to come will be the acid test of their good will, of their comprehension of her needs as distinguished from their own interests, and of their intelligent and unselfish sympathy.

VII. Belgium, the whole world will agree, must be evacuated and restored, without any attempt to limit the sovereignty which she enjoys in common with all free nations. No other single act will serve as this will serve to restore the confidence among the nations in the laws which they have themselves set and determined for the government of their relations with one another. Without this healing act the whole structure and validity of international law is forever impaired.

VIII. All French territory should be freed and the invaded portions restored, and the wrong done to France by Prussia in 1871 in the matter of Alsace-Lorraine, which has unsettled the peace of the world for nearly fifty years, should be righted, in order that peace may once more be made secure in the interest of all.

IX. A readjustment of the frontiers of Italy should be effected along clearly recognizable lines of nationality.

X. The peoples of Austria-Hungary, whose place among the nations we wish to see safeguarded and assured, should be accorded the freest opportunity of autonomous development.

XI. Rumania, Serbia, and Montenegro should be evacuated; occupied territories restored; Serbia accorded free and secure access to the sea; and the relations of the several Balkan states to one another determined by friendly counsel along historically established lines of allegiance and nationality; and international guarantees of the political and economic independence and territorial integrity of the several Balkan states should be entered into.

XII. The Turkish portions of the present Ottoman Empire should be assured a secure sovereignty, but the other nationalities which are now under Turkish rule should be assured an undoubted security of life and an absolutely unmolested opportunity of autonomous development, and the Dardanelles should be permanently opened as a free passage to the ships and commerce of all nations under international guarantees.

XIII. An independent Polish state should be erected which should include the territories inhabited by indisputably Polish populations, which should be assured a free and secure access to the sea, and whose political and economic independence and territorial integrity should be guaranteed by international covenant.

XIV. A general association of nations must be formed under specific covenants for the purpose of affording mutual guarantees of political independence and territorial integrity to great and small states alike.

DOCUMENT XXVI: LENIN'S REBUTTAL OF ARGUMENTS MADE BY KAMENIEV AND RIAZANOV, BOLSHEVIK OPPONENTS OF INSURRECTION, AS REPORTED BY JOHN REED

Source: John Reed. *Ten Days that Shook the World*. New York: International Publishers, 1934, 1967. Reprinted with permission.

1. Kameniev and Riazanov say that we have not a majority among the people, and that without a majority insurrection is impossible.

Answer: People capable of speaking such things are falsifiers, pedants, or simply don't want to look the real situation in the face. In the last elections we received in all the country more than fifty per cent of all the votes. . . .

The most important thing in Russia to-day is the peasant's revolution. In Tambov government there has been a real agrarian uprising with wonderful results. . . . Even Dielo Naroda (People's Cause) has been scared into yelling that the land must be turned over to the peasants, and not only the Socialist Revolutionaries in the Council of the Republic but also the government itself, has been similarly affected. . . .

2. We are not sufficiently strong to take over the Government, and the bourgeoisie is not sufficiently strong to prevent the Constituent Assembly.

Answer: This is nothing but timidity, expressed by pessimism as regards workers and soldiers, and optimism as regards the failures of the bourgeoisie. If *yunkers* and Cossacks say they will fight, you believe them; if workmen and soldiers say so, you doubt it. What is the distinction between such doubts and siding politically with the bourgeoisie?

Kornilov proved that the Soviets were really a power. To believe Kerensky and the Council of the Republic, if the bourgeoisie is not strong enough to break the Soviets, it is not strong enough to break the Constituent. But that is wrong. The bourgeoisie will break the Constituent by sabotage, by lockouts, by giving up Petrograd, by opening the front to the Germans. This has already been done in the case of Riga . . .

3. The Soviets must remain a revolver at the head of the government to force the calling of the Constituent Assembly, and to supress any further Kornilov attempts.

Answer: Refusal of insurrection is refusal of 'All Power to the Soviets.' Since September the Bolshevik party has been discussing the question of insurrection. Refusing to rise means trust our hopes in the faith of the good bourgeouisie, who have 'promised' to call the Constituent Assembly. When the Soviets have all the power, the calling of the constituent is guaranteed, and its success assured . . .

5. We're getting stronger every day. We shall be able to enter the Constituent Assembly as a strong opposition. Then why should we play everything on one card?

Answer: This is the argument of a sophomore with no practical experience, who reads that the Constituent Assembly is being called and trustfully accepts the legal and constitutional way. Even the voting of the Constituent Assembly will not do away with hunger, or beat Wilhelm. . . . The issue of hunger and of surrendering Petrograd cannot be decided by waiting for the Constituent Assembly. Hunger is not waiting. The peasants' Revolution is not waiting . . .

6. If the Kornilovisti make an attempt, we would show them our strength. But why should we risk everything by making an attempt ourselves?

Answer: History doesn't repeat. "Perhaps Kornilov will some day make an attempt!" What a serious base for proletarian action! But suppose Kornilov waits for starvation, for the opening of the fronts, what then? This attitude means to build the tactics of a revolutionary party on one of the bourgeoisie's former mistakes.

Let us forget everything except that there is no way out but by the dictatorship of the proletariat either that or the dictatorship of Kornilov. . . .

DOCUMENT XXVII: THE TREATY OF VERSAILLES

Source: Treaty of Peace between the Allied and Associated Powers and Germany, 1919. University of Alberta Libraries.

Article 22. Certain communities formerly belonging to the Turkish Empire have reached a stage of development where their existence as independent nations can be provisionally recognised subject to the rendering of administrative advice and assistance by a Mandatory [i. e., a Western power] until such time as they are able to stand alone. The wishes of these communities must be a principle consideration in the selection of the Mandatory.

Article 42. Germany is forbidden to maintain or construct any fortifications either on the left bank of the Rhine or on the right bank to the west of a line drawn 50 kilometres to the East of the Rhine.

Article 45. As compensation for the destruction of the coal mines in the north of France and as part payment towards the total reparation due from Germany for the damage resulting from the war, Germany cedes to France in full and absolute possession, with exclusive right of exploitation, unencumbered and free from all debts and charges of any kind, the coal mines situated in the Saar Basin.

Article 49. Germany renounces in favor of the League of Nations, in the capacity of trustee, the government of the territory defined above.

At the end of fifteen years from the coming into force of the present Treaty the inhabitants of the said territory shall be called upon to indicate the sovereignty under which they desire to be placed.

Alsace-Lorraine. The High Contracting Parties, recognizing the moral obligation to redress the wrong done by Germany in 1871 both to the rights of France and to the wishes of the population of Alsace and Lorraine, which were separated from their country in spite of the solemn protest of their representatives at the Assembly of Bordeaux, agree upon the following.

Article 51. The territories which were ceded to Germany in accordance with the Preliminaries of Peace signed at Versailles on February 26, 1871, and the Treaty of Frankfurt of May 10, 1871, are restored to French sovereignty as from the date of the Armistice of November 11, 1918.

The provisions of the Treaties establishing the delimitation of the frontiers before 1871 shall be restored.

Article 119. Germany renounces in favor of the Principal Allied and Associated Powers all her rights and titles over her overseas possessions.

Article 156. Germany renounces, in favor of Japan, all her rights, title and privileges . . . which she acquired in virtue of the Treaty concluded by her with China on March 6, 1898, and of all other arrangements relative to the Province of Shantung.

Article 159. The German military forces shall be demobilised and reduced as prescribed hereinafter.

Article 160. By a date which must not be later than March 31, 1920, the German Army must not comprise more than seven divisions of infantry and three divisions of cavalry.

After the date the total number of effectives in the Army of the States constituting Germany must not exceed 100,000 men, including officers and establishments of depots. The Army shall be devoted exclusively to the maintenance of order within the territory and to the control of the frontiers.

The total effective strength of officers, including the personnel of staffs, whatever their composition, must not exceed four thousand.

Article 231. The Allied and Associated Governments affirm and Germany accepts the responsibility of Germany and her allies for causing all the loss and damage to which the Allied and Associated Governments and their nationals have been subjected as a consequence of the war imposed upon them by the aggression of Germany and her allies.

Article 232. The Allied and Associated Governments recognize that the resources of Germany are not adequate, after taking into account permanent diminutions of such resources which will result from other provisions of the present Treaty, to make complete reparation for all such loss and damage.

The Allied and Associated Governments, however, require, and Germany undertakes, that she will make compensation for all damage done to the civilian population of the Allied and Associated Powers and to their property during the period of the belligerency of each as an Allied or Associated Power against Germany.

BIBLIOGRAPHY

Anderson, M. S. *The War of the Austrian Succession, 1740–1748*. London and New York: Longman, 1995.

Artz, Frederick Binkerd. *Reaction and Revolution, 1814–1832*. New York: Harper & Brothers, 1974.

Ashton, T. S. *The Industrial Revolution, 1760–1830*. Oxford and New York: Oxford University Press, 1997.

Becker, Jean-Jacques. *The Great War and the French People*, Trans. Arnold Pomerans. New York: St. Martin's Press, 1986.

Bergeron, Louis. *France under Napoleon*. Trans. R. R. Palmer. Princeton: Princeton University Press, 1981.

Bernard, Paul P. *Joseph II*. New York: Twayne Publishers, 1968.

Bridenthal, Renate, Susan Mosher Stuard, and Merry E. Wiesner, eds. *Becoming Visible: Women in European History*, 3rd. ed. Boston: Houghton Mifflin, 1998.

Cassirer, Ernst. *The Philosophy of the Enlightenment*. Trans. Fritz C. A. Koelln and James P. Pettegrove. Boston: Beacon Press, 1955.

Cook, Chris, and John Stevenson. *The Longman's Handbook of European History: 1763–1985*. London: Longman's, 1987.

Cranston, Maurice William. *Philosophers and Pamphleteers: Political Theorists of the Enlightenment*. Oxford and New York: Oxford University Press, 1986.

Crossick, C., and H. G. Haupt, eds. *Shopkeepers and Master Artisans in Nineteenth Century Europe*. London: Methuen, 1986.

Darnton, Robert. *The Business of Enlightenment: A Publishing History of the Encyclopédie, 1775–1800*. Cambridge, Mass.: Harvard University Press, 1979.

———. *The Literary Underground of the Old Regime*. Cambridge, Mass.: Harvard University Press, 1982.

de Luna, Frederick A. *The French Republic under Cavaignac, 1848.* Princeton: Princeton University Press, 1969.

de Madariaga, Isabel. *Russia in the Age of Catherine the Great.* New Haven: Yale University Press, 1981.

Doyle, William. *The Oxford History of the French Revolution.* Oxford and New York: Oxford University Press, 1990.

Elson Roessler, Shirley. *Out of the Shadows: Women and Politics in the French Revolution, 1789–1795.* New York: Peter Lang Publishers, 1996.

Fay, Sidney Bradshaw. *The Origins of the World War,* rev. ed., New York: Free Press, 1966.

Figes, Orlando. *A People's Tragedy: The Russian Revolution, 1891–1924.* New York: Viking, 1997.

Fischer, Fritz. *Germany's Aims in the First World War.* Trans. James Joll. London: Chatto & Windus, 1967.

Fussell, Paul. *The Great War and Modern Memory.* Oxford and New York: Oxford University Press, 2000.

Gagliardo, John G. *Enlightened Despotism.* New York: Crowell, 1967.

Gay, Peter. *The Enlightenment: An Interpretation.* New York: Norton, 1977.

Gildea, Robert. *Barricades and Borders: Europe 1800–1914.* Oxford and New York: Oxford University Press, 1987.

Goodman, Dena. *The Republic of Letters: A Cultural History of the French Enlightenment.* Ithaca, N.Y.: Cornell University Press, 1994.

Gray, John. *Liberalism,* 2nd ed. Minneapolis: University of Minnesota Press, 1995.

Greer, Donald. *Incident of the Terror during the French Revolution: A Statistical Interpretation.* Gloucester, Mass.: Harvard University Press, 1966.

Hamerow, Theodore S. *The Birth of a New Europe: State and Society in the Nineteenth Century.* Chapel Hill: University of North Carolina Press, 1983.

Hazard, Paul. *The European Mind: The Critical Years, 1680–1715.* Trans. J. Lewis May. Cleveland, Ohio: World Publishing Company, 1963.

Hobsbawm, E. J. *The Age of Empire, 1875–1914.* New York: Vintage, 1989.

———. *The Age of Revolution Europe: 1789–1848.* London: Weidenfeld and Nicolson, 1962.

Hudson, Pat. *The Industrial Revolution.* London and New York: E. Arnold, 1992.

Kafker, Frank. *The Encyclopædists as a Group.* Paris: Voltaire Foundation, 1996.

Kitson, Michael. *The Age of Baroque.* New York: McGraw-Hill, 1966.

Klaits, Joseph, and Michael Haltzel, eds. *The Global Ramifications of the French Revolution.* Cambridge, U.K., and New York: Cambridge University Press, 1994.

Langer, William L. *Political and Social Upheaval, 1832–1852.* New York: Harper & Row, 1969.

Lefebvre, Georges. *The Coming of the French Revolution.* Trans. R. R. Palmer. New York: Vintage Books, 1947.

Lindemann, Albert S. *A History of European Socialism*. New Haven, Conn.: Yale University Press, 1983.

Macartney, C. A. *The Habsburg Empire, 1790–1918*. London: Weidenfeld & Nicolson, 1968, 1971.

Mack Smith, Dennis. *Victor Emmanuel, Cavour, and the Risorgimento*. London and New York: Oxford University Press, 1971.

Magraw, R. *History of the French Working Class*. Oxford, U.K., and Cambridge, Mass.: Blackwell Publishers, 1992.

Marwick, Arthur. *Women at War, 1914–1918*. London: Croom Helm, 1977.

May, Arthur. *The Age of Metternich*. New York: Holt, Rinehart and Winston, 1963.

McPhee, Peter. *The French Revolution, 1789–1799*. New York: Oxford University Press, 2002.

Muller, Jerry Z. *Adam Smith in His Time and Ours: Designing the Decent Society*. New York: Maxwell Macmillan International, 1993.

Palmer, R. R., and Joel Colton. *A History of the Modern World*, 9th ed. Boston: McGraw-Hill, 2001.

Pflanze, Otto. *Bismarck and the Development of Germany: The Period of Unification, 1815–1871*. Princeton: Princeton University Press, 1963.

Pilbeam, P. M. *The Middle Classes in Europe, 1789–1914: France, Germany, Italy and Russia*. Basingstoke, U.K.: Macmillan Education, 1990.

Pinkney, David. *The French Revolution of 1830*. Princeton, N.J.: Princeton University Press, 1972.

Pipes, Richard. *Russia under the Old Regime*. New York, Scribner, 1974.

Plessis, A. *The Rise and Fall of the Second Empire, 1852–1871*. Trans. Jonathan Mandelbaum. Cambridge, U.K., and New York: Cambridge University Press, 1985.

Popkin, Jeremy. *A Short History of the French Revolution*. Upper Saddle River, N.J.: Prentice Hall, 2002.

Rawls, John. *Political Liberalism*. New York: Columbia University Press, 1993.

Remak, Joachim. *The Origins of World War I*. New York: Holt, Rinehart and Winston, 1967.

Ritter, Gerhard. *Frederick the Great*. Trans. Peter Paret. Berkeley: University of California Press, 1968.

Roche, Daniel. *France in the Enlightenment*. Trans. Arthur Goldhammer. Cambridge, Mass.: Harvard University Press, 1998.

Saville, John. *1848: The British State and the Chartist Movement*. Cambridge, U.K., and New York: Cambridge University Press, 1990.

Schama, Simon. *Citizens: A Chronicle of the French Revolution*. New York: Knopf, 1989.

Schmitt, O. *The Coming of the War, 1914*. New York: Charles Scribner's Sons, 1930.

Schroeder, Paul W. *Austria, Great Britain and the Crimean War: The Destruction of the Concert of Europe*. Ithaca, N.Y.: Cornell University Press, 1972.

———. *Transformation of European Politics, 1763–1848.* New York: Oxford University Press, 1994.

Shannon, Richard. *The Crisis of Imperialism, 1865–1915.* London: Hart-Davis, MacGibbon, 1974.

Sharp, Alan. *The Versailles Settlement: Peacemaking in Paris.* New York: St. Martin's Press, 1991.

Sheehan, James J. *German History, 1770–1866.* New York: Oxford University Press, 1989.

Shennan, J. H. *France before the Revolution,* 2nd ed. London and New York: Routledge, 1995.

Shukman, Harold, ed. *The Blackwell Encyclopedia of the Russian Revolution.* Oxford, U.K., and Cambridge, Mass.: Blackwell Publishers, 1994.

Sperber, Jonathan. *The European Revolutions, 1848–1851.* Cambridge, U.K.: Cambridge University Press, 1994.

Stearns, P. N., ed. *The Impact of the Industrial Revolution: Protest and Alienation.* Englewood Cliffs, N.J.: Prentice-Hall, 1972.

———. *1848: The Revolutionary Tide in Europe.* New York: Norton, 1974.

Venturi, Franco. *The End of the Old Regime in Europe, 1768–1776: The First Crisis.* Trans. R. Burr Litchfield. Princeton, N.J.: Princeton University Press, 1989.

Venturi, Franco. *The End of the Old Regime in Europe, 1776–1789.* Trans. R. Burr Litchfield. Princeton, N.J.: Princeton University Press, 1991.

Vyverberg, Henry. *The Living Tradition,* 2nd edition. New York: Harcourt Brace Jovanovich Publishers, 1988.

Weiss, John. *Conservatism in Europe 1770–1945: Traditionalism, Reaction, and Counter-revolution.* London: Thames and Hudson, 1977

Winks, Robin, et al. *A History of Civilization: Prehistory to the Present,* 7th ed. Englewood Cliffs, N.J.: Prentice Hall, 1988.

Winter, J. M. *The Great War and the British People.* Cambridge, Mass.: Harvard University Press, 1986.

Woolf, S. J. *Napoleon's Integration of Europe.* London: Routledge, 1991.

Yolton, John, et al., eds. *The Blackwell Companion to the Enlightenment.* Oxford, U.K., and Cambridge, Mass.: Blackwell Publishers, 1991.

Young, James D. *Women and Power Struggles: A History of British Working-Class Women, 1560–1984.* Edinburgh: Mainstream Publishing Company, 1985.

Zaller, Robert. *Europe in Transition, 1660–1815.* New York: Harper & Row, 1984.

INDEX

Abdul Hamid, sultan, 197
Abyssinia, 204, 212
academies, educational and scientific, 18–20, 21
Act of Settlement (1701), 43
Addison, Joseph, 21
Adrianople, 216
Adrianople, Treaty of (1829), 132
Afghanistan, 204, 209, 212
Africa, 61, 203–4, 212. *See also* individual African countries
Age of Louis XIV (Voltaire), 10
agriculture, 2, 31–35, 39, 63, 70–71; in Britain, 33–35, 117–18, 141; in the colonies, 61; in France, 94, 123; mechanization, 151; in Russia, 136, 199, 229–30, 232
d'Aiguillon, duc, 81
Aix-la-Chapelle, congress in (1818), 131
Aix-la-Chapelle, Treaty of (1748), 66
Albania, 195, 216, 241
d'Alembert, Jean le Rond, 11, 19
Alexander I, tsar of Russia, 109, 110, 112, 113, 115, 136, 137
Alexander II, tsar of Russia, 197–98
Alexander III, tsar of Russia, 198–99

Alexandra, empress of Russia, 228–29
Alexei (Romanov), crown prince of Russia, 229
Algeciras, conference (1906), 213, 215
Algeria, 203, 206
Algonquin (boat), 224
All-Russian Congress of Soviets, 234
All-Russian Union of Zemstva, 231
Alsace-Lorraine, 58, 181, 207, 209, 239
Amar, Jean-Baptiste, 95
American Revolution, 69–70, 72, 76
anarchism (political theory), 198
Anglo-Russian Convention (1907), 209
Angola, 204
anti-Semitism, 169, 186, 195, 237. *See also* Jews, Judaism
April Theses (Lenin), 232–33
Arabs, 204, 241
Arkwright, Richard, 38
armaments, build-up in Europe, 209–11. *See also* weapons
armies, 248n1; American, 226; Austrian, 50, 176, 195, 211, 220; conscription, 60, 183, 210, 246; French, 89, 92–93, 99, 109, 186, 211, 220; German, 211, 220, 240; growth of, in

Europe, 59, 209–10; Prussian, 48, 49, 174–75, 176; Russian, 52, 211, 220, 227, 231. *See also* mercenary soldiers; Red Army; warfare
Arouet, François Marie. *See* Voltaire
art and architecture, 26–28, 161–62, 163–64
artisans, 22, 39, 60, 71, 74, 75, 86, 90, 98, 125, 141, 146. *See also* guilds
Artois, Charles-Philippe, count, 87
Asia, 61. *See also* China; Hong Kong; Japan
astronomy, study of, 3
atheism, 17
Augustenburg, Christian Karl Friedrich, duke of Schleswig-Holstein, 175
Austria, 49–51, 65–66, 136, 239; constitution, 176–77; culture, 27, 30, 194–95; after Great War, 241; nationalistic concerns, 184, 193; and partitions of Poland, 69, 91, 101; population, 177; possessions in Italy, 149, 171–73, 192; reforms, 176, 193; refusal to join German nation, 146; relations with France, 89, 96, 100, 102, 109–11, 179; relations with Germany, 184; relations with Prussia, 132, 175; relations with Russia, 132, 213; revolution, 147–48; and Serbian unrest, 218; settlement after Seven Weeks' War, 176. *See also* Congress of Vienna
Austrian Netherlands. *See* Belgium

Babeuf, François-Noel, 100
Bach, Johann Sebastian, 30
Bacon, Francis, 2
Bailly, Jean-Sylvain, 80, 87
Bakewell, Robert, 34
Bakunin, Michael, 198
balance of power, global, 183

balance of power in Europe, 58–59, 65–66, 128
balance of trade. *See* trade and commerce
Balkan League, 216
Balkans, 208, 212, 216–18, 222, 241. *See also* Slavs; individual Balkan countries
Balzac, Honoré de, 158, 162
banking, 39, 41–42, 105, 118, 123, 192
baroque style: in art, 26; in music, 30
Bastille, 80
Bavaria, 65
Bayle, Pierre, 4, 18
Beagle (boat), 166
Beauharnais, Josephine de. *See* Josephine, empress, consort of Napoleon I
Bebel, August, 154
Beccaria, Cesare. *See* Bonesana, Cesare, marquis of Beccaria
Beer Street (Hogarth), 23
Beethoven, Ludwig von, 194
Belgian Congo, 206–7
Belgium, 49, 58, 65, 66; as a colonial power, 212; after Great War, 239; neutrality, 112, 219; occupation by France, 90, 96, 100; resistance to the Germans, 221; revolution, 134, 135
Benedetti, Vincent, count, 178–79
Bergson, Henri, 167
Berlin, Treaty of (1878), 213, 215
Berlin Academy, 20
Bernini, Gianlorenzo, 26
Bernstein, Eduard, 154
Bethmann-Hollweg, Theobald, 218
Bismarck, Otto von, 196, 218; appointed as chancellor of Prussia, 175–76; and German unification, 178–80, 188, 189; influence on European alliances, 207–8
Black Hand society, 216–17
Blanc, Louis, 138, 144

Czechoslovakia, 147; standard of
living, 118; victories against
Germany, 224
Great Northern War, 52, 57
Great War, 213–48; armistice, 238;
causes, 200–201; distribution of
German territories, 239–41;
economic impact, 246–47; impact
on civilians, 243; submarine
warfare, 224, 225, 227; supply lines,
222, 224, 225, 229; trench warfare,
221–22. *See also* names of individual
battles
Greece, 132–33, 195, 197, 216, 241
Grey, Edward, Lord, 219, 220
guilds, 37, 38, 39–40, 43, 49, 73, 84
Gustavus III, king of Sweden, 19,
47–48

Habsburg dynasty, 47, 49, 57, 58,
65–66, 136, 146–47, 177, 208
Hague conferences, 211
Haiti, 63
Handel, George Frederich, 30
Hanover dynasty, 43
Hard Times (Dickens), 162
Hardenberg, Karl August von, 110, 112
Hargreaves, James, 38
The Harlot's Progress (Hogarth), 28
Haussmann, Georges Eugène, 159
Haydn, Franz Joseph, 30, 194
health care, 155–56, 167, 183, 185,
201. *See also* famine and disease;
nursing, profession of
Hébert, Jacques René, 92
Hébertists, 96
Heligoland, 113
Helveticus, Madame, 19
Henslow, Steven, 166
Herzl, Theodor, 169
Herzogovina. *See* Bosnia-Herzogovina
Hindenberg line, 226

Hindenburg, Paul von, 222
Historical and Critical Dictionary
(Bayle), 4–5
History of England (McCauley), 15
*History of the Decline and Fall of the
Roman Empire* (Gibbon), 29
Hobson, J. A., 207
Hogarth, William, 23, 28
Hohenzollern dynasty, 48, 179, 189
Holbach, Paul, Baron d', 11, 17, 19
Holstein. *See* Schleswig-Holstein
question
Holy Roman Empire (Old), 102, 109,
113
Hong Kong, 203
House, Edward Mandell, 216
House of Lords. *See* parliamentary
government (Britain)
housing. *See* living conditions
Hubertusburg, Treaty of, 68
Hudson's Bay territory, 58
The Human Comedy (Balzac), 162
Hume, David, 17, 19, 58
Hungary, 49, 50, 71, 136, 239; within
Austrian empire, 176–77, 193–94;
after Great War, 241; population,
177; rebellion, 146–47
Huxley, Thomas Henry, 166

imperialism. *See* colonialism
Imperialism: A Study (Hobson), 207
*Imperialism: The Last Stage of
Capitalism* (Lenin), 207
Impressionism, 163
India, 65, 68, 203
Indian Mutiny, 203
Indochina, 204. *See also* Vietnam
Indonesia, 204
Indulgents, 96
Industrial Revolution, First, 38, 109,
117–27
Industrial Revolution, Second, 151–56

recreation, 23, 159
Red Army, 237
Reflections on the Revolution in France
  (Burke), 127
Reform Bill (Britain, 1832), 140–42
Reform Bill (Britain, 1867), 185
Reichstag. *See* Germany, government
Reign of Terror, 93–98. *See also* French
  Revolution
Reinsurance treaty with Russia (1887),
  208
relativity, theory of, 165
religion, 7, 17, 18, 20, 23, 24–25, 47,
  50, 128, 168, 185; freedom of, 9,
  81, 106, 129; as a motive for
  imperialism, 203; tolerance, 10, 29.
  See also names of individual
  denominations
Rembrandt, 26
Remembrance of Things Past (Proust),
  164
Renaissance, 2
Rennenkampf, Paul von, 222
Rerum Novarum (Of Modern Things)
  (Pope Leo XIII), 192
Reynolds, Joshua, 28
Richardson, Samuel, 29
Rilke, Rainer Maria, 164
Rimbaud, Arthur, 164
risorgimento, 148
The Rite of Spring (Stravinsky), 164
Robespierre, Maximilien, 87, 92, 95,
  96
Robinson Crusoe (Defoe), 28
rococo style, in art, 26–27
Romagna (Italy), 172
Roman Catholic Church, 21, 25, 168,
  185; in Austria, 49, 51; in France,
  72, 87, 105–6, 145, 178, 186, 187;
  in Germany, 188; in Italy, 191–92;
  social doctrine, 192. *See also* clergy,
  Inquisition, Jesuits

Romania. *See* Rumania
Rome (Italy), 173, 179, 191
Romanov dynasty, 230, 237
Rousseau, Jean-Jacques, 11–13, 22, 29
Royal Academy of Science (France), 4
Royal Society of London, 4, 20
Rubens, Peter Paul, 26
Rumania, 147, 195, 196, 208, 216,
  220, 223, 241
Russia, 51–57, 65; alliances with other
  European powers, 66, 101, 102,
  109–111, 115, 132; annexation of
  Finland, 113; annexation of
  Moldavia and Wallachia, 132;
  battles against the Austro-
  Hungarians, 222; battles against the
  Germans, 222–23; as a European
  power, 52, 57; expansion to the east,
  204; invasion by Napoleon, 110;
  involvement in Crimean War,
  169–71; involvement in Great War,
  218–19, 227–29; local governments
  following revolution, 232; reforms,
  197–98, 200, 231; relations with
  France, 208–9; revolution, 137,
  199–200, 227, 230–38; rise of
  socialism, 154; secret treaty with
  Germany, 208; supporter of Serbia,
  212, 215; threat to European
  alliance, 208; war with Japan, 200;
  war with Ottoman empire, 69, 91,
  196; westernization, 53–54. *See also*
  Moscow; Union of Soviet Socialist
  Republics
Russo-Turkish War (1774), 69
Rystaadt, Treaty of (1714), 40

St. Germain, Treaty of (1919) 239
Saint Matthew Passion (Bach), 30
Saint Simon, Henri, 138
salons, 18–19, 21, 46
Salvation Army, 168

ABOUT THE AUTHORS

Shirley Elson Roessler holds a doctorate in European and East Asian histories from the University of Alberta. Her fields of specialization include the history of France in the eighteenth and nineteenth centuries. She is author of the award-winning book *Out of the Shadows: Women and Politics in the French Revolution, 1789–1795* and she currently teaches in the Department of History and Classics at the University of Alberta, Edmonton, Canada.

Reny Miklos is a graduate of the University of Alberta in the faculties of Education and Arts and has taught social studies and history in Alberta high schools. He currently teaches in the college preparation program at the Northern Alberta Institute of Technology in Edmonton, Canada.